# The HISTORICAL JESUS and the MYTHICAL CHRIST

# The HISTORICAL JESUS and the MYTHICAL CHRIST

OR
NATURAL GENESIS AND TYPOLOGY OF
EQUINOCTIAL CHRISTOLATRY

GERALD MASSEY

Buffalo, New York
14209
eeworldinc@yahoo.com

Formally published by
A&B Publishers Group
Brooklyn, New York
ISBN 1-881316-04-1

**COVER CONCEPT:**
EWorld Inc.
**COVER ILLUSTRATION**
MSHINDO I.

**ISBN 978-1-61759-056-6**

**Published
by**

**EWORLD INC.**

**Buffalo, New York
14209
eeworldinc@yahoo.com**

4 3 2 1
Manufactured in the United States of America

## SKETCH OF THE LIFE OF GERALD MASSEY

Gerald Massey, an English poet, was born near Tring, Hertfordshire, in May, 1828. He was the child of a poor and illiterate couple, who lived in a hovel, and were barely able to feed and clothe their children. His whole education was confined to a few months at a penny school, where he learned to read and write; and at eight years of age he was sent to work in a neighboring silk mill, his weekly earnings, which never exceeded 1s. 3d., being deemed indispensable to eke out the subsistence of the family. From this unhealthful labor, which confined him 12 or 13 hours a day, he was released by the destruction of the mills; and soon after he was employed in straw plaiting—an occupation, if possible more unwholesome than the other. Living in a marshy region and deprived of opportunities for exercise, the whole family were sometimes prostrated by agues, and their life became a constant struggle with want and misery. Young Massey nevertheless contrived to read whatever books were accessible to him, and at the age of 15, when he went to London to seek employment as an errand boy, had made himself familiar with the Bible, the "Pilgrim's Progress," "Robinson Crusoe," and a few Wesleyan tracts. In the metropolis, while following his humble occupation, he read with avidity whatever came in his way, sitting up until two or three o'clock in the morning. At 17 years of age he fell in love, and under the influence of his passion felt the first impulses to poetical composition. "The first verses I ever made," he says, "were upon 'Hope,' when I was utterly hopeless; and after I had begun I never ceased for about 4 years, at the end of which time I rushed into print." Some of these early poems, dwelling upon the sufferings of the poor, and the "power of knowledge, virtue, and temperance to elevate them," appeared in the columns of a provincial journal; and subsequently a collection of them was published in his native town, Tring, under the title of "Poems and Chansons." The French revolution of 1818, by inducing him to look into the causes of poverty and misery and the anomalies of social life, and to view politics through the medium of such authors as Paine and Volney, "had the greatest effect on him of any circumstances connected with his life." Under the influence of the time, he started in conjunction with some fellow workingmen, in April, 1849, a cheap weekly newspaper called the "Spirit of Freedom," edited and half written by himself, and which became the vehicle of many articles from his pen of an ultra radical tone.

Mr. Massey has lectured extensively on Spiritualism, (in which he is a believer) and on literary topics in the United States in 1873. He has published the "Ballad of Babe Christabel" and other poems. For the last 12 years he has been preparing the matter and writing his great works "A Book of the Beginnings," and "Natural Genesis," which works will doubtless give him lasting fame.

They are the ripe fruit of long research and painstaking collation of authorities, and must be accepted in the years to come as the lever which has chiefly aided in the overthrow of the false system of historic Christianity.

In 1883-4 Mr. Massey lectured in various parts of the United States upon the Christian religion from the standpoint of Equinoctial Christolatry.

He also visited Australia in 1884-5 and repeated the lectures there. Mr. Massey is now (in 1886) a resident of London, England.

THE PUBLISHERS

## SUMMARY OF CONTENTS

Pre-Christian Christology—Persian Revelation—End of the Great Year—Fulfillment of Astronomical Prophecy—Cross type of the Equinox in the Bull, Ram, and Fishes—Pyramid of Har-Khuti—"Misery of the Seven Stars"—The God. A O. Equinox in Pisces—The Fish Man—Horus as Ichthys, the Christ—The Birthplace in Heaven—Its Localization on Earth—Egyptian Annunciation, Conception, Birth, and Adoration of the Babe—Khunsu and the Christ—Child born in the Cave of the Solstice—Decree of Augustus-Horus-type of the Christ—Ra-type—The Christ born of Seb or Earth—Iu-em-hept type of Christ—Two halves of Horus united to form the Christ—Khunsu the expeller of Demons as Christ—Anup and Horus the twins as John and Jesus—Osiris the Well of Life—The *Karast* or Mummy-Christ—The Mythos worked over twice—The two Dates of the Crucifixion—The Ass and the Colt, Lunar—John an earlier Messiah—Two Christs continued in Rome—The Seven Women who fed the Christ identified—The four Genii of the Mount—The Seven Fishermen—Origin of the four Gospels—Matthias, the Egyptian Mati—Gospel of Truth, Egyptian Types of Christ in the Catacombs—The Gnostic Link—Jehoshua ben Pandira—Paul the opponent of the Carnalizers—Why the A-Gnostics conquered—False Teaching and coming end of Equinoctial Christolatry.

### *EXPLANATORY*

"The Natural Genesis," contains the second half of *"A BOOK OF THE BEGINNINGS,"* and completes the author's contribution to the new order of thought that has been inaugurated in our own era by the writings of Darwin and Wallace, Spencer, and Huxley, Morgan and Mc Lennan, Tylor and Lubbock. It was written by an Evolutionist for Evolutionists, and is intended to trace the Natural Origines and teach the doctrine of development.

The total work is based upon the new matter supplied by the ancient monuments ranging from the revelations of the bone-caves and the records of the stone age to the latest discoveries of hieroglyphic inscriptions, the cuneiform tablets, and the still extant language of gesture signs. The work is not only one of original research, it is emphatically aboriginal, and the battle for evolution has here been continued amongst the difficult defiles and fastnesses of the enemy.

---

This book contains the entire section XIII of Gerald Massey's great work, "*NATURAL GENESIS*." The reader will find at the close of the book, the foot notes of the original work, a glossary of the unusual words, and an index of the subjects treated.

The publication of this work in cheap form is with the approval of Mr. Massey, who wishes that it may reach a wide circle of readers.

A careful study of the work will usually result in the conviction that Mr. Massey is correct in his conclusion as to the origin of Christianity.

DEDICATORY.

At times I had to tread
Where not a star was found
To lead or light me, overhead:
Nor footprint on the ground.
I toiled among sands
And stumbled with my feet:
Or crawled and climbed with knees and hands,
Some future path to beat.
I had to feel the flow
Of waters whelming me:
No foothold to be touched below.
No shore around to see.
Yet, in my darkest night,
And farthest drift from land,
There dawned within, the guiding-light,
I felt the unseen hand.
Year after year went by,
And watchers wondered when
The diver, to their welcoming cry
Of joy, would rise again.
And still rolled on Time's wave
That whitened as it passed:
The ground is getting toward the grave
That I have reached at last.
Child after child would say—
*"Ah, when his work is done,*
*Father will come with us and play—"*
'Tis done. And playtime's gone.
A willing slave for years,
I strove to set men free:
Mine were the labours, hopes, and fears,
Be theirs the victory.
GERALD MASSEY

## EXTRACTS FROM THE INTRODUCTION TO NATURAL GENESIS, BY GERALD MASSEY.

The writer has taken the precaution all through of getting his fundamental facts in Egyptology verified by one of the foremost of living authorities, Dr. Samuel Birch, to whom he returns his heartiest acknowledgments. He also sincerely thanks Captain R.F. Burton and Mr. George St. Clair, F.G.S., for their helpful hints and for the time and labor they have kindly given during the progress of this work. * * * * * The main thesis of my work includes the Kamite origin of the pre-Aryan matter extant in language and mythology, found in the British Isles, -the origin of the Hebrew and Christian theology, in the mythology of Egypt,—the unity of origin for all mythology, as demonstrated by a world-wide comparison of the great primary types, and the Kamite origin of that unity,—the common origin of the mythical Genetrix and her brood of seven elementary forces, found in Egypt, Akkad, India, Britain, and New Zealand, who became kronotypes in their secondary, and spirits or gods in their final psychotheistic phase,—the Egyptian genesis of the chief celestial signs, zodiacal and extra-zodiacal,—the origin of all mythology in the Kamite typology,—the origin of typology in gesture-signs,—and the origin of language in African onomatopoeia.

At least sufficient evidence has been produced to prove that all previous discussions, speculations, and conclusions concerning the genesis of language, mythology, fetishism, theosophy and religion are inadequate if only because the Kamite element has been hitherto omitted, and to show that the non-evolutionist could not possibly bottom any of the beginnings.

One object aimed at in these and the previous volumes is to demonstrate that the true subject-matter of "Holy Writ" belongs to astronomical mythology; the history first written in the book above, that was sacred because celestial; and that this has been converted into human history in both the Old Testament and the New. The "Fall in Heaven" was an Egyptian mythos previous to its being turned into a Hebrew history of man in the garden of earth. The Exodus or "Coming out of Egypt" first celebrated by the festival of Passover or the transit at the vernal equinox, occurred in the heavens before it was made historical in the migration of the Jews.

The 600,000 men who came up out of Egypt as Hebrew warriors in the Book of Exodus are 600,000 inhabitants of Israel in the heavens according to the Jewish Kabalah, and the same scenes, events, and personages that appear as mundane in the Pentateuch are celestial in the Book of Enoch.

It was my aim to be foundational and accomplish a work that should be done for the first and last time: to ascertain how the oneness in primitive thought bifurcated in duality and was differentiated in expression by visible and audible signs,—how natural gestures got stereotyped as ideography and hieroglyphics,—why the letter A should win the foremost place in the alphabet,—why mankind should come to worship a supposed divine being alleged to divide all things into three, as a mode of representing its own triune nature. All through, the object was to reach a root-representation of the subject-matter. Evolution teaches us that nothing short of the primary natural sources can be of a final value, and that these have to be sought in the Totemic and pre-paternal stage of Sociology, the pro-religious phase of mythology and the ante-alphabetic domain of signs in language.

One clue to the writer's mode of elucidation may be found in his treatment of mythology as the mirror of prehistoric sociology, and his beginning with the mould of the motherhood which preceded a knowledge of the individualized fatherhood, also, such phases as "*Serpent-worship*," "*Tree-worship*," "*Water-worship*," and "*Phallic-worship*" have but little meaning from the present stand-point. Nowhere did the Cultus originate in religion, but in a system of typology, a primitive mode of expression, a means of representation. The natural need of making signs by gesture-language led to the gradual adoption of certain things that were used as typical figures, a medium for the exchange of meanings, the earliest current coinage ever stamped and issued from the mint of mind. Such types were adopted for use, and became sacred in the course of time, the fetishtic or religious, being their final phase.

The present writer has sought for the natural genesis of the primitive mode of expression which created the types that were continued in the typology that is held to be fetishtic in Africa but religious in Europe. The oldest types, like the Serpent, Tree, or Water, were feminine at first, not because the female was then worshipped, but because the motherhood was known before paternity could be identified. The Serpent sloughed periodically, so did the female. The tree was the producer of the fruits as was the female. Water was the female fount of source.

The ancestral spirit that preceded the individual ancestor, which was represented as creating or continuing by transformation of itself, might come to be typified by the serpent that sloughed and renewed, because a type once founded could be variously applied, but the serpent was a feminine ideograph from the beginning, and *only the natural genesis of the type will enable us to interpret the later typology*.

Much of my matter has been fetched from far, and may be proportionably long in obtaining recognition. Being so remote from ordinary acquaintanceship, it could not be made familiar at first sight by any amount of literary skill. The appeal has to be continually made to a lapsed and almost lost sense of the natural genesis of ideas, customs, superstitions. Nothing short of the remotest beginnings could sufficiently instruct us concerning the origin of religious rites, dogmas, and doctrines, that still dominate the minds of men without being understood, and years of intense brooding had to be spent in *living back* to enter the conditions and apprehend the primary phases of the nascent mind of man, so as to trace the first laying hold of things by the earliest human thought of which the cave-dwellers of the human mind have left us any record; and the writer believes that no such sustained, or at least prolonged and an elaborate endeavor has hitherto been made, to interpret the mind of primitive and archaic man by means of the types—found to be extant from the first—which are herein followed from their natural genesis in phenomena to their final phase of application. To trace the natural genesis of mythology and typology is to write a history or present a panorama of man's mental evolution; and every type portrayed or traced in these pages proves the lowly status of the beginnings, and tends to establish the doctrine of mental evolution in accordance with the physical.

My work is written long and large, and the evidence is faithfully presented in every part for each conclusion drawn, so that the reader may test its truth. Indeed a certain absence of personal showmanship or explanation by the way, in marshaling the long array of data may be set down to a dominant desire that the serried facts should speak for themselves and tell their own tale as far as was possible.

A judgment of facts is now asked for, not belief in a theory; the judgment of those who have time and patience to study and the capacity to comprehend. Belief has no more to do with the reading of this book than theoretical speculation had to do with the writing of it. From the peculiar nature of the work it is almost inevitable that its critics will have to learn the rudiments of the subject from the volumes offered for review; and great patience may be needed to reach the root of the matter, or to perceive the author's drift through all the mass of details. Each section is complete in itself, but the serious student will find the whole of them correlative and cumulative. They are called sections to denote that they have not the continuity of narrative; but the are parts of a whole.

The claim now to be advanced on behalf of the work is that it sets forth a physical basis for the human beginnings in thought, language, and typology; shows the mode in which the primitive and archaic man attained expression in terms of external phenomena; demonstrates the natural genesis of signs and symbols, recovers the lost foothold of mythology in the phenomena of space and time, and traces the typology of the past into mytholatry of the present; that it represents the ancient wisdom, the secrets of the mysteries, numerical, physiological and astronomical, according to the mode in which the Gnosis was expressed: that mystical subjects, previously dabbled in, are for the first time sounded to the depth; that the foundations of the phallic cult are laid bare without the grin of the Satyr in Greece or the libidinous leer of the subject in its Italian phase, by a process as purely scientific as the origin was simply natural.

The writer has not only shown that the current theology *is*, but also *how* it has been, falsely founded on a misinterpretation of mythology by unconsciously inheriting the leavings of primitive or archaic man and ignorantly mistaking these for divine revelations. The work culminates in tracing the transformation of astronomical mythology into the system of Equinoctial Christolatry called Christianity, and demonstrating the non-historic nature of the canonical gospels by means of the original mythos in which the Messianic mystery, the Virgin motherhood, the incarnation and birth, the miraculous life and character, the crucifixion and resurrection of the Savior Son who was the Word of all Ages, were altogether allegorical.

During a dozen years the writer has put his whole life into his labor, fully facing the fact that the most important parts of his work would be the least readable, and the more thorough the research, the more fundamental the interpretation, the more would be its recognition and the fewer its readers. But the work is warranted to wait, and the author does not doubt that its comparatively few friends at first will be continually increased from many generations of genuine men and women.

# THE MYTHICAL CHRIST

When Herodotus visited Egypt and recognized the African originals of the Greek cities, he makes the sage remark that his countrymen, in their ignorance of the beginnings, counted the birth of their gods from the time when they first acquired a knowledge of them. So it was the "primitive Christians," in their ignorance of the natural genesis and past history of Christolatry.

They consisted of the knowing and the simple. The knowing ones kept back the esoteric explanation of the mythos, to let the untutored belief in the real history take root. The simple ones, like Bunyan, "fell suddenly into an allegory about the journey and the way to glory." which allegory they were led to believe was purely matter of fact.

The writer of the Ignatian Epistle to the Philadelphians represents their position. He observes:—"I have heard some say, 'Unless I find it in the ancient writings, (the originals or archives) I will not believe it to be written in the gospel.' And when I said to them: 'It is written!' they replied to me 'It is found written before;'" in what they called the uncorrupted originals, which Ignatius denounces as corrupt copies of his original gospel. "To me," he says, "Jesus Christ stands instead of all the uncorrupted monuments in the world, together with those untouched (or incorruptible) monuments, his cross, his death, his resurrection, and the faith which is in him."[1] The same standpoint was occupied by Professor Jowett, when he wrote:—"To us the preaching of the gospel is New Beginning, from which we date all things, beyond which we neither desire nor are able to inquire."[2]

Nevertheless, the fact remains to be faced that the gospel of Equinoctial Christolatry was written before with a totally different rendering, and that the sayings, dogmas, doctrines, types, and symbols, including both the Cross and the Christ, did not originate where we may have first made acquaintance with them. It was written before, in books of the secret wisdom, now searchable according to the recovered gnosis. It was written before, in the types which are here traced from the lowest root to the highest branch. It was written before in the incorruptible records of the past, inscribed on the starry heavens. The truth is that the real origines of the cult, here called "Equinoctial Christolatry," rather than Christianity, have never yet been reached, however suspected, because of the supposed New Beginning in human history, which was taken for granted by those who knew no farther, and who had no desire to know. The evidence, however, could not have been adduced before the mythology, typology, and Christology of Kam were discovered in the keeping of the mummies, and disinterred from the mausoleums of the dead.

The lost language of the celestial allegory can now be restored, chiefly through the resurrection of ancient Egypt; the scriptures can be read as they were originally written, according to the secret wisdom, and we now know how the history was first written as mythology.

THE BOOK OF REVELATION, FOR EXAMPLE, CONTAINS the oldest matter in the New Testament. This matter is fundamental, and as such lies at the foundations of the human history.

No Christolator doubts that the Jesus, or *A. Ω.* of this Scripture, is one with the Jesus of the Gospels. Those who adopted it as one of the natural bases for the New Beginning were too ignorant to know the origin and significance of the subject-matter. The Revelation assigned to John the Divine is the Christian form of the Mithraic Revelation. In the Parsee sacred books the original scriptures are always quoted and referred to as the "Revelation." "It says in Revelation," is the oft-repeated formula of authority. And the Bahman Yasht contains the same drama of mystery that is drawn out and magnified in the Book of Revelation. An application of the comparative method will prove this; and without such an application, all the works ever written on the Book of Revelation are as worthless as waste paper. The personages, scenes, circumstances, and transactions are identical in both. Each revelation relates to the Kronian allegory, and in both the prophecy is solely astronomical.

Zaratusht enters the state of trance to see the future; he remains in that condition during seven days and nights. John was in trance (in the Isle called Patmos), or in the spirit, on the Lord's (the seventh) day. Zaratusht is entranced by swallowing some (mesmerized?) water, by which the omniscient wisdom is communicated to him. John swallows a little book which he is commanded to eat and then to prophesy.[3] The vision of Zaratusht relates to the seven regions of the world founded on the heaven of the heptanomis; John's to the Seven Churches of Asia. These seven divisions in space and time are also typified by the tree of seven metals and seven branches. In John's vision the tree is represented by the seven candlesticks. In both, seven ages or passing periods of time are portrayed. In both, the world is described as being choked with its unburied dead. The people 'perish in the northern quarter,' i.e. in the celestial Egypt, the domain of death and Hades. In both, the beast from the pit appears, all the more furious because his time is growing short. In the one revelation the Azi-Dahaka or destroying serpent is said to swallow down "one-third of mankind, cattle, sheep, and other creatures of Ahura-Mazda;" in the other the great red dragon appeared as a wonder in heaven, "and his tail drew the third part of the stars of heaven, and did cast them to the earth."[4] The old Satan and the great harlot are to be cast out—the Persian whore being identified as Venus. It is said, "When the star Jupiter comes up to its culminating point, and casts Venus down, the sovereignty comes to the Prince."

The ancient genitrix is to be superseded by another "woman who becomes ruler," and who appears in revelation as the mother of the child, "a woman clothed with the sun, and the moon under her feet and upon her head a crown of twelve stars." At the coming of her child, the promised prince, born of a virgin, the signal is to be given by a star. "That a sign may come to the earth, the night when that prince is born, a star falls from the sky; when that prince is born, the star shows a signal." A star falls from heaven in both visions. The prince of thirty years is identical with the Horus, or Christ who manifests at thirty years of age. The "two witnesses" of the one revelation are "the two angels," the two especial messengers of Ahura-Mazda to mankind, called "Neryosang, the angel or friend, and "Sarosh the righteous," in the other. The apostate of the one revelation is the apostate dragon of the other.

In both the Persian scriptures and in Revelation the astronomical prophecies are fulfilled; the millennium arrives; the old heaven of the seven ( or seventy) divisions passes away. The tree of the heptanomis or primary heaven of seven divisions which are figured by the seven branches of the tree, not only seen by Zaratusht but also represented on the Assyrian monuments as well as in the Kamite planisphere, is superseded in the New Heaven of the twelve signs and seventy-two Decans by the Tree of Healing for all nations. Hushedar, son of Zaratusht, is born from lake Frazdan, and "the creatures become more progressing; he utterly destroys the fiend of serpent origin." The last of the prophets Soshyans, is born; he who is the latest to be "uplifted among the coporeal" (astvat-ereta), or incarnated, arises from the "water of Kansuya," in the "eastern quarter," for the restoration of the world;[5] so John preceded the Christ as last of the dead occurred. The drama of redemption was represented there and then, at the end of the age, cycle, or world.[6]

In the revelation of John this drama is dated, and the stellar scenery belongs to the time when the solar birthplace was in the sign of Aries which was symbolized by the Mithraic lamb of the Persians as the type of the manifestor, called the Messiah. This dates the time of the last pole-star in the dragon; of the end; the resurrection; the judgment; the new heaven and renewed earth of the "coming one," by the year 2410 B.C.

So in the Book of Enoch, the Son of Man takes the seat of the Ancient of Days at the end of the great year, and is the manifestor or Messiah of the cycle of 25,868 years. For this was the book of the revolutions of the celestial luminaries according to every year of the world, until the new work should be effected which will be eternal. Hence it is said that in the new heaven they shall not "enter upon the enumeration of time."[7] Here likewise the manifestor, the Kronian Christ, assumed the likeness of the eternal in a pychotheistic phase.

No competent scholar has ventured to date the Book of Enoch later than the century previous to the present era, and the subject matter is very ancient, yet in that, the Messiah had already come as the Son of Man or of God the Father, to supersede the son of the woman—just as it is in both books of Revelation.

Enoch the stellar and lunar logos, was superseded by the solar god. "The names of the Son of Man, living with the Lord of spirits, was exalted in the chariots of the spirit. From that time I was not drawn in the midst of them."[8] The end of the great year had come, the heavens were renewed; all the prophecy there ever was, according to the gnosis, had been realized; the drama of redemption was played out and the drop-scene let down, without any false claim that the mythos had been fulfilled in a human history.

The Æonian coming of the Kronian Christ, the promised redeemer, is not only prophesied by Esdras in one of the Books of Wisdom, but is likewise dated:—

"Behold the time shall come that these tokens which I have told thee shall come to pass, and the bride shall appear, and his coming forth shall be seen, that is now withdrawn from the earth. For my son Jesus shall be revealed with those that be with him, and they that remain shall rejoice within 400 years. After these years shall my son Christ die, and all men that have life. And the world shall be turned into the old silence seven days, like as in the former judgments: so that no man shall remain. And after seven days the world that yet awaketh not shall be raised up, and that shall die which is corrupt. And the earth shall restore those that are asleep in her, and so shall the dust, those that dwell in silence, and the secret places shall deliver those souls that were committed unto them.

And the most High shall appear upon the seat of judgment, and misery shall pass away, and the long suffering shall have an end."[9] The "day of doom" was the "end of this time." Here it is possible to identify the bride, whose starry image or soul was probably Sothis.

The New Jerusalem was portrayed as the bride coming down from heaven adorned for her husband; the bride that was the wife of the lamb.[10] In the next sign she would be the bride Ichthys, the fish. This would date the prophesy (255 + 400) by the year 655 B.C.

Surely if the prophetical and historical were combined anywhere, it must be here, where the subject-matter is explained according to the gnosis. Also the principles of the apocryphal tradition are undoubtedly identical in all the books of wisdom. Yet these books of Esdras are not even included among the canonical scriptures, but are held to be apocryphal in the modern sense of spurious.

How is it that the scriptures which contains the hidden wisdom and show that the gnosis relates to the fall of Adam, the loss of Paradise and the coming of Jesus Christ, as restorer, within 400 years, should be rejected in this manner?

*Because they prove too much, and are historical in the wrong sense.* They are historical solely in support of the allegory that was Kronian, and the Christ who manifested periodically and was forever Æonian. They show too plainly the way in which the records of Equinoctial Christolatry had been *written before*.

The last act in the drama of redemption is likewise performed in the "Gospel of Nicodemus" or the "*Acts of Pilate*," and called the "*descent of Christ in the underworld*." In this we find the astronomical prophecy is fulfilled on the scale of the great year, the cycle of Precession being completed by the Christ meeting and clasping hands with Adam.

It is related that the dead were lying in the dark places of Hades; all those who had fallen asleep from the first—when a great light suddenly shone in on them, and they awoke and saw one another. It was the coming of the Christ who was heralded by John, the last of the prophets.

The legend of the Tree is repeated. It is said that when Adam was sick unto death he sent his son Seth to the gate of Paradise to pray for a little oil from the tree of life to heal him. But the tree had vanished with the lost Eden. This tree of life and knowledge is represented as being restored in the shape of the cross, and the solar god who entered Amenti once a year is now depicted as doing the same thing at the end of the great cycle, as it was written in the "*first book of the seventy*" in a certain sacred volume said to have been preserved by the Jews.

The Seventy were the princes and rulers in the heaven of seventy divisions, preceding that of the twelve signs and seventy-two duodecans in which the lost tree of seven branches was replaced by the cross of the four corners, or the tree of twelve branches.[11]

In accordance with the nature of the whole subject, the Christ who joined hands with Adam could only be Kronian, and the cross that typified the returning tree of the lost paradise could be no other than the cross of the equinox.[12]

Virgil knew the nature, if not the date, of the cyclic renovation when he sang of the final period of fulfillment which the Sibyl had foretold; and of the grand series of ages that began afresh in the renewal of the great year; also when he asserted that "*there shall be another Ark, steered by another pilot, bearing the chosen heroes; there shall be other wars, and great Achilles shall be sent once more to Troy.*[13]

But those who continued the cult of Equinoctial Christolatry in its final phase were the men who did not know; they were A-Gnostics. They believed that at some indefinite period, afterwards dated, the Christ of chronology, the true Word, that founded the heavens on the periods of time, the word that manifested from the first, had taken flesh at last and manifested once for all in human form. The belief was false, but such is the foundation of the faith.

The sign of the Cross has been sufficiently identified as a figure of the equinox, and the Christ with the sun of the crossing. Upon this rests the cult of Equinoctial Christolatry. When the colure of the cross was in the sign of the Bull, the Apis, or the god Serapis, was the Christ that suffered and rose again as the typical Messiah. When, in the course of precession, the vernal equinox passed into the sign of Aries, the Ram of Sebek-Ra, and the Num-Ra, or the Lamb of Mithras typified the Christ that was sacrificed as savior of the world, at which time the crossing and the place or time of sacrifice were identified with the visible Southern Cross.

These forms of the solar victim who died and rose again were but very slowly superseded. Hence the Ram remained the Christ of the Equinox until the seventh century of our era, at which time it was finally replaced by a Christ on the cross, who was figured on the human likeness.

When the Persian astrologer announces that the parturient virgin bears the Messiah, the future mother of Zaratusht asks, "*How hast thou found out the circumstance and exact period of my pregnancy*?" and his answer is that he discovered it "*through the power of knowledge of the stars and the perusal of those ancient records which give an account of his auspicious existence*."[14] So the incarnations of Buddha were dated astronomically. His coming was indicated by the Messianic star of announcement or prophetic star of an incarnation, and the birthplace is known by astronomical signs. It belongs to the cycles of time, the ends of which were foreknown and prophesied from the beginning. The last of the Buddhas, who is designated "*all the Buddhas*," because, like the gnostic Christ called "*all things*" or Totum, he was the final flower of the whole pleroma perfected, is described as having advanced hitherward by *making seven steps toward each of the four cardinal points of the zodiac*. Therefore he had traversed the circle measured by the twenty-eight lunar asterisms.

We have seen that this was the course of the seven Rishis, the seven Manus (who are also known as the seven Buddhas), in fulfilling the cycle and following the path of precession: and Buddha is the manifestor of the pleroma of seven primary forces, faculties, spirits, or gods, which is shown by his symbol of the eight-rayed star, the sign of Assur in Assyria and of the Christ in Rome. Agni also had been the manifestor of the seven ever since the entrance of the vernal equinox into the sign of the Ram. This is shown by the god being portrayed upon his Ram with *the sign of the Ram* on a banner borne in front of him, which identifies him with Aries in the zodiac. Agni likewise embodied the seven powers; these are typified by his figure with seven arms. In an address to the god it is said; "*Agni! seven are thy fuels; seven thy tongues; seven thy holy sages; seven thy beloved abodes; seven ways do seven sacrificers worship thee; thy sources are seven.*"[15] These are the Seven that began as Elementaries in external nature and afterwards became Planetary and Eschatological.

The Ram is an Egyptian ideograph of a soul, and seven rams are equivalent to the seven souls of the solar god, or the seven spirits in the pleroma of gods now localized in the sign of Aries. The old Samaritans at Nablous still sacrifice seven lambs at their passover or festival of the vernal equinox. These are identified with the cross by being spitted upon it,[16] and also with the cross erected in the zodiacal sign of the Ram or Lamb. This type of the seven souls or spirits is continued in the seven lambs of the Christian iconography grouped about the mount or throne upon which stands the Christ, even as the seven stand *as spirits* round the throne of the Lamb in "Revelation."[17] The seven sacrificed lambs took the place of the seven bullocks offered upon the seven altars of Balak that point back to the time when the vernal colure was in the sign of the Bull. Moreover, the eye is an emblem of reproduction. As such it was figured as a constellation in the replace of birth; and the Lamb with seven eyes in Revelation is a sevenfold type of the birthplace in the sign of Aries and the station of the seven powers, the pleroma whose manifestor was the Lamb, the Horus, Buddha, Mithras, Sebek, *IAO*, or the Christ.

In typology nothing can be more important than the types. The cult of Equinoctial Christolatry is founded on the mythical types, however interpreted; and this typical seven with its eight-rayed star of the manifestor is all-important in proving the identity and continuity of the mythical Christ, in conjunction with the Seven powers in their final psychotheistic phase.

The birthplace of the "*coming one*" as it passed from sign to sign was indicated by the typical "*star in the east,*" and the Star in the East will afford undeniable data for the mythical and celestial origin of the gospel history. When the divine child is born, the wise men or magi declare that they have seen his star in the east. The wise men are identified as the Three Kings of other legends who are not to be derived from the canonical gospels. The three kings or three solar representatives are as ancient as the male triad that was first typified when the three regions were established as heaven, earth, and nether-world, from which the triad bring their gifts; and the three rulers were impersonated for example in the *red* Atum, the *black* Kâ and *white* Hu who accompany the god Har-khuti in the scenes of the hades. When the birthplace was in the sign of the Bull, the Star in the East that arose to announce the birth of the babe was Orion, which is therefore called the star of Horus. *That was once the star of the three kings*; for the "*three kings*" is still a name of three stars in Orion's belt; and in the hieroglyphics a three-looped string is a symbol of *Sahu, i.e.* the constellation Orion.[18] Orion was the star of the Three Kings which rose to show the time and place of birth in heaven some 6,000 years ago, when the vernal equinox was in the sign of the Bull. When the colure passed into the sign of the Ram, 2,410 B.C., the triangle or pyramid of Har-khuti became the Star in the East that rose in the decans of Aries to show the solar birthplace during 2,155 years.[19] Here it might be argued that the Great pyramid built in Egypt with power to demonstrate the ending of the great year and the final overthrow of the dragon, was set in the planisphere to mark the point of recommencement in the circle of precession. The name of the great pyramid is khuti or the Lights. The lights, whether as constellations or planets, are seven in number, and the pyramid is a figure of 7 which unites the square and triangle in one. Horus of the triangle is Horus of the pyramid, Har-Sapti or Sebti (*i.e.* Seb. = 5; ti = 2). Sut-Anup is called "*Lord of Sapt in Nerau*;"[20] and Sapt is the place of the Seven; the place of the pleroma and its manifestor, which shifted according to the colure of the equinox. Har-khuti is Lord of the Lights that were seven in number, the perfect Star of the gnostic pleroma; Soul of the Seven spirits, Breather of the Seven Breaths, Word of the Seven vowel-sounds, Bull of the Seven cows, Stone of the Seven eyes, Ram of the Seven horns, Player of the Seven pipes, on the planetary scale of Seven tones. He is portrayed in the dreams of the Ram, holding the pyramid or triangle as his Star in the East. This god was a survival of the ancient Sut-Horus. Those Egyptologists who have been unable to follow the development of the astronomical mythology have looked upon the cult of Har-khuti as a later importation into Egypt whereas it belonged to a continuation of the mythos by those who wrote history in the stars of heaven. Horus of the pyramid above was the Horus of the great pyramid at Ghizeh, the Horus of the Shus-en-Har; and this Lord of the Seven Lights is identical with the *IAO*-heptaktis of the Chaldeans, the *IAO*-Chnubis or Panaugria of the Gnostics, and *AΩ* the All in Revelation.

The "*Mystery of the Seven Stars*" relates to the new heaven established when the vernal equinox entered the sign of the Ram or Lamb, and the pyramid or triangle of Horus became the Star in the East that beckoned the wise men, magi, or gnostics to the birthplace of the Messianic babe.[21] Here the god of the Seven Lights, Rays, Powers, or Planets is the *AΩ* of the Seven Eyes, Seven Lamps of Fire, Seven Golden Candlesticks, who *has seven stars in his right hand*, just as Har-khuti holds the stars of the pyramid, the figure of 7, in his right hand, and the sign of the rule in his left.[22] This then is the Jesus of Equinoctial Christolatry in the Book of Revelation, who was the Lord of Seven Lights in the astronomical allegory from the year 2,410 B.C.

Amongst other philological fallacies is the current assumption that the Greek name of Ιγοϖ was *derived* from the Hebrew Jehoshua. Philology is indefinite in such matters without the typology, and the natural genesis in phenomena. "*Ie*" or "*Iu*" in Egyptian means the *Coming One*, the duplicator who is of a plural nature. Har-*iu*, the reduplicative Horus, was a title of Osiris in this sense. *Iu*-em-hept, the second Atum, called the Son, the Word, or Logos of God, the Father, was the *Coming One*, he who came with (or as) Peace, and brought good luck and happiness. The calf-headed god *Au*, whose name denotes the past, present, and future of being; the Hebrew *Iaho*, the Phoenician, Chaldean, and gnostic *Ιαω* the British *Iau*, Manx *Ie*, Delphian Apollo, designated *Ie*, were forms of this *Iu*, the ever-coming one, who was personified as the divine child, that is the *Su* (Eg.), whence *Iusu* (Gr. Jesus) is the coming child whose mother's name in one cult is *Iusaas*. Jehoshua and Jesus are two names derived on two different lines from one original root; and the name has to be determined by the nature of the type. The Kamite *Iu* and Chaldean *Iaw*-heptaktis, gods of the Seven Rays or Lights, were continued as the *AΩ,* who is Jesus in the Book of Revelation. As already shown the one god called *Iu* or *Iao* became the solar representative of the pleroma of Seven Powers, Lights, or Spirits, that were expressed by this divinity in the human image of the Trinity, composed of the mother, child, and virile male in unity. Thus the divine hebdomad and the human triad were combined in a tenfold totality, and the *Iu* or *AΩ* is a personal equivalent of the 10 (ten) in numbers.

This god of the seven spirits or breaths was represented by the ineffable name which consisted of the sevenfold vowel as the summit of all previous attainment in sound, and both are coproducts traceable to conscious evolution; seven elements of the consummated deity being expressed by the seven vowels in one sound, like A, I, O, or a diphthong.

Amongst other mysteries declared by Marcus he taught that the *restitution of all things* occurred when all the numbers of the ineffable Name mixing in *one letter should utter one and the same sound.* Irenaeus, says Marcus, "*imagined that the emblem of this utterance was found in 'Amen' 'which we pronounce in concert.* Marcus did not imagine—*he knew*, being a Gnostic. "*Amen*" in revelation is a title of the God $A\Omega$ and in Egyptian both *Amen* and *Iu* mean "*come*' the "*coming one.*" *Iu* (Eg.) was originally written *aa*, and the pyramid or Triangle is *aa* by name. As a triangle this sign is threefold, as a pyramid it united the square and triangle and is sevenfold, therefore it could be a sign of the ten-total, which was also figured thus

as a pyramidal ten by the Pythagoreans, an image of the All composed of seven elementary forces expressed in threefold human form.

The Name could be uttered by a single sound or sign as it was by the Hebrew Jad =10, or two hands; the Egyptian pyramid the Chinese Δ, the British Cyfriu, (A, I, still, at Lloyds) or the Coptic I with inherent U, which has the numeral value of 10. *This was a mode of expressing the representative of divine Unity* (comprising the seven elementary powers, together with the human trinity, in a ten-total,) *by one sign and a single sound*; and this I, Iu, Δ, or $A\Omega$ is a symbol of the name of *Iusu* (*i.e.*, *Iu* the duplicative or dual one), the Greek *Iesous*, as the $A\Omega$ in Revelation.

The pyramid (triangula) is the letter A in stellar form; and the divinity Har-khuti, Har-Sebti the Iu, $A\Omega$ or Iao is the primary one—answering to the A at the head of the alphabet—who as the child or son Su (Eg.) is Iusu, Iesous, Iso, or Jesus. The name of Horus (Har, Eg.) also has the meaning of No. 10, and Har-khuti of the Seven Lights is the God One = ten, of the triangle (trinity) and pyramid (hebdomad), the symbol of the three and the seven. Lastly, this God One=three=seven=ten, whose title was a length expressed by the first and final letter of the Greek alphabet, $A\Omega$ is the pubescent male who was born of the virgin mother without the fatherhood, third in advent, but placed first in series, as the representative of all the powers, whose natural genesis has been traced to lunar phenomena, and who in the solar mythos was the opponent and vanquisher of the *Beast* with *ten horns*, which represented the total of the opposing Typhonian powers.

The seven breaths are assigned to the Holy Spirit, by Justin. Macrobius also affirms that the soul of the world is of a sevenfold origin; the seven continued from the Elementaries of chaos.

The Hindu Agni was at times portrayed with two faces, three legs and seven arms, as a form of this one total god of a duplicative nature, twin in sex, triadic in form, and manifestor of the seven-primary powers.

Thus the name Jesus can be traced to *Iu* the coming one, and *Su* the child of either sex who grows up with the attributes of both into the *Deus trinus unus*, the typical manifestor, under various names, of the Seven Elementaries, Seven Kronotypes, Seven Spirits, Planets, Lamps, or Lights, which constituted the pleroma of powers from the first; and such is the *mystery of the seven stars.*

According to the Syriac version quoted by Bunsen, in the concluding passage of the Epistle of Ignatius to the Ephesians, "*Three Shouting Mysteries*" were connected with the star of annunciation in heaven. The passage reads, "*From the moment that the star appeared, and thus the son was manifested upon the spot, the reign of darkness, of magic, of death, ceased; and the earthly development of God's own eternal kingdom began.*"

The three shouting mysteries are so ancient in the celestial allegory that they are also extant as the Chinese sign of the "*Three Lights*," denoting the supernatural, mystery, and revelation; also as the "*Three Shouts*" of the British Barddas which are symbolized by the triple sign of their triune Being, named *Iao*, the younger, as they were also represented by the three stars of constellation, *Triangula* in the dreams of the Ram, which was the typical star in the east after the year 2410 B.C.

About 255 B.C. the sun, or, more correctly, the Colure of the Vernal Equinox entered the sign of the Fishes. Thenceforth for 2155 years that asterism became the station of the cross and the birthplace of the solar Christ. Here we find the pleroma of seven powers as the seven great gods of Assyria. That is, the month associated with this sign is dedicated to the pleroma of seven gods of which Assur was manifestor. *It is of course impossible for this to have commenced as such for the first time with the year* 255 B.C.

It is sufficient however for the present purpose to know that with the re-entrance of the vernal equinox into the sign of the Pisces, the solar birthplace was once more in the quarter of the beginning, that of the waters and of the great fish, hippopotamus, or other type of this mouth, or uterus, the *Piscina* of creation, the place of emanation and point of re-emergence from the waters of the abyss, out of which issues the river of the Waterman, the fish from the river, and the manifestor born form the fish.

This was in the Egyptian *Anna* or celestial Heliopolis, which had retained the name of the Fish, *An* (Eg.) originally represented by the Great Fish, the ketos, the water-horse or dragon of the deep. The star Fomalhaut, for example, is still the "*mouth of the fish*," that marks the place of emanating from the waters which was continued as the *piscina*, or *vesica piscis*, the Roman emblem of Mary; the ru of the mother who was *Ma* or *Mu* (Eg.) by name. Thus, when the solar birthplace (at the time of the vernal equinox) passed once more into the zodiacal sign of Pisces, it had come round to the primordial point of emanation from the quarter of the Waters in the beginning. The genetrix, under the fish-type as Hathor, Atergatis, or Semiramis, was at last figured in the sign of the Fishes, where she brought forth her divine child as her fish. Hence the fish-goddess and her young one were portrayed as the two zodiacal Fishes, instead of the earlier *one*, who had represented the sign 25,868 years earlier. The Messiah who manifested in this sign was foreordained to come as Ichthys the fisherman, or, doctrinally, the fisher of men. In the backward cycle of precession, Pisces is the first of the three water-signs. Hence, it was foretold that the Christ, under various names, was to ascend from the waters. The earliest mode or form of emanation being from the waters, the great mother first brought to birth as the water-element or under some water-type. the primordial manifestor in Chaldea was the *Oan* of fish-man.

In one account there are four of these fish-men or Annedoti, and there are seven altogether; these two groups are identical with the four genii, and the total family of seven in the Egyptian *Ritual*. The fish of Horus and Sevekh is the crocodile—the fish itself being an earlier type than the fish-man. The fish is *An* in Egyptian; the fish-region, Annu, is the solar birthplace, and Ichthys, the fish, had been continued from this beginning. Hence, the manifestor was the one who was born of the waters; who came forth from the celestial deep; who crossed the waters as the fish, or inside of it; who was personified as the Oar (as was Horus), and the Steersman, the Lord of the Boat or Ark that saved souls from the abyss and the deluge. "*Rising from the great water is my name*," says the Osirified in the character. This is the manifestor who is foreseen by Esdras coming up out of the sea as the "*same whom God the highest hath kept a great season, which by his ownself shall deliver his creature*;" the character assigned to the Christ of the gospels.

The fish-man Oannes only came up out of the Erythraean Sea (the pool of Pant in the *Ritual*) to converse with men and teach them in the daytime. Then the sun set, says Berosus, it was the custom of this being to plunge again into the sea, and abide all night in the deep; for he was amphibious. In like manner the man who comes up out of the sea is visible only by day. "*Even so can no man upon earth see my son or those that be with him but in the daytime.*" This is parodied or fulfilled in the account of Ichthys, the Christ, who instructs men by day, but retires to the lake of Galilee where he demonstrates his solar nature by walking the waters at night. The Son of Man who "hath not where to lay his head" goes on board the boat to sleep, which is also a parallel to the Oan going down into the sea for the night. We are told that the disciples being on board ship "*when even was come*," "*in the fourth watch of the night Jesus went unto them walking on the sea.*" Now, the fourth watch began at three o'clock, and ended at six o'clock. Therefore this was about the proper time for a solar god to appear walking upon the waters, or coming up out of them as the Oannes.

Oannes is said to have taken no food whilst he was with men. "*In the daytime he used to converse with men; but took no food at the season.*" So Jesus when "*his disciples prayed him saying, 'Master, eat said unto them, 'I have meat to eat that ye know not of. My meat is to do the will of him that sent me.*"[23] This is the perfect *replica* of the character of Oannes, who took no food, but whose time was wholly spent in teaching men. Moreover, the fish-man is made to identify himself. When the Pharisees sought a "*sign from heaven*," Jesus said, "*there shall no sign be given but the sign of Jonas." "For as Jonas became a sign unto the Ninevites, so shall also the Son of Man be to this generation.*" The sign of Jonas is that of the Oan or fish-man of Nineveth, whether we take it direct from the monuments or from the Hebrew history of Jonah who was inside the fish during three days and nights; it is equally the fish-man, or the man emaned as Vishnu, is from the fish in the Hindu drawings, and as the man-child is brought forth in the sign of the Fish by the fish-goddess in the year 255 B.C. Assuredly there was no other sign than that of the sun reborn in Pisces. The voice of the secret wisdom says, those who are looking for signs can have no other than that of the returning fish-man, Ichthys, Oannes, or Jonas—who could not be made flesh.

The Valentinians maintained that the *dispensational* Jesus was identical with *Pan* (Pan in the Greek version being *Christus* in the Latin text) because he included the names of all those *who had produced him*. And Pan, as manifestor, may be seen in the decans of the Bull sign.[24] He was portrayed with a face of fire, holding seven circles in his left hand. But the extant evidence shows that the great starting point for modern Equinoctial Christolatry was with the sign of the Ram, and the next stage with the Fishes. This fact is patent in the iconography of the Roman catacombs. The two signs are 2,155 years apart in time, yet they are connected by indissoluble links, the Christ having been both a ram and a fish before he was depicted in the human likeness.

In a grotto or grave of the ancient necropolis at Cyrene there is a fresco in which the Good Shepherd or Christ is portrayed. He is accompanied by seven lambs, and seven fishes are arranged in a semicircle over his head.[25] This figure is supposed to represent the Christ in the two characters of the Good Shepherd and the Fisherman. What it does signify is the solar Messiah, the manifestor of the seven powers who is identified with the sign of Pisces by the seven fishes, the two types having been combined in one representation through the course of precession, and blended in the consequent imagery.

The passage of the cross from the sign of the Lamb into that of the Fishes, together with the change in the type of sacrifice, is very palpably portrayed in a symbolical scene discovered in the catacombs and copied by De Rossi.26 In this, seven persons are seated in a semicircle, with two fishes and eight baskets of bread set out in front of them. According to Lundy, the "*seven persons obviously denote the complete number of God's elect in the communion of saints*," whatever that may mean![27] But according to the present view, if the scene represents a sacramental feast, the seven figures would typify the seven spirits or gods of the pleroma now localized in the sign of the fishes. The scene is evidently zodiacal, because the sacrifice of the lamb—now superseded by the fish—is portrayed on the *left and inferior hand*, the crossing being denoted by a human figure making the sign of the cross. On the other hand, the sacrifice of the fish is being performed, and here the sign of the cross is made by a female figure, the Orante or bride of Christ, who has now transferred her affections from the Lamb in Revelation to Ichthys the Fish; or in other words, the mother of Messiah now brings forth the divine child in the sign of the Fish and the House of Bread instead of the previous sign of the Ram.

The fish, in a long, upright form, with a forked tail, is also carved on an Irish cross at Kells in the county of Meath, with seven figures bowed before it as if in adoration.[28]

When the spring equinox passed into Pisces, the fish which is carried over the head of Horus was not only a zodiacal sign of the Christ, but was made eucharistic; it is not merely portrayed with the bread, but a living fish is represented as the bearer of the bread and wine of the sacramental rite.

Ichthys, the fish, was the child of Atergatis, the fish-tailed goddess of Syria, whose portrait may be seen in the zodiacal sign of Pisces, where she brought forth her child at the epoch of 255 B.C. from the waters represented by the lake at Ascalon.[29] This sign in the Hermean zodiac is called *Ichthon*; and the mother is depicted in the act of holding up the child in her left hand; he who wears the rod of iron in his hand. Ichthon is identified by jamblichus with god *Emphe*, that is with *Iu-em-hept* (the Greek Imothes or Æsculapius), whose father is Atum and whose mother's name is Hathor-*Iusaas*, she who was great with Iusa, Iusu, or Jesus, the coming son (from *Iu* to, come, *Sa*, the son, and *As*, to be great, a name of Isis), who was born or incarnated for the last time when the equinox entered the sign of the Fishes, 255 B.C., from which time "Ichthys" became the sign of salutation for the Equinoctial Christolaters, who were called *Pisiculi*.

[Horus, in Egypt had been a fish from time immemorial, and when the equinox entered the sign of Pisces, Horus, was portrayed as *Ichthys* with the fish sign over his head.[30] This engraving has been called Jesus Christ in the character of Horus, but it is simply the Egypto-Gnostic Horus, the Christ who was born as the fish of the perfected solar Zodiac in the year (or thereabouts) B.C. 255.]

This imagery is too late for the Egypt of the Pharaohs, but the gnosis survived, and it was continued by the Graeco-Egyptian gnostics; hence we find Iu-em-hept (*i.e. Iu* the *Su*, or Iusu) re-born is Ichton in Pisces; he who had been the Æonian bringer of peace, the "divinity" whom Jamblichus calls the "One God," who must have been a most ancient form of the "*coming one*" in the Kamite mythology, as, in the pedigree of architects traced by Brugsch Pasha, Imhotep (*i.e.* Iu-em-hept) is the name of an ancestor of Khnum-ab-Ra, who lived in the time of the third dynasty.[31]

Bishop Munter, in his *Sinnbilder*, remarks that in the Talmud the Messiah is called Dag, the fish. "*The Jews connected him with the astronomical sign of the Fishes, and the conjunction of the planets Jupiter and Saturn in this constellation*—WHICH INDICATED THE LAND OF JUDEA—*was to announce his birth. Arbanel, in his commentary on the prophet Daniel, positively says that this is derived from ancient sources of authority, as in the highest degree probable. And the learned John Frischmuth, in his work on the Christian religion, as against the Jews, remarks on the madness and infatuation and obstinacy of that people that they themselves have concluded that the time of the Messiah's advent was indicated by the conjunction of the planets, Jupiter and Saturn in the constellation of the Fishes, and yet when that conjunction actually took place at Christ's birth, the Jews rejected him.*"[32] This shows the Jews were not only in possession of the astronomical allegory, but also of the tradition by which alone it could be truly interpreted. There is a reference to the Kronian manifestor in the Gemara, which states that the war of the Thaninim or the fishes shall precede him and announce his coming. The supposed prophecy relates to the entrance of the vernal equinox into the sign of Pisces, 255 B.C., and not to any planetary conjunction at a period more suitable to the later reckoning.

It has been shown how the celestial scenery was localized and represented on earth. Khnum-hept speaks of "*setting up landmarks like the heaven.*"[33] Thebes was called the "*Heaven on Earth,*" the *August Staircase of the Beginning of Time.*"[34] The mount of seven steps, the four quarters (and lastly the twelve signs), was still the earlier type. Such imagery was localized in all lands where the mythos is to be found. For example, Meru, the mount of the birthplace in the north, is still extant at *Meru*, a town in Picardy, *i.e.* in the *north* of France, with a castle seated near the source of a brook that runs into the river Oise. Hence the birthplace of the Messiah in the sign of the Ram or the Fishes already belonged to the geography of various countries. In the astronomical prophecy of Micah, the Æonian manifestor, who, according to the Chaldee Paraphrast, is the Messiah, was to be born in Bethlehem-Ephratah; and it was through this announcement that the chief priests and scribes were enabled to tell Herod where the child should be born.[35]

BETHLEHEM MEANS THE HOUSE OF BREAD-CORN, GRAIN or wheat.[36] In the houses of the zodiac, that of Virgo is the place of the seed for sowing, and the opposite sign, Pisces, is the house of the gestator who brings forth the corn, as Siton. These two are the signs of the Virgin and Matrona. Aphrathah signifies fruitfulness of the wife or of the gentrix.[37] who was Aphrodite, Hathor, Atergatis, Semiramis, Parmuti, or Venus-Pisces, each of whom was a form of the bringer-forth in the house of Breadcorn, fish, and fruit, first set in heaven in accordance with the seasons of Egypt. The Hebrew Messiah was to be born in Bethlehem-Ephratah because the birthplace above was localized in that city of Judea, the land of the solar birthplace in the sign of the Fishes. And so the Christ that was born in heaven was landed on earth as the fish in place of the Lamb.

THE FATHERS OF THE CHURCH HELD THE FISH TO BE THE Christ. Prosper Africanus calls Christ that "*great Fish who fed from himself the disciples on the shore, and offered himself as a fish to the whole world*" In the last chapter of the gospel according to John, where we are told that, if all which Jesus did should be written, "*even the world itself could not contain the books*," the Christ appears to the Seven and feeds them on the broiled fish. "*The broiled fish is Christ*," says Augustine. It was so after the equinox had entered the sign of Pisces, 255 B.C.

The *actual* birthplace of the carnalized Christ was NEITHER BETHLEHEM NOR NAZARETH, BUT ROME! It was there that the cult of Equinoctial Christolatry was continued by conversion. Rome was the refoundry of the ancient religion. And according to astronomical prophecy, Rome was another of the localities in which the Messiah was expected to appear. That is, Rome on earth, Rome of the seven hills, represented a Rome in heaven, just as Jerusalem below was the replica of Jerusalem above, or Bethlehem had been named from the celestial House of Bread-corn. In the Jerusalem Targum, the coming out of Egypt is identified with the advent of Messiah. It is affirmed that Moses shall go forth from the midst of the desert, and "*king Messiah from the midst of Rome. The one shall speak on the top of the cloud, and the other shall speak on the top of the cloud, and the Word of the Lord shall speak between them.* "*Coming out of Egypt*" is a Kamite expression for ascending from the lower to the upper heavens, which were divided in the equinoctial signs.[38]

The birthplace in Rome is likewise found in the Babylonian Talmud, where the Manifestor is represented as sitting amongst the sick and destitute poor.[39] Rabbi Jehoshua Ben-Levi asked Elijah, "*When does Messiah come?*" He replied, "*Go and ask himself.*" "*But where does he wait?*" "*At the Gate of the City.*" (*i.e.* Rome). The Sibyl was also credited with a prophecy to the effect that the Messiah was to come when Rome should be the ruler of Egypt. "*When Rome shall rule Egypt, then shall dawn upon men the supremely great kingdom of the immortal king, and a pure sovereign will come to conquer the sceptres of the whole earth unto all ages.*" This was the Egypt of the allegory; "*Egypt, where also our Lord was crucified.*"[40] The Rome signified was celestial. The prophecies were astronomical. The Gate of Rome was the sign of the Fish, and Rome became the ruler of this Egypt when the equinox entered Pisces, 255 B.C.

*Annu* (Eg.), the typical Heliopolis is the region of the Fish. Another Egyptian name of the fish is *Rum* or Rema, which is identical with the name of *Roma*, the goddess, the river, the city of Rome. Rama was a form of the gentrix as the fish, like Semi-*Ramis*, or Semu-*ramat*; and the emaning mouth of the fish (os tineae) is still preserved in the mitre of the Pope of Rome. Also, the ring of investiture placed on the Pope's finger at the time of his election which is afterward used as his letter-seal, is the sign of the fish. It is pretended that this was the ring of Peter the fisherman. It is called *Annulus Piscatorius*, but the symbolism over the head of the fisher points to the two fishes of the zodiac.[41] Thus when the Roma (or Judea=Pisces) was the birthplace above for the Messiah, 255 B.C., the mythos had its localization in Rome of the seven hills,[42] as well as in Annu, Mat, or Maturea, Judea, Bethlehem, or Nazareth (from Natzer the branch, the offspring, descendant, or child).

We learn from the writer of the *Clementine Homilies*, that as late as the reign of Tiberius there was a rumor current concerning the "*vernal equinox*," connected with the prophecy that at the *same season* a king would arise in Judea, who was to work miracles—make the blind to see, the lame to walk; heal every disease, including leprosy, and raise the dead. He also limits the ministry of this *kurios* to one year. Now a king whose advent depended on the shifting of the vernal equinox, and whose time was limited to one year, called his ministry, could be no other than the solar god; could be no other than the mythical Messiah whose birth was due in Rome as in Bethlehem in the year 255 B.C.

One of the most perfect representations of the end of an old cycle at the birth of the new Messiah that has come down to us is contained in the gospel of James. This scripture belongs to the "*Apocrypha*," which are looked upon as spurious history; but they contain the history according to the gospel of the mythos, or preserve somewhat of the secret gnosis midway between the true mythos and a fabulous history. The attendant circumstances connect the new advent with the birth of the other Manus, Messiahs, and Repas, that have personated the eternal in time at the end and rebeginning of the great cycle.

When the pains of her travail came upon Mary, Joseph is described as finding shelter for her in the cave and going forth in search of a midwife. Then follows the arrest and standstill of all things by which the event was represented in mythology, sometimes as the petrifying of living forms into stones whilst in the act of dancing or making the circle. "*And I, Joseph, walked, and I walked not; and I looked up into the air, and saw the air violently agitated; and I looked up at the pole of heaven and I saw it stationary, and the fowls of heaven still. And I looked at the earth and saw a vessel lying, and workmen reclining by it and their hands in the vessel, and those who handled did not handle it, and those who took did not lift, and those who presented it to their mouth did not present it, but the faces of all were looking up. And I saw the sheep scattered, and the sheep stood, and the shepherd lifted up his hand to strike them and his hand remained up; and I looked at the stream of the river, and I saw the mouths of the kids were down and not drinking, and everything which was impelled forward in its course was arrested.*"

All things were caught at this culminating point which marked the end of a cycle in the heavens as though the universal motion were catalepsed into the solidity and stillness of stone. It is a description fit to have been carved by the pyramid builders.

The sign given by the angels for the shepherds to know that the Savior, Christ the Lord, was born at Bethlehem, was, "*Ye shall find the babe lying in a manger.*" The manger is also celestial, zodiacal, and *the actual birthplace of the Messiah in Egyptian mythology*. The typical birthplace was designated Apt or Aptu, whence the name of Abydus. *Ap* (Eg.) means to manifest and expose to view, also to guide; *Apt* is the place or person. Apt, as person, was the most ancient genitrix who first brought forth from the waters as the fish, crocodile=dragon or hippopotamus, hence Aptu is the mythical fish. *Apt* as place was also the pool of two truths, the *Piscina* of the beginning, which was made zodiacal at last in the sign of Pisces. The pool, fish, uterus, crib, are all types of the birthplace named *apt*, and *the apt* (Eg.), is *also a Manger*. The manger, *apt*, is a sign of the birthplace in Thebes, as in Aptu (Abydus). Thus the hieroglyphics will explain why the divine child as Ichthys was born in a manger.[43] One position of the "manger" can be identified by the asterism called *Proesepe*, in the sign of Cancer, which was at one time the place of birth at Summer Solstice. The manger at Bethlehem had been the birthplace of the divine babe in a far earlier cult. Hieronymus describes the Syrian Adonia, extant in his time (A. D. 331-420), and says that in place where the redeemer cried in the manger, the lament of the women mourning for Adonis had been heard *even in later times*,[44] as it assuredly had been in the pre-Christian period. According to the chronicle of Alexandria,[45] the Egyptians not only consecrated the nativity of the babe born of the virgin mother, they likewise had the symbolical custom of exposing a child in a crib to the adoration of the people. When king Ptolemy asked why this was done, he was told that it was an ancient mystery. The crib or *apt* being identical with the manger, this was the same babe in the manger that was born in the *apt* above. "*The loss of the manger of Bethlehem*," says Dean Stanley, "*is a witness to the universal significance of the incarnation.*"[46] On the contrary, we claim that the discovery of the manger (*apt*) in the solar birthplace is a testimony to its never having been other than celestial or mythical, and therefore it is universal.

We shall find that the gospel history was "*written before*" from beginning to end. The story of the divine Annunciation, the miraculous Conception (or incarnation), the Birth, and the Adoration of the Messianic child, had already been engraved in hieroglyphics and represented in four consecutive scenes upon the innermost walls of the holy of holies in the temple of Luxor which was built by Amenhept 111., a Pharaoh of the eighteenth dynasty.[47] In these the maiden queen Mut-em-Ua, the mother of Amenhept, her future child, impersonates the virgin mother who bore without the fatherhood, the mother as the solar boat, the mother of the Only One.

DESCRIPTION OF THE SCENE ON THE NEXT PAGE.

The first scene on the left hand shows the god Taht, the lunar Mercury, the divine Word or Logos, in the act of hailing the virgin queen, announcing to her that she is to give birth to the coming son. In the next scene the god Kneph (in conjunction with Hathor) gives life to her. This is the Holy Ghost or Spirit that causes conception; Kneph being the spirit. Impregnation and conception are made apparent in the virgin's fuller form. Next the mother is seated on the midwife's stool, and the child is supported in the hands of one of the nurses. The fourth scene is that of the adoration. Here the child is enthroned, receiving homage from the gods and gifts from men. Behind the deity Kneph, on the right *three* men are kneeling and offering gifts with the right hand and life with the left. The child thus announced, incarnated, born, and worshipped was the Pharaonic representative of the Aten sun, the *Adon of Syria*, and Hebrew Adonai, the child-Christ of the Aten cult, the miraculous conception of the ever-virgin mother personated by Mut-em-Ua.

The moon at full with the solar child of light was the great determinative of the equinoxes. In the planisphere of Denderah the child Horus is portrayed within the disk of the full moon just over the sign of the Scales at the Autumn equinox. In the same map of heaven the luni-solar god, Khunsu, is depicted in the disk of the full moon of the Vernal equinox. But instead of being in the decans of the Ram and *vis-a-vis* with the full moon of the Autumn equinox it *appears in the sign of the Fishes*, and is another witness to the bringing on of the reckonings which *proves that in repeating this zodiac the place of the Vernal equinox was shifted into the sign of the Pisces, whilst the place of the Autumn equinox was left unadjusted in the Scales*. Khunsu will supply one of our most perfect types of the Kronian Messiah and announcer of the sign of the Fishes. He is mentioned here,

Scene from the Temple of Luxor at ancient Thebes in Egypt, built by Amenhept III., about 1600 B. C., described on page 33.

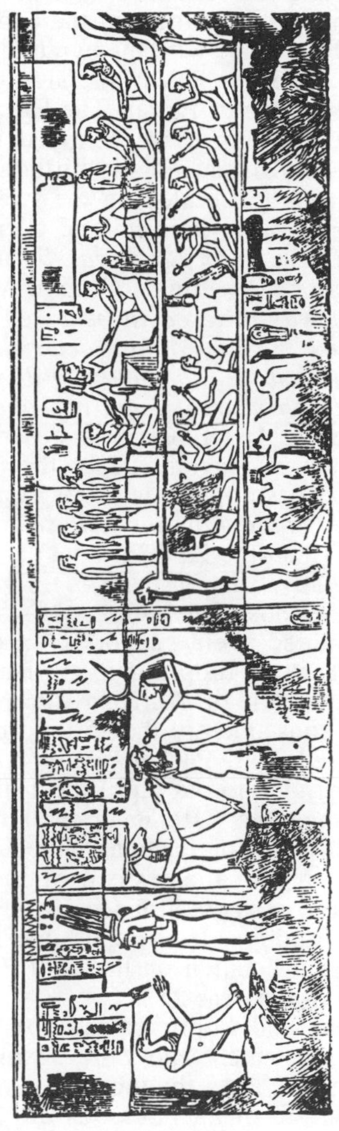

SCENE FROM THE TEMPLE OF LUXOR AT ANCIENT THEBES IN EGYPT, BUILT BY AMENHEPT III., ABOUT 1600 B. C.

however, to point out that he stands in the disk of the full moon of the Vernal equinox holding a pig in his hand, which may be called the pig of Easter; and Khunsu with the pig in the full moon is the manifestor and announcer of the equinox in the sign of the Fishes, just as Har-Khuti with his pyramid had been in the sign of the Ram, and Orion or Pan in the sign of the Bull. The pig is still a well-known type of Easter. The Egyptian origines of the Christ in relation to Khunsu are betrayed in a remarkable manner. The festival of Khunsu, or his birthday, at the vernal equinox, was at one time celebrated on the twenty-fifth day of the month named after him *Pa-khunsu*. And Clement Alexander, the Egyptian, asserts that "*our Lord was born in the twenty-eighth year* (of the era of the battle of Actium, Aug. B.C. 31, 32) *when first the census was ordered to be taken in the reign of Augustus; and there are those who have determined not only the year of the Lord's birth but also the day, and they say that it took place in the twenty-eighth year of Augustus, and on the twenty-fifth day of Pachons*."[48] Dr. Lauth has observed with much simplicity that this date of Pachons 25 of the lunar *fete* of the (σελζϖεζα) moon-worshippers is very remarkable. "*The Egyptians*," he says, "*could not have chosen another date in their whole calendar* (than the 25th Pachons) *if they intended to make the Lord's birthday coincide with the most striking lunar festivity*."[49] Thus have those Egyptologists, who are above all things Bibliolaters, added their support to prop the reversed pyramid and keep it from toppling over. But the month of Pachons began on the 26th of April in the Alexandrian year (introduced B.C. 25) consequently the 25th corresponded to our May 21st. In the sacred year, Pachons commenced March 17th when the 25th corresponded to our April the 11th, and this is the only year which brings the date near enough to the Vernal equinox to identify the 25th of Pachons with the festival of the full moon at Easter, or with the festival of the second Horus, whom Plutarch calls the *afterbirth* of Isis, which was celebrated just after the Vernal Equinox. It is impossible for the equinox and Easter festival to have fallen on the 25th Pachons since the calendar was changed in the year 25 B.C.!

In the old Egyptian and Coptic calendar the 8th of Pachons is marked as the day on which "*our Lord Jesus Christ went up on high into the heavens*."[50] As the month began on March 17th in the sacred year, the 8th of Pachons was *our* March the 25th, the day of the equinox upon which the sun crossed the line, came out of Egypt, or went up into heaven.[51] The day of the equinox was the fact of facts fixed forever in relation to the solar resurrection, whilst in the celestial allegory or mythical representation, the birth, rebirth, resurrection, and ascension were four forms of one and the same event. When the Alexandrian year or new style was introduced during the reign of Augustus Cæsar, in the year 25 B.C., this date of Pachons 8th=March 25th, sacred year, had *already receded* to the 4th of May. From Pachons the 8th (our March 25th) to May the 4th is exactly forty days, so that *the ascension into heaven that was celebrated by the Coptic church according to the later calendar was the day of the equinox in the calendar of the second year.*[52] Thus the two different days of the resurrection and ascension, which are some three thousand years of tropical time apart, resolve into one and the same day of the equinox, and the ascent of the solar Christ or luni-solar Khunsu, whose birthday had been celebrated according to the ancient calendar some 3,000 years before it was readjusted by Augustus Cæsar 25 B.C. when March 25th old style was represented by May 4th new style. This means that nearly 5,000 years since "*our Lord*" ascended into heaven on the day of the Vernal equinox; and this date had been continued by the Coptic Christians without change. The fact is further shown by the entry for Pachons 14th (May 23rd, 1878) stating that "*The sun enters Gemini*"—instead of the Bull—that being one whole sign behind time in consequence of non-readjustment. The difference of forty days between the calendar of the sacred year and that of the Alexandrian year is shown by September 18 = October 28; November 17 = December 27; February 15 = March 27; June 15 = July 25. These forty days may now be compared with those in the "Acts of the Apostles." In this book it is declared that the risen Christ "*showed himself alive after his passion by many proofs, appearing unto them by the space of forty days,*" at the end of which "*he was taken up, and a cloud received him out of their sight.*" Here the difference of forty days between the resurrection and ascension, which are one in the solar mythos, is identical with that in the two Egyptian calendars. Further, it appears possible that the change in the reckoning from old style to new may have a bearing on the impossible history recorded by Luke, who says, "*It came to pass in those days that there went out a decree from Augustus that all the world should be taxed,*" or enrolled, and it was at the time when Joseph and Mary were on their way to be taxed that Mary brought forth the child. The writer continues, "*This was the first enrollment made when Quirinus was governor of Syria.*"[53] Justin Martyr in his *First Apology* tells the Romans, with all the impudence of ignorance, that they may *assure* themselves of the birth of Jesus of Bethlehem, by *means of the census made in the time of Quirinus the first procurator in Judea!* Whereas *history proves that Quirinus was not governor until some years after the date given for the birth of Jesus.*

It was not until the 37th year from the battle of Actium, A. D., that Quirinus was sent by Cæsar to look after the Hebrew contribution to the imperial revenue and take an account of the substance of the Syrians, in which year the taxings were made.[54] But there *had been a decree issued by Augustus Cæsar*, if not to all the world, yet to a portion of it most important for the present purpose. It was in the year 25 B.C., in his reign, that the Alexandrian year was introduced into Egypt and the calendar corrected; the vague year was then converted by Augustus into an exact year, which the Copts have handed down to our own times. This was the date of a half-phoenix period, a phoenix having appeared in the year 275 B.C., and the previous half-phoenix fallen in the year 525 B.C.,[55] A fresh census of population, or enrollment of those who paid taxes, was probably taken at this time. Be this as it may, there *was a change of forty days in the date for collecting the taxes*. According to the Coptic church and the old Egyptian calendar the 28th of Kyhak is the end of *Saumel Milâd,* the Christmas fast, and the next day, Eedel-Milâd, is the "*birth-day of our Lord Christ*," the 29th of Kyhak being our Christmas day.

THE CHRISTIAN FATHERS IDENTIFIED THE BIRTH OF CHRIST BOTH WITH THE TIME OF THE VERNAL EQUINOX AND THE WINTER SOLSTICE.

Cassini had demonstrated the fact that the date assigned to the birth of Christ is astronomical. It is calculated, according to the tradition of the Roman church, by an astronomical epoch, in which, as shown by the modern tables, the middle conjunction of the moon with the sun happened on the 24th of March, according to the Julian form (re-established a little after by Augustus), at half-past one o'clock in the morning, at the meridian of Jerusalem, the very day of the middle equinox. The day following the 25th was the day of the incarnation according to tradition of the church as represented by Augustine,[56] but which was the time of birth according to Clement Alexander. Here the incarnation coincides with the conjunction of the sun and moon at the end and rebeginning of the equinoctial year. Nine months after this conjunction of the solar father and lunar mother, who are portrayed in the earliest known picture of the crucified, the divine child was born in the Winter solstice, December the 25th, the date assigned to the birth of the young sun-god Mithras, and to Horus the child in Egypt. Plutarch tell us that the virgin mother Isis was *delivered of Harpocrates* (*i.e.* Horus considered as the child of the mother alone) *about the Winter tropic, he being in the first shootings and sprouts very imperfect and tender. Which is the reason, as the Egyptians say, that when the lentils begin to spring up they offer him their tops for first fruits*. They also observe the festival of her afterbirth (the Hebrew *Shiloh*), or Horus, the son of the father, after the Vernal equinox. These two astronomical dates were continued *faute de mieux*, by the Equinoctial

Christolators, who could not account for them in the absence of the gnosis, hence the solstice and spring equinox are *both assigned as the time of the one birth*, which is impossible as human history, but is true to the mythos and the two Horuses The birthday of Mithra, the invincible one, was celebrated as an ancient festival, on the 25th of December, the day of the solstice, our Christmas day. He was born in a cave, and wherever Mithra was worshipped, the cave was consecrated to him; as the "*highly-mysterious cavern*" was sacred to the sun-god in Egypt.

In the gospel of James, the child Jesus was born in a cave.[57] The gospel of pseudo-Matthew says Mary entered the "*cave below a cavern in which there was never any light*" to bring forth the light of the world, and on the third day she "*went out of the cave and entering a stable, put her child in a manger*."[58] In the *History of Joseph the Carpenter* the Christ affirms that his mother gave birth to him in a cave[59] According to the Arabic *Gospel of the Infancy*,[60] the birth occurred in a cave.[61] The cave of Mithras was that of the sun born in the Winter solstice when this occurred in the sign of the Sea-goat. *Abba Udda*, the Akkadian name of the tenth month, answering roughly to December, the month of Capricorn, denotes the Cave of Light. The cave, or Winter solstice in Capricorn, was the birthplace of the Mithraic Messiah from 2410 to 255 B.C., and this was continued as the cave or birthplace of the Christ after it ceased to be applicable to the solar god. Justin says that Christ was born on the same day that the sun was reborn *in stabula Augiae*;[62] and the stable of Augias, cleansed by Herakles in his sixth labour, corresponds to the cave in the Sea-goat. Thus the cave and the stable are two types of the birthplace at the solstice. Justin, determined to include both, asserts that Christ was *born in the stable and afterwards took refuge in the cave*. No Messiah, however, whether called Mithras, Horus or Christ could have been born in the stable of Augias after the date of 255 B.C., because the solstice had passed out of that sign into the asterism of the Archer.

The supposed historical Christ had no other birthday than that of the solar god, the birthday of the year, whether reckoned from the solstice or the equinox, and, as a specimen of the way in which the apostolic institutions were derived, take what Chrysostom says, who wrote on the nativity of Christ, in Antioch, about A.D. 380. He declares, "*It is not yet ten years since this day was made known to us*." He says, further, "*Among those inhabiting the west, it was known before from ancient and primitive times, and to the dwellers from Thrace to Cadiz* (Gadeira) *it was previously familiar and well known*." But this birthday of the Lord was not known in the east, at Antioch, where the name of Christian was said to have been first adopted, on the verge of the Holy Land itself![63] We also learn that as late as the fifth century

Leo the Great was compelled to rebuke the "*pestiferous persuasion*" of those Christians who were found to be celebrating Christmas day *not for the birth of Christ, but for the resurrection of the sun*. The actual origines of Equinoxtial Christolatry were not then superseded.

Now, at the time when the calendar was changed in Egypt by the decree of Augustus, the date of the solstice and the festival of the youthful sun-god was brought forward into the month Toubeh (Tebi), so that the general collection of taxes then coincided with the date assigned to the birthday of the Christ who is held to have fulfilled the law in being circumcised on the 6th day of the month Toubeh, or the eighth day after Christmas. the collection of taxes was an ancient institution, but *it was newly associated with the month Toubeh in consequence of this decree of Caesar Augustus, which introduced a change of calendar into the Roman empire; and possibly this was the world*, which was connected by tradition with the birth of Christ.

Amongst other features in the common likeness between the stories of Krishna and the Christ, there is one relating to the time of taxing. When Vasudeva is carrying away the newborn child from the clutches of Kansa, the Herod of Purana, who slays the children of Devaki in his endeavor to kill Krishna, he meets with Nanda and his companions the cowherds, who are coming *to pay their taxes of a yearly tribute to Kansa* (a toll paid to the Devil,) *which was just then due*.[64] In both legends the time of taxing or paying tribute is like our Christmas quarter-day, coincident with the birth of the solar god; and this date was changed by the decree of Augustus Cæsar, which probably necessitated a new enrollment or census in Egypt, and thus a tradition relating primarily to the child Horus may have survived in connection with the child Christ in the gospel according to Luke.

## PARALLELS BETWEEN JESUS, HORUS AND RA.

The youthful Messiah who was the manifestor of the Seven Powers in the sign of the solar birthplace was one in phenomena, but he had several personifications and names in the different cults. He was Horus in the Osirian mythos; Har-khuti in the Sut Typhonian; Iu-em-hept in the cult of Atum; and several characters have been reproduced in the Christ of the canonical gospels.

The Christ is the good Shepherd. So was Horus.
Christ is the Bread of Life. So was Horus.
Christ is the truth and the Life. So was Horus.
Christ is the Fan-bearer. So was Horus.

Christ is the Door of Life. Horus was the Path by which the dead travel out of the sepulchre; he is the god whose name is written as the Road.

The Jesus of the gospels is the coming one, "*He that should come*;" "*He that cometh*; as was the Egyptian Jesus, Iu-em-hept.

It is said of the future manifestor, "*Then shall they see the Son of Man coming in a cloud with power and great glory. But when these things begin to come to pass, look up, and lift your heads; because your redemption draweth nigh.*"[65]

And of Osiris coming in the clouds of heaven we read: "*The Osiris passes through the clouds, turns back the opposers, gives life to the ministers of the sun. The face of the Osiris is rendered great by his crown. Lift up your heads! pay ye attention! make way for your Lord.*"[66]

Jesus came in the name of the Lord. Horus was the Lord by name.

The Jesus of Paul is the second Adam. The Egyptian Jesus was the second Atum.

The "Litany of Ra" is addressed to the solar god in a variety of characters, many of which are assigned to the Christ of the gospels. Ra is the "*supreme power, the beetle that rests in the empyrean, who is born as his own son.*"[67] This is the God in John's gospel, who says, "*I and my father are one*," and who is the father born as his own son; for he says in knowing and seeing the son "*from henceforth ye know him and have seen him*,"[68] *i.e.* the father. Ra is the "*soul that speaks.*"[69] Christ is the "Word." Ra as the god of earth, Tanen, makes his own members, is the only one who fashions his own body, and is earth-born and self-embodied.[70] In like manner Jesus fashions his own body without human father. "*Ra calls his gods to life when he arrives in his hidden sphere*," "*he imparts the breath of life to the souls in their place.*"[71] "*They receive it and develop.*" Jesus "*came unto his own, and as many as received him, to them gave he power to become the sons of God*," Thus he "calls his Gods to life." Khepr-Ra is twin-born. he is *Khepr who becomes two children.*" These are the Sut-Horus or the double Horus. They reappear in the gospels as John and Jesus, who are announced by the same angel, and who are six months apart, like the Horus of the double equinox. The relationship of Jesus to John could not be more perfectly expressed than by the description of Ra as the "*Supreme power! He who always goes towards him who precedes him*;" and "*he whose head shines more than he who is before him.*"[72] The first action of Jesus in this gospel is to "*go towards him who precedes him*," that is John; and then his head "*shines more than he who is before him*," with the Spirit descending on it from heaven like a dove, which abode upon him. This was in the scene of the baptism; and Ra is called, "*the brilliant one who shines in the waters.*"[73] Ra is the "*Master of the Light, who reveals hidden things, the spirit who speaks to the gods in their spheres.*"[74] Such is the claim of Jesus.

In one character Ra is the transformer.[75] Christ is the same on the mount of transformation. Ra is the destroyer of venom.[76] Jesus says, "In my name they shall take up serpents, and if they drink any deadly thing it shall not hurt them."[77] Ra is also the god who "makes the mummy come forth." Jesus makes the mummy come forth in the shape of Lazarus; and in the Roman catacombs the arisen Lazarus is not only represented as a mummy but *is* an Egyptian mummy which has been eviscerated and swathed for the eternal abode. Thus Lazarus is the typical mummy-figure which would be signified if the name were derived from Laz (or Ras, Eg.), to be raised up, and aru (Eg.), the mummy shape; which with the Greek terminal ς, would be Lazarus the risen mummy. The supposed historic Christ who raises Lazarus in the Christian monuments[78] is identical with Hours (or Ra) who raises or bids the mummy to "*come forth.*" Jesus cries "*Lazarus, come forth*; and in the monuments Lazarus does come forth a mummy. Moreover, Sut-Anup, the earliest Mercury, the attendant on the dead, who is often seen embracing the mummy, appeared in the same picture in the Greek form of Mercury.

In the character of Aperto the god is said to be he "*who furnishes the inhabitants of the empyrean with funeral things.*" The Christ says Mary had kept the ointment of spikenard against the day of his funeral.[79] Aperto, or Aper, is Anubis, the god of things funeral, whose double holy house is in Annu; the house being the Beth, and Beth-Annu, may be compared with Bethany. As Senekher, Ra is "*shining face*;" both the Anointed and the Anointer. "*The spirit who anoints the body, his form is that of shining face.*"[80] Christ is the Anointed; his divinity rests on that; he is also represented as the shining face, when "*his face did shine as the sun.*" "*Shining-face*" is the "*great walker who goes over the same course.*" Jesus in the character of "shining face," went up into a mountain apart. Ra, the supreme power, is the *Master* of souls "*who is in his obelisk*"— the "*chief of the confined gods.*"[81] Jesus is taken prisoner by Satan and carried to the top of the mount and the obelisk or pinnacle of the temple, where he shows his mastery. Ra is also associated with the "*double obelisk.*"[82] This is apparently reproduced in the two elevations of the Christ on the high mountain and upon the pinnacle. Ra is "*the spirit who is raised upon the two mysterious horizons.*" These two horizons appear perplexingly in the gospels as those of Judea and Galilee. The very works said by one writer to be done in the one region, another writer localizes in the opposite country. The "mysteries of the two horizons," and of the dual deity Har-Makhu, are greatly increased in the gospels. Origen confessed that the attempt to reconcile these opposite statements made him giddy. Ra manifests as the weeper,

Remi. The suffering god passes through "*Rem-Rem*," the place of weeping, and thus conquers on behalf of his followers. The Osirified in this character exclaims, "*I find no escape from weeping on the Week of Abtu*," the place of the second birth,[83] the Passion Week of Osiris. In the *Ritual* the god says, "*I have desolated the place of Rem-Rem*."[84] Jesus also sustains the character of Remi the weeper, the "*timid one who sheds tears in the form of the afflicted*." THE WORDS OF JOHN, "JESUS WEPT," are like a carven statue of Remi. Ra manifests as the "*timid one who sheds tears; his form is that of the afflicted*,"[85] and Christ, the Weeper, is the afflicted one, born to suffer.[86]

## JESUS AND RA BOTH HIDE THEMSELVES.

Under the form of *Netert*, Ra is "*the spirit that causes his disappearance*."[87] Jesus is caught up by the spirit that drives him into the wilderness and causes his disappearance.[88] Ra's "*form is that of the hidden body*;" "*he who hides his body within himself*," and who in the next line is "*more courageous than those who surround him*." Jesus, when surrounded by those who took up stones to cast at him, "*hid himself and passed invisibly through their midst*;" his "*form is that of the god with the hidden body*," he too is the power who "*hides his body within himself*."[89] Ra manifests as "*the burning one*;" he who "*sends destruction*" or "*sends his fire into the place of destruction*;"[90] "*he sends fire upon the rebels*,"[91] his form is that of the "*god of the furnace*,"[92] Christ also comes in the person of the burning one and sender of destruction by fire. He is proclaimed by Matthew to be the baptizer with fire.[93] He says "I am come to send fire on the earth."[94] He is portrayed as "god of the furnace" which shall "burn up the chaff with unquenchable fire."[95] He is to cast the rebellious into "a furnace of fire,"[96] and send the condemned ones into "everlasting fire."[97] Ra is the god who "opens pathways in the sarcophagus, his form is that of the god who makes the roads." He "makes the road in the empyrean."

The risen god "causes the development of his body in the empyrean. His form is that of the inhabitant of the empyrean."[98] "His form is that of the eternal essence," as penetrator of the empyrean.[99] In effecting this "he shines and he sees his mysteries." He is likewise named the splendid one who lights up the sarcophagus in the form of Shepi.[100] He "raises his soul and conceals his body" (as Herba; her, to rise up, ba, the soul) "in its place." So Jesus is the resurrection and the life, the door, the tomb-breaker, road-maker, and establisher of a foot-hold in the empyrean. In the vanishing vision of the risen Christ, "he was taken up, and a cloud had received him" as the inhabitant of the empyrean.[101] The "Litany" collects the manifold characters that make up the total god (Teb-temt), and the gospels have gathered up the mythical remains; thus the result is in each case identical. IT WILL BE PROVED THAT THE HISTORY OF CHRIST IN THE GOSPELS IS A LONG AND COMPLETE CATALOGUE OF LIKENESSES TO THE MYTHICAL MESSIAH. In one version of the gospel according to John,[102] instead of the "*only begotten son*" of God, the reading is the "*only begotten God;*" and it has been declared impossible for the "*sacred writer*" to have employed the phrase "*only begotten God.*" It is said to be contrary to the genius of the gospel and opposed to the general teaching of the New Testament. These things, however, can only be determined by the doctrines and the gnosis that were pre-extant. Of course the current Christology knows nothing of any such possible variant as the "*only begotten God,*" because the Kamite origines have been left out of the reckoning. But the "only begotten God" was an especial type of mythology, and the phrase recovers the divinity whose emblem is the beetle. This was Khepr-Ptah, who, like Atum, was reborn as his own son, Iu-em-hept, the Egyptian Jesus. "*To denote an only begotten or a father,*" says Hor-Apollo,[103] the Egyptians "*delineate a scarabaeus.* And they symbolize by this an only-begotten because the scarabæus is a creature self-produced, being unconceived by a female." This was in a cult which tried hard to dethrone the female, and exalt the male god as the only one. The "only-begotten god" is a well-known type, then, of divinity worshipped in Egypt as Khepr-Ptah and Khepr-Atum, and in each cult the Messiah-son and manifestor was the only-begotten god Iu-em-hept, and Iu the son (Su), whether of Ptah or Atum, is Iusu or Jesus. This, according to the text, is the Christ, the Word, the Manifestor in John's gospel. Of course the reading is totally opposed to the historic interpretation, and is therefore good evidence of its authority as an original reading. This god is the express image of the Christ of John's gospel, who begins in the first chapter, without father or mother, and is the Word of the beginning, the opener and architect, the light of the world, the self-originated and only-begotten God. The very phraseology of John is common in the Egyptian texts, which tell of him who was "the Beginner of Becoming, from the first," "who made all things, but was not made."[104] There were Christian traditions which support this identification of the "only-begotten god," who is extant in this genuine reading of John's gospel, with Khepr-Ptah. Some of the Fathers, Ambrose, for instance, knew that the beetle was a symbol of the Christ. Augustine also identifies the Christ with, or as,. the good scarabæus: "Bonus ille scarabæus meus, non ea tantum de causa quod unigenitus, quod ipsemet sui auctor mortalium speciem induerit sed quod in hâc nostra fæce sese voluntaverit et ex hâc ipsâ nasci voluerit."[105]

In accordance with this continuation of the Kamite symbols, it was also maintained by some sectaries that Jesus was a potter, not a carpenter. The AGnostics made the most of the fragments of the mythos which they had collected, but knew not how to interpret. The truth is that this "only-begotten god," Khepr-Ptah, was the Potter personified, who is portrayed sitting at the potter's wheel, forming the egg or shaping the vase-symbol of creation.

When Osiris the saviour comes down to earth as the child Horus to cross it "as a substitute," he exclaims; "The gates of earth open to me. Seb has opened the bolts, he has opened the chief or lower abode wide. The Osiris comes. He prevails over his heart, he prevails over his hand, he prevails over the meals, he prevails over the waters, he prevails over the streams, he prevails over the pools, he prevails over everything done against him in hades, he prevails over what he has been ordered to do on earth. The Osiris is born like, or as a Word. He lives!—then it is off the bread of Seb."[106] Half the history of Christ on earth is contained in this passage. He comes to earth as a substitute. He is born as the Word. He is the great prevailer over the waters as the worker of miracles. He also prevails over the meals by working three different miracles, and is very possibly born into the house of Seb, represented by Joseph.

Seb is the god of earth, god the father of earth, therefore the especial father of the sun-god in the earth; and as he is also a god in time or Kronus in person, he is the divine father on earth of the Messiah-son who manifests in time. Thus Seb is the father of Osiris or Horus on earth. "My father is Seb, my mother is Nu, I am Horus," i.e. as son of earth and heaven[107] When on earth he is in the dwelling of Seb." In the same way, house and food for the Christ are found by Joseph. Now the iconography of the catacombs continually furnishes a bridge from Egypt to Rome, by which we can pass over, independently of the alleged history. In certain sculptures of the "first ages of Christianity," the Christ or Horus is depicted, without a nimbus, and with his feet resting on a scarf that is upheld by a naked female, who is identified by Didron and others as a personification of earth. But, in other sculptures the supporter of the youthful Christ is an aged man with a beard, who undoubtedly represents the earth god Seb. In each case the head and shoulders only of the figure are shown ; and the earth was called the "back of Seb." Seb's back sometimes opened female-fashion, as the bringer-forth on earth and in time, hence Seb was a mother as well as the father. Seb is the opener of the earth for the solar god. The consort of Seb is the mother heaven, named Nu ; but *Meri* is also an Egyptian name for heaven as well as of the genitrix. Thus Seb and Meri (Nu) for earth and heaven would afford two mythic originals for Joseph and Mary as parents of the divine child. It is more likely, however that the female figure is the mother heaven (Nu or Meri), and Seb the father earth. This typology was continued in Rome, and can be identified by the Kamite mythology ; but it cannot be pretended that these allegorical figures portray the human parents[108]

In another and following chapter there is a variant of Seb, written Aseb, given as a title to the father Osiris. It is said : "Osiris, the good opener, is Aseb ; Aseb is the brother of Isis." Aseb, then, is a variant of Seb, the opener of earth, the father of Horus on earth, and there is nothing improbable in the suggestion that the name of Joseph renders the Egyptian *Aseb*. *Aseb* is the name of a typical seat or throne of rule, in accordance with the Hebrew *Iosheb*, to sit, to be enthroned, and *Iazab*, to set firmly in place. This seat or throne was personated by Seb, and is likewise portrayed by the bearded old man who supports the youthful Christ,[109] as the God on earth. So Amenhept IV says he rises and appears on the throne of Seb (i.e. on earth) to assume the functions of Atum, the sun of the lower world. The Christ, as Horus or the Osiris in the *Ritual*, has four different places and kinds of birth in the course of making his transformations.[110] In the mythical Abtu (Abydos) there are "*Four Places of New Birth*" for the Osiris or the Osirified:

(1) *The Great Place of Birth.*
(2) *The Typical Place of New Birth.*
(3) *The Creative Place of New Birth.*
(4) *The Good Place of New Birth.*

Thus the god or Messiah has one place of birth and three of rebirth ; and these four are repeated for the Christ in the gospels. Jesus is born in Bethlehem as the "*great place of birth.*" (This is glossed by Matthew "thou Bethlehem art not the least ;" with reference to Micah. V. 2). The "*typical place of new birth*" is in the water of Jordan. The "*creative place of new birth*" is on the mount of transfiguration, where the voice from heaven again said, "*This is my beloved son.*" The fourth and final place, the good place of rebirth, is the grave from which he rose again. This the Egyptians called "*the good dwelling.*"[111]

Considered as those of a human being, the character and teachings of the Christ in the gospels are composed of contradictions and opposites impossible to harmonize. In fact, the three hundred sects of Christians who are to-day engaged in formulating and defining the theology of their assumed founder and denying each other's interpretation, do but inevitably represent the organic disunity from the beginning, and reflect the fragmentary nature of the origines. Christ is the Prince of peace. He is born to bring peace on earth. He says : "*Peace I leave with you : my peace I give you.*" "*Peace unto you.*"[112] But he also asserts that he is not the bringer of peace. "*Think not that I came to send peace on earth : I came not to send peace, but a sword.*"[113] And not only can these two opposite characters be explained according to the mythos, they constitute the one being of a dual nature who is the bringer of peace by name in one character as Iu-em-hept, and a sword personified in the other. In this aspect the god says, "*I am the living image of Tum, proceeding from his body* (or person) *a sword.*" And in the dual character he can affirm of himself, "*I am the first Child, the great disturber, the great tranquilizer, whose name is the root of Osiris* (cf.. the root of Jesse), *by which he spares thy life.*"[114] This is said by the elder Horus, the sun in the west, who was the warrior-god that had to descend and cut his way through a world of opposing powers, and who emerged on the horizon of the resurrection as the conqueror of death and darkness, the way-maker through the tomb, the bringer of that peace which is brought by the re-arisen Iusu or Jesus. "*The god Contention is then as the god Peace, with the great hold he has in his hand,*" by which the Osiris lives and is at rest.[115]

In one of the quotations from the *Gospel of the Egyptians*, made both by Clement of Alexandria and Clement of Rome we are told that the *Lord having been asked by Salome when his kingdom would come, replied, "When you have trampled under foot the garment of shame* (or modesty) : *when two shall be one, when that which is without shall be like that which is within, and when the male with the female shall be neither male nor female.*"[116] This doctrine is virtually expressed in the 17th chapter of the *Ritual*, which is entitled the Egyptian gospel or faith. Osiris is an androgynous being ; the one god who includes the biunity of both sexes (or of the double Horus). During his "*bloody flux*," Osiris *tesh-tesh* suffers in his feminine phase, and is called the sun in linen ; he may be said to wear the "*garment of shame*," or modesty. But "*Osiris goes into Tattu and he finds the soul of the sun there.*" Here his two halves or souls are united in one to form the perfect being. These two halves are otherwise represented by the two Horuses, the child (epicene) and the virile male ; also by the soul of Shu and the soul Tefnut, who are male and female. That which has to be trampled under foot is described in the *Ritual* as the failing which has to be cut clean away before the soul in its two halves is made one in Tattu, and the Osiris, as Horus, is no longer male nor female in the new kingdom of the coming one which came every year.

The more hidden the meaning in the history the more satisfactorily is it explained by the mythos ; the more mystical the doctrine, the more obviously is it mythical. The two halves of Osiris are—Horus the child of the virgin only, the mystic word, and Horus Ma-Kheru, the word made truth or become law ; the one who *did* what the other *said*. In like manner Khunsu, the Good Peace or Comforter. These are the two characters of Christ and the Paraclete. Christ is the word made flesh (as the first Horus had the human form) the sayer solely, the speaker in parables only. In the second phase he will tell the disciples "*plainly of the father*."[117] In this he will send the comforter, Helper or Nefer-Hept,—also the "spirit of truth"[118] or (Ma-Kheru),—as the god in the second character, in which he came to them after the resurrection, the bringer of *peace*.

The "*spirit of truth*" is identified with Ma-Kheru, the word that becomes law, as he who will be sent to "*convict the world in respect of Sin, and of Righteousness, and of Judgment*."[119]

The two halves of Horus were also continued in the *Agia Psyche* and *Agion Pneuma* of the Greeks, as two more abstract forms of the Holy Ghost. These had their followers in two different and opposed sects of Christians : the one being the *υχι* οι(Psychikoi), the worshippers of the Holy Spirit as *αγια ψυχη*; the other the *πνευματι οι,* who held the Paraclete to be the more perfect form of the revealer.

The peculiar Egyptian doctrine of the Word that *makes*, *enacts*, or *does the truth* is perfectly expressed in the passages ; "*If we* DO *not the truth*,"[120] and "*He that* DOETH *the* TRUTH *cometh to light*."[121] So is it in the Apocrypha : "*In the Word of the Lord are his Works*."[122] The two characters of the Sayer and Doer in the mythos constitute the double foundation of the Gospels. Papius tells us that Matthew first wrote the Words of the Sayer, and Mark added what Jesus did ; and this twin record of the Sayer and Doer is distinctly visible, as two or more collections of Sayings and Doings obviously unconnected in the gospels according to Matthew and Mark.

## JESUS AND HORUS AT 12 AND AT 30 YEARS OF AGE.

The first was the child, who always remained a child. In Egypt the boy or girl wore the Horus-lock of childhood until twelve years of age. Thus childhood ended about the twelfth year. But although adultship was then entered upon by the *Sherau*, and the transformation of the boy into manhood began, the *full adultship was not attained until thirty years of age*. The man of thirty years was the typical adult. The age of adultship was thirty years, as it was in Rome under the Lex Pappia. The *homme fait* is the man whose years are triaded by tens, and who is Khemt. As with the man so it is with the god, and the second Horus, the same god in his second character, is the Khemt or Khem-Horus, the typical adult of thirty years. The god up to twelve years was Horus the son of Isis, the mother's child. The virile Horus, the adult of thirty years, was representative of the Fatherhood, and this Horus is the anointed son of Osiris. These two characters of Horus the child and Horus the adult of thirty years are reproduced in the two phases to which the life of Jesus is limited in the gospels.

John furnishes no historic dates for the time when the Word was incarnated and became, flesh, nor for the childhood of Jesus, nor for the transformation into the Messiah. But Luke tells us that the child of twelve years was the wonderful youth, and that he increased in wisdom and stature.[123] This is the length of years assigned to Horus the child ; and this phase of the child-Christ's life is followed by the baptism and anointing, the descent of the pubescent Spirit with the consecration of the Messiah in Jordan, when Jesus "*began to be about thirty years of age.*" It has been sufficiently explained that the earliest anointing was the consecration of puberty ; and here at the full age of the typical adult, the Christ who was previously a child, the child of the virgin mother, is suddenly made into the Messiah, the Lord's anointed. And just as the second Horus was regenerated and this time begotten by the father, so in the transformation scene of the baptism in Jordan the voice of the father authenticates the change into full adultship with the voice from heaven, "*This is my beloved son, in whom I am well pleased*";[124] the spirit of pubescence or the *Ruach* being represented by the descending dove, called the Spirit of God. Thus from the time when the child-Christ was about twelve years of age until that of the typical *homme fait* of Egypt, which was the age assigned to Horus when he became the adult god, there is no history. This is in exact accordance with the Kamite allegory of the double Horus. And the mythos alone will account for the chasm which is wide and deep enough to engulf a supposed history of eighteen years. Childhood cannot be carried beyond the twelfth year, and the child-Horus always remained the child, just as the child-Christ does in Italy and in the German folk-tales. The mythical record, founded on nature, went no further, and there the history consequently halts within the prescribed limits, to rebegin with the anointed and regenerated Christ at the age of Khem-Horus, the adult of thirty years.

As we have seen, the Christian Father, Clement Alexander, identifies the birthday of Christ with the great luni-solar festival of the youthful god Khunsu, which was determined by the full moon of Easter ; and Khunsu appears to be the mythical prototype that is more particularly reproduced in the gospel according to Luke. In his description of the "*heavenly host praising God and saying, 'Glory to God in the highest, and on earth peace and good will toward men,'*" various authorities read "*peace, good pleasure amongst men.*" This conveys a perfect rendering of the title of Khunsu, the "Nefer-Hept," or divine child. *Nefer* signifies good, and *hept* means peace, luck, happiness and therefore good pleasure.

The Nefer-hept, or Iu-em-hept, was the youthful manifestor who represented the peace and good luck, pleasure or felicity, promised to men at his advent, and he is portrayed as the *coming* youth, a slim and lissom figure, always in a marching attitude.[125] The double Horus or twin Sut-Horus type of deity was unified in the one god as *Khunsu-nefer-hept* who is the *good peace* in person. At times he is called Khunsu-Ra, and at others Khunsu-Taht, in consequence of being the child of both the sun and moon. He is said to unite the two Lots of Horus, the son of Isis, in one, and is designated the Lord *Horus at the centre of the double earth,* which he unites in one and thus abolishes the mid-wall of partition as god of full moon at the Easter equinox.[126] Khunsu might have been the Kamite prototype of the Christ set forth by Paul. "*For he is our peace who hath made both one, and hath broken down the middle wall of partition, . . . for to make in himself of twain, one new man, so making peace.*"[127] Not only were the twin brothers blended in him, he is also the God of gods who was especially entitled to say, "*I and my father are one.*" He is called the "*illustrious seed of the entire Lord, the issue of Kamutf,*"[128] the male-mother, a mystical title of his parent Amen-Ra. He is the registrar of the decrees of this god, whose name signifies the hidden.[129]

He was also the soli-lunar reckoner of time by the year, who carries the stylus and palm-branch in his hands, and on his head the full-moon of Easter which determined the festival of the resurrection in Egypt, as it still does in the cult of Equinoctial Christolatry. Khunsu is the calculator of the length of life. He is said to give years to whom he chooses, to increase the length of life for those who obey his will ; he asks years for whomsoever he pleases. *Life issues from him and health is in him.* He was likewise the divine healer *par excellence* amongst other healers and saviors, especially as the opponent of obsessing demons, and the caster-out of evil spirits. In the inscription of the "Possessed Princess" he is expressly called the "Great God, driver away of possession," or of obsessing spirits that enter the body. He has two characters, the *Sayer*, and the *Doer*, or the Word and the Word made Truth, as the dual divinity was described in his two aspects which are represented in the gospel of Luke as the "Word and the Power."[130] He is denominated the "*Giver of Oracles*" in one phase, "*Expeller of obsessing spirits*" in the other. In the Stele of the "Possessed Princess" the image of this is sent for by the chief of Bakhten that the god in effigy may come and cast out an obsessing spirit from his young daughter, Bentrash, who has "*an evil movement in her limbs.*" Then

Khunsu, the giver of oracles and expeller of demons, described as Khunsu-nefer-hept, having imparted "*his divine virtue fourfold to Khunsu the giver of oracles*"—his other self—the god sets out for the land of Bakhten. He exorcised the evil spirit and cured the maiden. *The demon recognizes the deity and says to Khunsu the bringer of peace, "Thou hast come in peace, great God! driver away of obsessors ; I am thy slave, I will go to the place whence I came to give peace to thy heart on account of the journey here.*"[131]

This character of Khunsu the exorcizer of evil spirits is especially reproduced in the Christ of Luke's gospel. Following his investiture with the Messiahship and the conflict with the devil in the wilderness, he begins to teach and utter forth the logia ; and it is recorded that "*they were astonished at his doctrine, for his Word was with Power.*" The proof of this follows in the performance of the healer's first miracle. "*There was a man which had an unclean devil.*" This devil likewise recognizes the divinity as the holy one of God. "*And Jesus rebuked him, saying, Hold thy peace, and come out of him.*" The evil spirit being cast out, the amazed witnesses said, "*What a word is this!*" or "*What word is this?*" the rendering being difficult in the absence of the doctrine, which was known, for example, to Faustus, the Maichean, who affirmed that the *power* of Christ dwelt in the sun and his *wisdom* in the moon, which identifies him with the soli-lunar Khunsu-nefer-hept ; it might mean in Oriental style, what work is this?

When the obsessing demon departs from Bentrash it is on condition that the god will cause the prince of Bakhten to "*make a great sacrifice before* (or to) *that spirit.*" This was done. "*He made a great sacrifice before Khunsu and that spirit upon a good day for them.*"[132] The sacrifice stipulated for is not described, but it can be ascertained elsewhere.

## THE PIG OF EASTER.

Khunsu was the divinity of the month Pachous or Pa-khuns, the month of Khunsu, which began March 17 in the sacred year, or April 26 in the Alexandrian year. In the zodiac of Denderah, Khunsu is portrayed standing in the disk of the full moon of Easter, after a vernal equinox had passed into the sign of Pisces. Here he is represented *in the act of offering the pig,* which he holds out straight in his extended left hand. Once a year only did the Egyptians eat the pig, and then as a sacrifice offered up at the full moon of Easter. Herodotus declined to give the reason for this custom. The pig, however, had been a type of Typhon as Rerit, the sow, and was continued as the sacrifice offered up by Khunsu for a propitiation or devil's Tax to Typhon. When the luni-solar god had won the annual triumph over the powers of darkness, the pig of Typhon was offered up and eaten as the typical sacrifice. This was the custom, ages before the picture was set in the decans of Pisces, to coincide with the year 255 B.C. The festival of the pig in the full moon was the one by which the Egyptians had long regulated the Apis period, there being a great lunar celebration every twenty second year.[133]

The pig of the equinox passed into the later boar of the solstice. Khunsu standing in the disk of the full moon of Easter offers the pig as a sacrifice when he has attained the horizon of the resurrection at the Vernal equinox, the exact date of which is determined by the full moon. Thus the sacrifice to be offered to Khunsu and Typhon on a good day, in the land of Bakhten, would naturally be that of the pig.[134]

## THE DEVILS AND THE SWINE.

So when the exorcist of demons casts out "legion" there is a great sacrifice of swine. The devils entreat Jesus not to bid them depart into the abyss, but as a herd of swine were feeding on the mountain they ask permission to enter into these. "*And he gave them leave*." Then the devil came out of the man and entered the swine, which ran down into the lake,[135] —exactly as it is in the Egyptian scenes of the judgment, where condemned souls are ordered back into the abyss, and they make the return passage down to the lake of primordial matter by taking the shape of swine. Horus also in the *Ritual* causes the transformation into the pig. "*Says Horus to the gods, When I sent him to his place, he went, and he has been transformed into a black pig!*" "*Hateful is the pig of Horus, turning his shape into the abomination of a great pig*."[136] Such a transformation originated in the lunar phases being represented by the sow, pig and boar, as a typical trinity consisting of genitrix (Typhon or Menat), Sut, Horus.

This character of the mighty exorcist and chaser away of demons portrayed in the god Khunsu and the Christ of Luke's gospel is not represented in the gospel according to John, which alone does not contain the story of the demons entering the swine to rush down into the abyss. John's gospel is here as much of a blank as is the *Ritual* in regard to Khunsu, who is only mentioned once.[137] No case of possession is to be found in it. There is neither the "*certain man*" who "*had devils*" this "*long time*."[138] Nor the child possessed with a devil.[139] Nor the "*blind and dumb*" possessed with a devil.[140] Nor the woman having an issue of blood twelve years.[141] These miracles are not performed by the Christ of John's gospel. But how is it they do not appear in the gospel that is supposed to have been published last? It does give the miracles of the loaves and fishes, turning the water into wine, raising the dead, walking the waters, giving sight to the blind, but not the miracles of Khunsu. The answer is that the Christ of the canonical gospels had several mythical prototypes, such as Horus, Iu-em-hept, or Khunsu, and sometimes the copy is derived from one original and sometimes from another. We shall find that, as fast as the historic Christ of the four gospels disintegrates and falls to pieces, the mythical prototypes reclaim and gather up the fragments for their own as with the grasp of gravitation.

## THE DOVE OF JORDAN.

One of the mysteries in the *Ritual* is called the "*secret of Horus in Annu, and how his mother made him in the water.*"[142] Annu is the region of fishes, which became zodiacal in the sign of Pisces. In this sign the fish-goddess as Hathor or Atergatis brought forth the adult Horus out of the Jordan, Eridanus, or Nile ; he who had transformed in the waters from which he was reborn. The dove is also a type of Hathor, and is borne in the hand of the fish-goddess.[143] When the equinox had passed into this sign of the Fish and Dove, it was the place where Horus received his soul of pubescence, the *ruach*. The scene and scenery are represented in the baptism of Jesus in Jordan or "*in Bethany beyond Jordan.*" John the witness to the Christ says, "*He that sent me*" "*said unto me, Upon whomsoever thou shalt see the Spirit descending, and abiding upon him, the same is he that baptizeth with the Holy Spirit.*" "*And John bare record, saying, I saw the spirit descending from heaven like a dove, and it abode upon him.*"[144] Here the dove, which had been Egyptian as the bird of Hathor, and was continued by the Mitharists, is a type of the rebegetting spirit, the *ruach*, in place of the divine hawk into which Horus transforms when he becomes a soul. But both signify the descent of the pubescent spirit of the anointed one.

The dove was continued as feminine type of the Holy Spirit in Rome, as it had been in Greece, Babylon, Syria, and Egypt. In the *Legenda Aurea*, at the assumption of Mary, the Christ addresses his mother as his dove and says, "*Arise, my mother! my dove! tabernacle of glory, vase of life, celestial temple*," and thus identifies the genitrix with the dove.[145] But in the tenth or eleventh century the Holy Ghost began to appear in Christian art as a little child, next as a youth, and lastly as a man; and the female nature, which had been first, was finally excluded from the trinity.

JOHN THE BAPTIZER WITH WATER SAYS OF JESUS the coming one, "*He shall baptize you with the Holy Ghost and fire, whose fan is in his hand, and he will thoroughly purge his floor.*"[146] The fan is an Egyptian ideograph of spirit, called the *khu* or *khukhu*, carried in the hand of Horus, and borne by the Bak-hawk, a bird of soul and of the solar fire. The baptism of Christ is followed by the contest with Satan during forty days in the wilderness. The original of this contention, which occurs in many forms of the mythos, may be traced in the solar phase to the annual battle between Horus and the evil Sut, the Egyptian Satan, which was preceded in the lunar stage by the struggle for supremacy between Taht and Sut, or Horus and Anup. In the "Inscription of Shabaka" (rendered by Goodwin), the struggle between Horus and Sut occurs immediately after the baptism or immersion in the river. Whether fought yearly or monthly, the battle was between the Lord of Light and the devil of darkness, as it has gone on ever since the twins were born.

Goodwin translated an account of the battle in which the twins are said to have transformed themselves into wild beasts and remained in that state during three days.[147] Here the period of conflict tallies with the three days of the moon in the underworld. In the solar mythos the battle extended over the typical forty days which are still memorized in Lent.

Both the baptism and the contest are referred to in the *Ritual*. "*I am washed with the same water in which the good Opener* (Un-Nefer) *washes when he disputes with Satan, that justification should be made to Un-Nefer, the Word made Truth* ;"[148] or the word that is law.

The chapter of "*Coming out to the heaven*" follows immediately after Horus has been *made* or transformed in the water. The speaker says "*I was great yesterday among the chiefs. I transformed. I have shown my face to the Only One, opening the form of darkness. I know the spirits in Annu. The greatly-glorious does not pass over unless the gods give me the word.*" "*I knew that eye, the hair of the man was on it.*"

So Jesus "showed himself" to John, the hairy man, the Only One crying in the wilderness who opens the darkness and bears witness to the light. The gods give him the *Word* in the shape of the descending dove. He makes his transformation into the Messiah.

"*Says the sun at the words of the king to him who was before him, 'let him stand unchanged for a month.' Said by the sun to him who is before him, 'received the weapon for the issue of men.' 'The weapon it is made,' is said by him who is before him ; the* TWO BRETHREN *make it, they make the festival of the sun.*"

This is paralleled in the scene with Christ and John, the precursor "who is before him." The "two brethren" who are disciples of John, and who became followers of the Lamb of God ; or "the weapon for the issue of men" may be compared with the "stone" of the new name given to Simon. In the same chapter of the *Ritual* [149] it is said, the Osirian "does not rest from making his transformations." He proceeds to make himself known to "the lady with the long hair, which is Annu, chasing those who belong to the race of this country. The chase made in Annu is after the race of his race. The greatest of its spectacles is when a chase is made by him to the greatly-glorious, as a son does to his father.[150] He drinks out of the pools to take away his thirst."[151] He also says "I am creating the water. I make way in the valley, in the pool of the great one. Make-road (or road-maker) expresses what I am." "*I am the path by which they traverse out of the sepulchre of Osiris.*"[152]

## JESUS AND THE WOMAN AT THE WELL.

In John's version the "greatly-glorious" makes himself known to the woman at the Well of Sychar. She does not chase him perhaps, but the distinction of race is brought out : "How is it that thou being a Jew asketh drink of me, which am a woman of Samaria? for the Jews have no dealings with the Samaritans." The Messiah reveals himself to her as the source of living water, "that springeth up unto everlasting life." Later on he says "*I am the way, the truth, and the life.*"[153]

"*I am creating the water ; discriminating the seat,*" says Horus.

Jesus says, " The hour cometh when ye shall neither in this mountain nor yet at Jerusalem worship the father."

Osiris both appears at the Well and personates the water. He pours out the water of life from a far earlier time, but in the Osirian cult the male type of the waterer took precedence in the scene of the Christ and the woman at the well. The five consorts who are not husbands answer to the five gods born of Seb and Nu.

Jesus is represented by John as being the well of the water of life, or the water that is a well of life. "He that believeth on me out of his belly shall flow rivers of living water.

"If any man thirst," says Jesus, "let him come unto me and drink." Jesus claims that this well was given to him by the father.

In the *Ritual* it says "*He is thine, O Osiris. A well or flow comes out of thy mouth to him!*[154] Also the paternal source is acknowledged in another text: "I am the father inundating when there is thirst, guarding the water. Behold me at it." Moreover, if we identify Salem with Shiloam, then the well of water in the *Ritual* is one with the pool of Siloam or Salem, for the speaker says, "The well has come through me. I wash in the pool of peace," Not only is the pool described at which the Osirified are made pure or healed; not only does the angel or god descend to the waters, the "certain times" on the fourth hour of the night, and the eighth hour of the day, saying," "pass away hence" to him who has been cured.[155] Bethesda in Hebrew is rendered the House of Mercy, but in Egyptian *Eshta* or *Ushta* means to absolve, acquit, propitiate. It must also denote healing, as *Usha* signifies the doctor, hence the name of the *Essenes,* which is equivalent to that of the Therapeutæ in Greek. It has been admitted by Eusebius that the canonical Christian gospels and epistles were the ancient writings of the Essenes or Therapeutæ reproduced in the name of Jesus.[156] In another version of this chapter of "*coming out of heaven, of passing the court and knowing the spirits of Annu,*" [157] the Osirified says, "*I am he who is in the midst of the eye. I have come. I have given truth to the sun. Welcome to Sut-Anup. by the brood of the red asps, by the blessing of Seb in the ark, by the sceptre of Sut-Anup, I have welcomed the chief dead in the service of the Lord of things*"

## THE FIELDS WHITE FOR HARVEST.

Anup takes the place of John. The Osirian gives him the greeting of welcome, and it is by the authority of Anup, who is the guide through the wilderness of the underworld, that he is able to welcome the great spirits called the chief dead in the divine service. He exclaims, "*I am the Lord of the fields when they are white,*" *i.e.* for the reapers. So the Christ now says to his disciples," Behold I say unto you, lift up your eyes and look on the fields the are white already unto harvest. He that reapeth receiveth wages and gathereth fruit unto life eternal, that he that soweth and he that reapeth may rejoice together." In the *Ritual* the speaker says, "I have welcomed the chief dead in the service of the Lord of things," and Jesus welcomes the disciples in the work of the harvest, in the same character of "*Lord of the fields when they are white.*"

Much of the meaning in the *Ritual* has a dim drowned look as it lies far below the surface, yet the dead face preserves the living likeness, and here, in two or three brief chapters, we find crowded together the likenesses to Christ and John, the scene of transformation, the descent of the Word, the "*two brethren,*" the precursor, the woman at the well, the living water, the "*discriminating of the seat*" of worship, the "*Lord of the fields when they are white,*" the chief spirits (called the dead) in the service of the Lord of things who are welcomed to the work of the harvest.

In the *Ritual* and the *Book of Hades* the scenes are in the other world, whereas in John's gospel they have been transferred to this, but it needs no large amount of comparative faculty to recognize their original identity.

An epitome of a considerable portion of John's gospel may be found in another brief chapter of the *Ritual.* "Ye gods come to me to be my servants. I am the son of your Lord. Ye are mine through my father who gave you to me. I have been among the servants of Hathor. I have been washed (by thee, Oh) attendant! As Jesus was baptized by John.

Jesus as Lord of the Harvest or Savior of Souls, is first described as beginning with the "two brethren," Simon and Andrew, for his followers or disciples.

To these John and James are added by Matthew and the four agree with the brethren who are the genii of the four corners; the four gods who are the brethren of Horus their Lord, the whole family being the five gods by Seb (time) or Sebekh.

The twelve are introduced by Matthew as reapers of the harvest.

"Then said he unto his disciples; the harvest is truly plenteous, but the laborers are few. Pray ye, therefore, the Lord of the harvest, that he send forth laborers into his harvest. And he called unto him his twelve disciples."[158]

"And his disciples came unto him, saying, DECLARE UNTO US THE PARABLE OF THE TARES OF THE FIELD."

He answered and said unto them : "He that soweth the good seed are the children of the kingdom ; but the tares are the children of the wicked one : the enemy that sowed them is the devil ; the harvest is the end of the world ; and the reapers are the angels. As therefore the tares are gathered and burned in the fire , so shall it be in the end of this world. The Son of man shall send forth his angels, and they shall gather out of his kingdom all things that offend, and them which do iniquity, and shall cast them into a furnace of fire ; there shall be wailing and gnashing of teeth. Then shall the righteous shine forth as the sun in the kingdom of their Father."[159] In addition to this there is another scene in which the Lord of the harvest appears with the twelve who are fed on ears of corn.

The mythical harvest is in the fields of heaven, the Aahenru, which are denominated, "the producers of grain for the gods behind the chest."[160]

Now, if we turn to the *Book of Hades,*[161] *the harvest, the Lord of the harvest, and the reapers of the harvest are all portrayed.; the twelve are also there. In one scene they are preceded by a god leaning on a staff, who is designated the master of joy ; a surname of the Messiah Horus when assimilated to the soli-lunar Khunsu*. The Twelve are "*they who labor at the harvest in the plains of Nuter-kar*." A bearer of a sickle shows the inscription—"*These are the reapers*." The twelve are divided into two groups of five and seven—the original seven of the Ashenru ; these seven are the Reapers. The other five are bending towards an enormous ear of corn—the image of the harvest, ripe and ready for the sickles of the seven. The total twelve are called the Happy ones, the bearers of food. Another title of the twelve is that of the Just ones. The god says to the reapers, "*Take your sickles! Reap your grain! . . . Honor to you, reapers.*" "*Offerings are made to them on earth as bearers of sickles in the fields of hades.*" On the other hand the tares, or the wicked, are to be cast out and destroyed. It is said to the avengers, "*let them not escape from your hands ; let them not fly from your fingers, being enemies. Watch over the massacre, according to the orders you have received from the founder.*"

## THE PARABLE OF THE LOAVES AND FISHES.

In the chapter on "Celestial Diet the Osiris eats under the sycamore tree of Hathor. He says, "*Let him come from the earth. Thou hast brought these seven loaves for me to live by, bringing the bread that Horus* (the Christ) *makes.*" "*Thou hast placed, thou hast eaten rations : let him call to the gods for them, or the gods come with them to him.*"[162] This is suggestive of the miracle performed when the multitude was fed upon seven loaves. The seven loaves are here, together with the calling upon the gods. In the next chapter is a scene of eating and drinking. The speaker who personates the god says, "*I am the Lord of Bread in Annu. My bread at the heaven was that of Ra ; my bread on earth was that of Seb. By the cabin I come into the house of the great God of Annu.*"[163] The seven loaves represent the Bread of Ra. Elsewhere the number prescribed to be set on one table as an offering is five loaves.[164] These are also carried on the heads of five different persons in the scenes of the underworld.[165]

Five loaves may be the Bread of Seb, as Seb is No. 5 and his gods are five. Thus five loaves would represent the bread of earth, and seven the bread of heaven. Be this as it may, both the five loaves and the seven are sacred regulation numbers in the Egyptian *Ritual*. And in the gospel of Matthew the miracles are wrought with five loaves in the one case, and seven in the other, when the multitudes are fed on "celestial diet."

In the gospel narrative there is a lad with the five barley loaves and two fishes.[166] In the next chapter of the *Ritual* we possibly meet with the lad himself, as the miracle-worker says, "*I have given breath to the said youth.*"

The Gnostics asserted truly that celestial persons and scenes had been transferred to earth in the gospels, and it is only within the pleroma, or in the zodiac, that we can at times identify the original of both. Thus when the equinox had entered the sign of Pisces, the solar birthplace was in Annu, and that word denotes the Fishes. The zodiacal Fishes are twins, and this will account for the "*two fishes*," as miraculous food, or celestial diet. Ichthys the Fish here feeds his followers in that dual form, which in the zodiac represented the fish-goddess and her child. It is noticeable that in the gospels the two fishes are coupled with the five loaves only ; a "few little fishes" being mentioned with the seven loaves.[167] But in the cemetery of Priscilla, Rome, there is a scene in which seven figures are kneeling with seven loaves accompanying two fishes, seven basketfulls of food being arranged in front of the loaves and fishes.[168]

There are other mythical data here which can be astronomically identified. As the latest form of the manifestor was in the heaven of the twelve signs, that probably determined the number of twelve basketfulls of food remaining, when the multitude had all been fed. "*They that ate the loaves were five thousand men* ;"[169] and five thousand was the exact number of the celestials, or gods, in the Assyrian heaven before the revolt.[170]

## WALKING ON THE WATERS.

The scene of the miracles of the loaves and fishes is followed by an attempt to take Jesus by force, but he withdrew himself ; and this is succeeded by the miracle of his walking on the waters and conquering the winds and waves.[171] So in the *Ritual*. Chapter 57 is that of the "*Breath prevailing over the Water in Hades*."

The speaker, having to cross over, says :—*O Hapi! let the Osiris, prevail over the waters, like as the Osiris prevailed against the taking by stealth the night of the great struggle. Let the Osiris pass by the great one who dwells in the place of the inundation."*

The disciples were afraid when they saw Jesus ; and they did not recognize him, but he said, "*It is I, be not afraid!*" In the *Ritual* it says, "*While they conduct that great god they know not his name,*" *i.e.* in the passage of the waters, "*the Osiris passes through wherever he wishes, and sits there..*"[172] Jesus is represented in one aspect of mystery, as if the mortal could become impalpable at will, and spirit-like elude the grasp of those who would lay hands upon him. This is the Christ of the Docetæ. He passes through the midst of his enemies as if suddenly masked.

## JESUS HIDES HIMSELF.

When the Jews took up stones to cast at him, "Jesus was hidden, and went out of the temple."[173] "They sought again to take him : and he went forth out of their hand.[174] The character is in accordance with that of the Osiris called "*hidden-face*."

In the chapter entitled, "Things to be done on the daylight of a festival,"[175] the Osiris is in the "fields of peace,"—the Kamite equivalent to the porch of Solomon or peace. He is in the midst of those who "watch to capture" him. But the Osiris remains "sound like the rock of the horizon of heaven." The

Osiris is placed in the halls of the horizon. The gods holloa to stop him ; dirt is thrown at him ; the snare does not catch him ; the Guardians of the halls do not injure him, for he is the Hidden-Face within the palace, and in the midst of the shrine of the god who is lord of the gates at the place of the gates. The Osiris is not caught. The Osiris makes way. He sends truth to the sun. He corrects the Apophis. The Osiris passes through the clouds, turns back the opposers, gives life to the ministers of the sun. The Osiris has made a good passage in the boat, (as) lord of the oar.[176]

The festival in John's gospel is the feast of Dedication at Jerusalem. "Jesus was walking in the temple in Solomon's porch." These agree with the fields of peace, and the "Shrine of the God." Jesus extols the father (sends truth to the sun) and rebukes the Jews (corrects the Apophis, or evil powers). They took up stones again to stone him, and sought to capture him, but he escapes out of their hands, and like the Osiris "*is not caught*." He "makes way" and has a "good passage in the boat ," or "went away again beyond Jordan into the place where John was at the first baptizing ; and there he abode."[177] The "rock of the horizon" in Luke's gospel becomes "the brow of the hill on which the city was built," to which the Jews brought Jesus "that they might throw him down headlong. But he passed through the midst of them and went his way."[178] he had escaped in the character of *Hidden-Face*. The Osirified, when on his way to the festival in the fields of *peace*, says "I am he who is staying away a while from all his earthly sports ;" and the Christ, on his way to the feast of the passover in Jeru-*salem*, says to his brethren, "Go ye up unto his feast : I go not up yet unto this feast, for my time is not yet fulfilled.[179]

THE GNOSTICS TRULY DECLARED THAT ALL THE supernatural transactions asserted in the gospels "*were counterparts* (or representations) *of what took place above.*"[180] That is, they affirmed the history to be mythical, the celestial allegory made mundane. Thus in the gospels the mythical is continually reproduced as miracle. That which naturally pertains to the character of the sun-god becomes supernatural in appearance when brought to earth. They identified the doings of the Christ in the gospels as those of their own Christ who was not made flesh, and who performed the same things within the pleroma or in the nether world, the Nuter-kar of the Egyptians. Into this world of the dead the sun-god descended as the restorer to life and liberty. It is in this region that the miracles are wrought and the transformations take place. Here the evil spirits are exorcised from the mummies, the stains of life are purified, the dead are raised, and the lamed and maimed are made to get up and go. In the "*reconstruction of the deceased*," one of the first acts of the revivifier is to give the dumb dead a mouth. The chapter is called that of "*A person having his mouth given to him in hades.*" This, when reproduced on mundane ground, becomes the miracle of making the dumb to speak. The deceased says Atum has "*made for me my hands to put forth* ;" Atum is also the god who makes the deaf to hear. Eyes are given to the blind. One text says, "*Seb has opened the blind* or closed) *eyes of the deceased.*"[181] This "*reconstruction of the deceased*" is transferred to the earth-life, whereupon "*the blind receive their sight, and the lame walk, the lepers are cleaned, the deaf hear, and the dead are raised up*," at the coming of Christ.

Another exemplification of this fact may be cited. According to the Kamite expression, the dead, or the spirits are those *who are on the mountain ;* the mount of the horizon a type of the ascension. The contest between the Christ and Satan takes place on an exceeding high mount. Jesus went up into the mountain to deliver the "sermon" and to utter the logia ; the fifth, sixth, and seventh chapters of Matthew are spoken on the mount. He also "went up into the mountain apart to pray, and when even was come he was there alone."[182]He *went up into the mountain and sat there*,"[183] when he performed his great miracles in healing the lame and maimed, the blind and dumb, including the miracle of the loaves and fishes. It was in "a high mountain apart" that he was transfigured, and his divine sonship was audibly authenticated. [184] He sat on the mount of Olives when the disciples sought him secretly to be instructed by him in the mysteries.[185] And from the mount called Olive, Jesus vanished into heaven, [186] —Olivet being a typical Mount of the equinox from which the solar god ascended.[187]

THE SCENE ON THE MOUNT OF TRANSFIGURATION IS obviously derived from the ascent of Osiris into the mount of the moon. The sixth day was celebrated as that of the change and transformation of the solar god in the lunar orb, which he re-entered on that day as the regenerator of its light.[188] With this we may compare the statement made by Matthew, that "after six days Jesus" went "up into a high mountain apart ; and he was transfigured," "and his face did shine as the sun, and his garments became as white as the light."[189] There the voice of God the Father was heard from the overshadowing cloud proclaiming, "This is my beloved son," who had been rebegotten of the moon! And as he came down from the mountain Jesus commanded the Three to tell the vision to no man, until the Son of man should have risen from the dead.[190] Mark says, "They kept the saying, questioning among themselves what the rising again from the dead should mean." This follows immediately after the vision in which Elijah and Moses had appeared to them, and they had thus been shown what rising from the dead did mean. One scene on the mount has here been mixed up with another connected with the "Sermon on the mount." The seventh Book of Hermes is entitled, "His secret sermon in the mount of regeneration, and the profession of silence." Tat the son of the god whom he calls his father, is described as going up into the mountain, where the father speaks with him and discourse concerning the salvation by means of regeneration or transformation. Tat entreats the father to unfold to him the argument of regeneration, that is, the spiritual form of rising from the dead or renewing, as he had promised to do when he, the son, had sufficiently estranged himself from the world (Jesus went up into a high mountain apart from the world). The suggestion of the vision or trance is apparent in the words of Heroes, "*Thou seest, O son, with thine eyes ; but though thou look never so steadfastly upon me with thy bodily sight, thou canst not see nor understand what I am now* (he says he had been begotten in mind and passed into an immortal body). *I would that thou also wert gone out of thyself like them that dream in their sleep.*

## THE THREE TABERNACLES OF PETER.

Amongst other things Hermes instructs Tat in the nature of the "*tabernacle of the zodiacal circle*"—Peter wanted to make three tabernacles—and he says, "*This is regeneration, O son, that we should not any longer fix our imagination upon the body, subject to the three dimensions*" (of space). Having instructed Tat in the nature of the mystery of this rising from the dead (which was described also as a rebirth of the moon) the father charges his regenerated or newborn son to *keep the secret in silence*, and "*impart unto no man, O son, the tradition of regeneration lest we be reputed calumniators*."[191] This is an important contribution, because Elijah is identified as John the Baptist, and, in other traditions, with Hermes, *i.e.* Sut-Anup, the predecessor of Taht, who is here called son. The mythos was continued in the divine Pymander or shepherd of Hermes in an Egypto-Gnostic and psychotheistic phase. Also the name of his Hermean work was continued in the *Shepherd of Hermas* which was one of the elementary scriptures accepted by the church before the Christ had been completely carnalized by the *Sarkolatrae.*[192] Irenæus quotes it as canonical scripture. Clement of Alexandria held it in reverence. Origen mentions it as writing divinely inspired.

## THE VIRGIN AND CHILD.

The Christ or Horus was born as child of the mother alone called the virgin, she who came from herself, and whose peplum had never been lifted by any male. Her child was the unbegotten or the self-begotten one. The virgin mother was called by coarser names in later language. She was the harlot and the whore. Now, Jesus is not only born of the Virgin Mary as the fatherless, the "Mamzer" of the Hebrews, but his descent on the maternal side is traced in accordance with this origin of the mythical Christ. The four female ancestors of Jesus who are enumerated in the genealogies of Matthew are not only non-Hebrews, they are all four forms of the harlot. Thamar played the whore with Judah to become the first female ancestor of Jesus, or the Lion of Judah. Rahab of Jericho is frankly designated the harlot, and she is second female ancestor. Ruth, the Moabitess, whose history is so tenderly told, is the third. The fourth is Bathsheba, wife of Uriah the Hittite, the prostitute of David. This history does not show that illicit human intercourse was the natural mode of the divine descent. Nor does it imply unparalleled profligacy ; it only proves the mythos. By this means the true character assigned to the most ancient genitrix was preserved and continued according to the cult in which the Kronian Messiah had been brought to birth independently of the human fatherhood. Judah was the Lion-god ; Pharez was one of the twins, and David was the lunar Herakles. The genealogies of the youthful son-god were not human, but divine ; and this line of descent from the harlot on the female side demonstrates the divinity of Jesus the Christ, as the child of the ever-virgin mother, who had a four-fold representation in heaven as goddess of the seven stars, goddess of the moon, goddess of the sun, and goddess of the planet Venus.

This character of the divine and eternal child of the mythos, he who rebegot himself as the representative of lunar or solar phenomena is very plainly portrayed in the statement of Jesus, who is made to tell the Jews— "*Your father Abraham rejoiced to see my day; and he saw it and was glad;*" and this he caps with the further statement that he existed before Abraham was born, "*Before Abraham was born* (Greek) *I am.*"[193] Here it is immaterial whether Abraham be considered mythical or human. He was expressly *the father* to the Jews ; and the sonship in mythology, as it was in nature and sociology, is prior to the institution of the individualized fatherhood. The Christ as the divine son claims to have existed before the typical father of the Jews was born. This the Gnostics will explain. They tell us (in a passage previously quoted) that it was the work of Monogenes or Nous, who alone was in communion with the father, to reveal the nature of the fatherhood and sonship to the rest of the æons,—that was within the pleroma.

In the gospels this has been transferred to mundane ground, where the auditors of Monogenes are Jews. Now, whether Abraham be considered as the father god in an allegory of the two covenants, as Paul implies, or the typical progenitor of the Jews, he was the supreme father in Israel, and is quoted as such. Abraham saw the fatherhood established in the second covenant which was sealed by circumcision, and, consequently, the sonship assigned to the fatherhood in place of the earlier motherhood. But the sonship was prior to the fatherhood! The son of the virgin mother or feminine Holy Ghost was before Abraham. And here the instructor of the æons in these mysteries claims to be that pre-paternal son, the *Apator* of the Gnostics.

The son who preceded the father is—like the virgin mother—an institution solely mythical. Primitive sociology had deposited the types, but the types could never more be humanized.

The Osiris is portrayed as the sun of light overcoming all the powers of darkness. "*His actions are the actions of the sun in heaven.*" [194] and the actions of his opposers are those of the dwellers in hell, the Apophis, the viper of Sut, the red-haired monster, the strangling snakes, the lord of gore, the devourers of the dead, the worm that never dies, the eater of millions, the demon-dog, and the devils in general. This character is likewise assigned to the Christ, in consequence of which the Jews become the devils, vipers, and other Typhonian types. "*Ye offspring of vipers,*"[195] he calls them ; he tells them, "*Ye are of your father the devil,*" who "*was a murderer from the beginning.*"[196] "*Ye are from beneath, I am from above.*"[197] He was Horus ; they derived from Sut. And Christians marvel that these victims of an allegory should remain a people apart

## THE WOMAN WITH THE ISSUE OF BLOOD.

The Gnostics identified the Christ of the gospels with their own Horus in the act of teaching the mystery that occurred among the twelve æons with the pleroma out of which the mother Achamoth (or Sophia) wandered with her ailment or issue of blood, until the "Christ above" took pity on her forlorn condition, and by extending himself beyond the boundary-fence of the pleroma he sought her out and gave form (the masculine imprint) to her amorphous substance. "*They explain the wandering sheep to mean their mother, by whom they represent the church as having been sown.*"[198]

This poor lost mother they said was the sheep that had gone astray, as set forth in the parable of the lost sheep.[199] The main mission of the Christ, according to Matthew is that of the Gnostic

Horus. He also had extended himself beyond the pleroma as Stauros to save that which was lost according to the mythos. He comes solely to save the lost sheep of the House of Israel, saying, "*I was not sent but unto the lost sheep of the House of Israel.*"[200]

The House of Israel on earth or in heaven is a type of the twelve, equivalent to the twelve æons, the twelfth of which was the strayed, wandering, and lost one whom Horus came to recover.

When Sophia had been restored by the Christ the pleroma of the twelve æons was complete ; and it happens that on the spot, immediately after restoring the daughter of Jairus, Jesus "*called the twelve together, and gave them power and authority over all devils and to cure diseases ; and he sent them forth.*"[201]

## MARY MAGDALENE AND HER SEVEN DEVILS.

According to Irenæus, Simon Magus the Samaritan, who declared that he impersonated the power of God, was in the habit of carrying about with him a certain woman named Helena, whom he was said to have redeemed from slavery in Tyre. This Helena proclaimed to have been the mother of all. She descended into the lower regions of space, or had the fabled fall, and could not return upwards. She passed from one female form to another and suffered contumely and insult in each. until at last she became a common prostitute.[202] This was the great mother who had several characters, beginning as the virgin and ending as the harlot. Simon as representative of the male divinity, professed to have come into the world to seek and to save her. But this was also the rôle of the Christ ; and the great mother whom he does redeem is Mary Magdalene, out of whom he cast seven devils, and who accompanied with him as Helena did with Simon.

Irenæus also shows the Gnostics claimed the woman suffered from an issue of blood to be their own Sophia who was healed by Horus the Christ. They related that Sophia had made an impracticable and impossible attempt to create, but brought forth a substance that was amorphous and imbecile, such as her female nature was capable of producing ; that is, the flesh-making substance which needed the male to impress and imprint it with form. She was flowing away, "*flowing into immensity*," and in danger of perishing, when the Christ dwelling on high took pity on her, and *having extended himself* through and beyond Stauros (the boundary fence of the pleroma) he *imparted a figure to her,* but *merely as respected substance, and not as to convey intelligence.* By Horus she was purified and established. This woman with the issue of blood they said was their twelfth æon, and this number was represented by the twelve years. They also pointed out that the boundary fence of Stauros was the hem of the garment worn by Horus the Christ.[203] In the apocryphal gospels the woman who had the issue of blood is identified as Veronica, she who received the likeness of the Lord pictured on a napkin or kerchief, which is still on view in Rome. Veronica, as Vera-iconica, indicates the true likeness, but the Gnostics, who were the authors of the Christian Icons, knew better. The Christ imparted a figure to her, but not a living likeness, and this corpse-like portrait has been preserved by the Italian and Spanish painters.[204] It was further affirmed by the Gnostics that

THE DAUGHTER OF JAIRUS, WHOM JESUS RAISED FROM the dead when *she was about twelve years of age,*[205] was likewise a form of the same twelfth æon who was restored by Horus the Christ. It is remarkable that Jesus being on his way to raise the one from the dead performs the miracle of healing on the other.

The Gnostics explained the miracle of the man who had been born blind and whose sight was restored by the Christ[206] as being their mystery of the æon who was produced by Monogenes as the sightless creature of a soulless creator. Irenæus cachinnated with his usual ghastly hilarity over the Word that was born blind.[207] Yet the gnostic mystery continued the Kamite myth of the double Horus, one of whom was the blind Horus, who says in his blindness, "*I come to search for mine eyes;*" and whose sight is restored by the second Horus, the Light of the World.[208]

The mystery of Christ and the church of which Paul says, "*this mystery is great,*"[209] is identical with that of the gnostic Anthropos, the Son of man, and Ecclesia, who produced twelve æons, the first of which was the Paraclete (Paracletus), the advocate,[210] or comforter; the same whom Christ promises that the Father will send to the disciples in his name.[211] The Gnostics professed to be the men who knew, and the mythos and typology now recovered, vouch for their knowledge of the mysteries that lurk beneath the parables, events, and teachings that have been gathered up in the gospels, and at the same time show that those who collected them for reissue in an historic narrative were unaware of their real nature. Hence the Gnostics were denounced for "*striving to adapt the good works of revelation to their own wicked inventions,*" in the sheerest ignorance of what had been preserved by the petrifying Past.[212]

The mythical nature of the Christ, and his doings and sayings, recorded in the gospels, are not only shown in the psychotheistic and doctrinal phase of Gnosticism, but can be traced to the natural history of the phenomenal solar god, who as the sun of day and night was depicted in the course of navigating nightly through the lower regions during the twelve hours of darkness. Twelve gates enclosed twelve portions of space. Through these the god passes one by one, generally having the blessed at his right hand and the damned upon his left. The twelve gates correspond to the twelve hours of the night assigned to the sun in the lower hemisphere. "*The way of absolute darkness is that of the sun during the twelve night hours.*" The name of the place in the twelfth hour means "*production of darkness ; the rise of births.*" The "*great god is reborn in it, he goes out of the abyss and reunites himself to the body of Nut,*" the mother-heaven. The drama of the midnight mysteries contained the scenery of this passage of the sun below the horizon. Har-khuti, the Lord of Lights and of the spirits or Glorified Elect ones, the *Khu*, is an especial form of the divinity who descends and passes through the twelve doors of the twelve hours of the night : and there is a formula found on at least six doors to this effect :—"*The great god reaches and enters this porch ; the great god is worshipped by the gods who are there.*" They salute him :—"*Let our doors be thrown aside ; let our porches open for Ra-Har-Khuti. O Ra, come to us, great god, mysterious image.*" "*Sa says to Tek-Her, Open thy door to Ra, throw aside the leaf of thy door for Khuti. He shall illumine the darkness of the night, and he will bring light into the hidden dwelling. The door closes after the entrance of this great god, and those who are in this porch cry out when they hear this door shut!*"[213] One verse reads, "*The secret dwelling is in darkness in order that the transformation of this god may take place. The door is closed after the entrance of this god, and the dwellers of the earth cry out when they hear the door shut.*"[214] This is very suggestive of the *parable* of the ten virgins and the bride-groom who comes by night. Har-khuti is the lord of lights and the Elect spirits. He too comes at midnight, and the righteous were supposed to help him through the darkness by having their lamps ready against his coming.

THE TEN VIRGINS WITH THEIR TEN LAMPS ARE POSSIBLY reproduced from the "*Ten Uraei upright in the basin of the Uraei,*"[215] as in one place it is said of each Uræus, "*its flame is for Ra,*"[216] these being among the magnifiers of the god, "*emitting globes of fire for Ra.*" The Uræus is a type of *Renen*, whose name signifies the virgin, so that ten Uræi emitting globes of flame are at least equivalent to ten virgins with their lamps of light. Thus we can see how certain scenes in the hades were represented in parables. Now in the book of the solar passage and the scenes in the lower hemisphere, rendered by M. Deveria,[217] it is said that the myth of its mysteries of the lower heaven is so hidden and profound it is not known to any human being. At the fifth gate it is asserted that "*one cannot make known nor see nor understand this myth of Horus.*" But the transaction in the *sixth hour* is expressly inexplicable. In the gospel we read, "Now from the sixth hour there was darkness over all the land unto the ninth hour."[218] The sixth hour being midnight, that shows the solar nature of the mystery which has been transferred to the sixth hour of the day in the gospels.

It is in the Seventh Hour the mortal struggle takes place between Osiris and the deadly Apophis, or the great serpent Haber, 450 cubits long, that fills the whole heaven with its vast enveloping folds. The name of this seventh hour is that which wounds the serpent Haber. In the conflict with the evil power thus portrayed, the sun-god is designated the "*conqueror of the grave,*" and is said to make his advance through the influence of Isis, who aids him in repelling the Serpent of Darkness.

In the gospel, Christ is likewise set forth in the supreme struggle as "Conqueror of the grave," for "*the graves were opened and many bodies of the saints which slept arose.*"[219] It is said of the great serpent "*there are those on earth who do not drink of the waters of this serpent Haber,*" which may be compared with the refusal of the Christ to drink of the vinegar mingled with gall.[220]

When the god has overcome the Apophis serpent, his old nightly annual and eternal enemy, he exclaims "*I come, I have made my way! I am Horus, the defender of his father. My mother is Isis. I have slashed the Accusers in the bend of the Great Void. I have passed through the darkness, O Hailers! I have made my way. I come for the protection of Osiris. I am Horus, his beloved son. I have come like the sun through the gate of the one who likes to deceive and destroy, otherwise called Viper. I have made my way ; I have bruised and have passed pure.*"[221]

But the more express representation in the mysteries was that of the annual sun, the elder Horus or Atum. As Julius Fermicus says in the solemn celebration of the mysteries, all things in order had to be done which the youth either did or suffered in his death.[222] The youth represented the sinking, diminishing sun, that was portrayed as dying or transforming into a future life.

Diodorus identified the "*whole fable of the underworld,*" that was dramatized in Greece as having been "*copied from the ceremonies of the Egyptian funerals.*"[223]

Damascius[224] says "In a manifestation which one must not reveal, . . . there is seen on a wall of the temple a mass of light which at first appears afar off. It is transformed whilst unfolding itself into a visage evidently divine and supernatural, of an aspect severe but with a touch of sweetness. Following the teachings of a mysterious religion, Alexandrians honor it as Osiris or Adonis." But the total nature of the transformation was not to be revealed. One part of this mystery was the portrayal of the suffering in a feminine phase.

Luke describes the Lord in the Garden of Gethsemane as being in great agony, "and his sweat was as it were great drops of blood falling to the ground."[225] This experience the Gnostics identified with the suffering of their hemorrhoidal Sophia whose passion is the original of that which is celebrated during Passion week, or the week of weeping in Abtu, and which constitutes the fundamental mystery of the Rosy Cross and the Rose of Silence.

In this agony and bloody sweat the Christ fulfills the character of Osiris *Tesh Tesh,* the sun-god that suffered his agony and bloody sweat. *Tesh*(Eg.)means the bleeding, red, gory, separate, cut, and wounded; *tesh-tesh* is the inert form of the god, whose suffering, like that of Adonis, was represented as feminine, which fact alone attains a natural origin for the type. He was also called *Ans-Ra,* or the sun bound up in linen.

Blood or red was the color of the sun that suffered in the underworld. Atum, who set from the land of life, was the red sun; and red was also the color of the suffering Christ preserved by tradition and extant as late as the fourteenth century. In a manuscript of that time,[226] Jesus is represented on the cross as the old and ugly Christ; the "old child" of Egypt; entirely naked, and the *color of his skin is red.* When the body of Christ was not painted of that color, the hair and beard were constantly depicted red. It was a common popular tradition that the Christ was of a red complexion, and this as already shown was the proper hue of the suffering sun-god, and of Osiris in his body sweat, or Adonis in his feminine phase.

Atum, the red sun is described as setting from the land of life in all the colors of crimson in Pant, the red pool. This clothing of colors is represented as a "gorgeous robe" by Luke; a "purple robe" by Mark, and a robe of "scarlet" by Matthew.

The suffering or crucified Christ of the true mythos is the sun of Autumn, and the cross of his suffering is that of the equator and meridian. Plutarch tells us how the 22nd of Paophi (Sept 10th in the sacred year) was celebrated by the Egyptian as *the nativity of the props or supports of the sun*, which they observe after the Autumn equinox (it had become Oct 20th in the Alexandrian year) intimating thereby that he now wanted as it were a prop and stay, because he suffered a great diminution of light and heat as he declined and moved *obliquely* away.[227]

## THE CROSS.

This stave, stake, prop, or stay of the suffering sun was the Stauros, which was primarily a stake for supporting, shaped as a cross. Thus Horus the crosser was called Staurus by the Gnostics. The serpent was an emblem of the Autumn sun personated by Harpocrates, and the serpent lifted up on the cross in the later symbolism was a sign of this suffering, transforming, and renewing Christ, not as a cross of death but of life and substance. The cross was the shape taken by the prop and stay, with which those who were grateful for the life of light and heat of the sun sought to uphold him typically when he was waning in lustre and growing weak and childish. They did not crucify their god. The cross was their prop of support. The serpent signified renewal. This sympathy with the sun in its loss of power, as with the moon in the darkness of her eclipse, is very touching and human. At the Vernal equinox the cross, like the crosser, was changed in character and became a sign of divine support for men, as the symbol for the conquering sun. The difference between the two characters is visibly figured in the Roman and Greek forms of the cross. The sinking sun-god "sets with his arms drooping."

This attitude is imaged by the Roman cross, ×, which is the sign of the god who decussates and *duplicates.* The Greek cross, +, with arms stretched out denotes *"over and above"* (or plus), and is the sign of the re-arisen god who has crossed; the gnostic Horus, the Kamite Khem-Horus, the risen Christ, or Atum as the *Iusu*. These two crosses, however, can have no basis in an historic crucifixion, and the equinoctial Christolators did not know what to do with both ; they never were able to determine which of the two was the true type of the crucified. The ex-cross × was (and still is) considered to be a sign of death ; the Tau T, the cross of life and symbol of salvation ; the significance in both cases having been derived from the phenomena thus figured in external nature. In the *Ritual* the solar god Atum who goes down at the western crossing or on the cross (for *am*, the west, is also the cross) is described as "setting from the land of life with his hands drooping."[228] It is said to him ;— "Glory to thee, O Tum, in thy course perfected, crowned, prevailing : thou has traversed the heaven, thou hast perambulated the earth ; thou hast purified the chiefs, thou has created the life of the earth for them. Thou hast been addressed as the lord of heaven, ruler of hades, clasped by thy mother, Nu. Seeing in thee, her son, the Lord of Terror, the greatest of the terrible, setting from the land of life, she became obscure."

*Nu* is the firmament. In this passage the god sets from the land of life with hands drooping. There is a great darkness, as at the crucifixion described by Matthew, where the passing of the lord of terror is rendered by the terrible or loud cry of the synoptic version. The sun-god causes the dead or those in the earth to live as he enters the underworld.

In some legends the end of the age or world was caused or accompanied by earthquakes. The festival of Quetzalcoatl was a solemn preparation for the end of the world, which was to happen on the day of the four earthquakes, of which the people lived in daily dread.[229] Earthquakes likewise mark the crucifixion of Christ in Matthew's gospel.[230] In the Johannine gospel there is no account of the three hours' darkness, nor of the rending of the temple-veil in twain, nor of the graves opening for the resurrection of the dead—as if the collector might have had access to the Egyptian gospel or faith and other fragments of the *Ritual*, but knew nothing of the "Manifestation as the day." The darkness over all the land was enacted in the mysteries by the practice of extinguishing the lights. "He fell down and died, then we all overthrew the lights," says Esdras.[231] So it was at the death of the sun-god. The custom of putting out the candles in the Roman churches just before the *Miserere* is a survival from the most ancient mysteries. Then the torch of the new life was lighted, and we find the other world described as the "torch-lighted shores."[232]

THE SUN-GOD WAS BETRAYED TO HIS DEATH BY THE Egyptian Judas on the night of the "taking by stealth," the "night of the great struggle."[233] The god is "waylaid by the conspirators who have watched very much." They are said to smell him out "by the eating of his bread."[234] So the Christ is waylaid by Judas, who "knew the place, for Jesus often resorted thither,"[235] and the Jew had long watched to take him. The smelling of Osiris by the eating of his bread is remarkably rendered by John at the eating of the last supper. The *Ritual* has it, "They smell Osiris by the eating of his bread, transporting the evil of the Osiris." "And when he had dipped the sop he gave it to Judas Iscariot, and after the sop Satan entered into him."[236] Then said Jesus to him into whom the evil or devil had been transported, "That thou doest, do quickly," The *Ritual* says, "Osiris was the same, beseeching burial."[237]

IT IS DEMONSTRABLE THAT HEROD IS A FORM OF THE APOPHIS SERPENT CALLED THE ENEMY OF THE SUN.

In Syriac Herod is a red dragon. Herod in Hebrew signifies a terror. *Her* (Eg.) is to terrify, and *herrut* (Eg.) is the snake, or typical reptile. The blood of the divine victim that is poured forth by the Apophis serpent at the sixth hour on "the night of smiting the profane" is literally shed by Herod as the *Herrut* or Typhonian serpent. The speaker in the *Ritual* asks : "Who art thou then ? Lord of the silent body ! I have come to see him who is in the serpent, eye to eye and face to face !" "Lord of the Silent Body" is a title of Osiris. "Who art thou then? Lord of the silent body!" is asked and left unanswered.[238] This character also is assigned to the Christ. The high priest said unto him, "Answerest thou nothing?" "But Jesus held his peace."[239] "Herod questioned him in many words but he answered nothing."[240]

## THE WOMEN AT THE SEPULCHER.

The death of Osiris in the *Ritual is* followed by the *"night of the mystery of the great shapes,"* and it is explained that "*the night of the mystery of the great shapes is when there has been made the embalming of the thigh, leg and foot (?) of Osiris, the good being justified for ever."*[241] In the chapter on "the night of the laying out" of the dead body of Osiris, it is said that "Isis rises on the night of the laying out of the dead body, to lament over her brother Osiris;[242] and again "the night of the laying out" (of the dead Osiris) is mentioned, and again it is described as that on which Isis had risen to "make a wail for her brother."[243] But this is also the night on which he conquers his enemies and "receives the birthplace of the gods."[244] "*He tramples on the bandages they make for the burial."*[245] So the Christ is found to have unwound the linen bandages of burial, and they saw the linen in one place and the napkin in another.[246] Of the rearisen sun-god it is said : "*All his enemies fall down stabbed."* He is justified, and wears the crown of life: "the gods having repeated the good fact of the justification of the Osiris for ever and ever."[247] This is closely paralleled in John's gospel where it is Mary Magdalene who rises in the night and comes to the sepulcher "while it was yet dark;"[248] to find the Christ arisen as the conqueror of death.

In John's version, after the body is embalmed in a hundred pounds' weight of spices, consisting of myrrh and aloes, we have the "night of the mystery of the shapes." For, while it was yet dark, Mary Magdalene, coming to the sepulchre and peering in, sees two angels in white sitting one at the head and the other at the feet, where the body had lately lain.[249] And in the chapter of "*how a living being is not destroyed in hell, or the hour of life ends not in hades,"*[250] there are two youthful gods, "*two youths of light"* (Shu), who "*prevail as those who sees the light."* The vignette shows the deceased walking off ; he has risen. Matthew has only one angel, or splendid presence, whose "appearance was as lightening,"[251] like the *Shepi,* the splendid one who "*lights the sacrophagus,"* as a representative of the divinity.[252]

The risen Christ, who is first seen and recognized by Mary, says to her, "Touch me not, for I am not yet ascended unto my father." The same scene is described by the Gnostics when Sophia rushes forward to embrace the Christ, who restrains her by exclaiming "*Iao."* [253] In the last chapter of the preservation of the body in hades there is much mystical matter that looks plainer when written out in John's Gospel. It is said of the regerminated or risen god, "*May the Osirian speak to thee? The Osirian does not know. He* (Osiris) *knows him. Let him not grasp him."*[254] The Osirified "*comes out sound, immortal is his name.*

*He has passed along the upper roads"* (that is, as a risen spirit). "*He it is who grasps with his hand,"* and gives the palpable proof of continued personality ; as does the Christ who says, "See my hands and my feet, that it is I myself." In his presence it is said, "*Their countenances burn, their hearts are agonized at the Osiris ; he rules his seat ; he passes at the time ; he is guided on the road."* This is like the scene on the way to Emmaus.[255] In the *Ritual* it is the last day of the preservation of the body in the underworld, and in the gospel it is the first day of the risen body.

Now when the Vernal equinox was in the sign of the Bull, the constellation Orion was a stellar image of Horus, who had risen from the underworld in his glorified body. Hence the body of the risen Horus is said to *shine in the stars of the constellation of Orion, on the bosom of the upper heaven.*[256] In the *Ritual* the reconstructed and rearisen mummy says, "*I am the great constellation Orion* (Sahu), *dwelling in the solar birthplace in the midst of the spirits."* That is, he rises as Orion, the Star in the East that once showed the place where the babe lay, or where the reborn god arose on the horizon of the resurrection. The name of Orion as the Sahu is also that of the erect mummy, the type of the risen dead. The word means *incorporate*, or *incorpse;* but the Sahu constellation showed the mummy the *Karast,* or Christ. To *Karas* (Eg.) is to embalm the dead and make the mummy, whence the mummy figure is the *Karast* by name, the image of the dead who has attained a soul or starry self in the second life, which was typified by Orion, the constellation of Horus.[257]

At that time the Southern Cross, on the opposite side, was a figure of the Autumn crossing, the sign of the sacrificial offering, the crucified of the solar allegory, so far as the suffering, descending, diminishing sun was ever represented as the crucified; and every time Orion the conqueror of darkness rose, the Cross of Autumn set; and the Scorpion over it, that had given the death-wound to Messiah in the Osirian mythos, was hurled into hades by Orion the *Sahu*, the glorified body of the risen mummy, or Christ, the starry *eidolon* of immortality. Speaking of the deceased in their coffins, the Osirian says it is well with them : "*All the dead shall have passages made for them through the embalmment of Osiris :* that is in consequence of his becoming and being the *krast,* or mummy-type of the future life,[258] the image of the resurrection. The dead in their graves are to rise again, because Osiris has been *karast* or embalmed, and made the Christ of Egypt, who became the Anointed in Greek. Now *it is in this image, as the actual mummy, the physical type, the Sahu or incorporate body of the Egyptians, that the Christ of the Gospels rose again and reappeared.* When he "stood in the midst of them," as the Good Peace (Nefer-hept), and said, "Peace unto you," it was emphatically as the *corpus-christus, or* the *karast* mummy of the monuments.

There is always something extant to illustrate the continuity of the mythical types, this of the karast included. In a Roman scene of the Madonna and Babe, the child-Christ is portrayed as the mummy of the young solar god.[259] when Christ reappeared,

THE CHILD-CHRIST AS AN EGYPTIAN MUMMY.

the apostles supposed it was a spirit, but this is denied and repudiated : "A spirit hath not flesh and bones, as ye behold me having; and when he had said this he showed them his hands and his feet." "See my hands and my feet," he exclaims.

THE NAILS ON THE FEET AND HANDS OF JESUS.

He was the complete man of twenty nails, which nails were covered with gold-leaf in the mummy Christ or karast of Egypt; the genuine mummy that was embalmed for the purpose of rising again. It has been shown that the nail marks on the hands and feet of cruciform figures, male or female, are signs of a second life, the phase of pubescence, gestation, or resurrection, just as the Horus lock of hair was emblematic of the reappearing one. It is also noticeable in this connection that the nails of the body bear the name of the mummy-Christ, or *Sahu,"* and that these were gilded as a type of pubescence, of renewal coming of itself, and of rising again. Thus the preserver of men and saviour of the world conforms to the image of the most perfectly preserved mummy of the Egyptians, and the reappearance as a proof of immortality is in accordance with that of the mummy which was carried round whilst they sat at feast and sang the song, and shouted the name of "Maneros," or Men-Horus, the *karast*, the mummied Christ,[260] whose soul or starry self arose in heaven as Orion, representative of the sun and equinox in the sign of Taurus.

THE RESURRECTION OF CHRIST WAS OBVIOUSLY FOUNDED on that of the mummy, and ever since, the resurrection of the dead has been dependent upon the rising again of the mummy, which is no longer preserved to last for 3,000 (or more exactly 2155) years, as it was when the doctrine had any real significance for men.

## THE CROWN OF THORNS.

The sun-god of Autumn sets from the land of life, but, being a divinity, he does not die; he makes his transformation and emerges again upon the horizon or the resurrection at the Vernal equinox. It is said in the *Ritual*, "*Atum himself made his transformation into his Anbu. He transformed, he spiritualized, he grew against them* (the opposing powers), *he was the only one they let forth. He came forth from the horizon with them, they made him the terror of the gods and spirits transformed with him, the only one of millions, creating all that is made.*" This transformation of Atum into his "*Anbu*" has been alluded to before.[261] The word *Anbu,* which signifies eyelashes, or hair that surrounds, is also a name for *Thorns*.[262] Here Atum in his second character transforms into his thorn; and this offers an origin for the crown of thorns worn by the Christ. The crown of thorns did not originate as a symbol of suffering and death, or of derision. The Mexican Messiah was crowned with the thorns of the Maguey tree, a tree of life, the thorn of which was a prick of power. In his *ascension* Witoba is portrayed as a cruciform figure extended in space, with the nail marks on his hand which betoken the virile divinity who was potent enough to rise again ; and the nails are the symbol of his pubescent potency. This view is confirmed by the fact that in the Dekkan, Witoba is held to be an avatar of Siva the lingaic,[263] as the god who rose again, or was what the *Ritual* calls re-erected. There can be no doubt that Orion was once a phallic type, with the three stars for the male emblem. These are still known in North Britain as the rod or staff of his power.

When Atum had made his transformation, he reappeared on the horizon of the resurrection as his own son,—the renewal being represented by human likeness and relationships,—whose name is Iu-em-hept, or *he who comes as peace,* and who was the prince of peace. Another of his titles, Nefer-Hept, is that of the Good Peace. This is the character in WHICH THE CHRIST REAPPEARS AFTER HIS RESURRECTION . "When the doors were shut, Jesus came and stood in the midst, and saith unto them, 'Peace be unto you.' Jesus said to them again, 'Peace be unto you.' And when he had said this, he breathed on them, and said unto them, "Receive ye the Holy Ghost." Jesus is here portrayed as the breather of peace, and Nef (Eg.) is breath ; *Nefer* is the heat emitted, therefore breathen, from the mouth of Sekhet ; and in breathing thus, and saying "peace," the Christ acts the character of Nefer-Hept, the breather as well as the bringer of peace. Nefer also denotes a blessing, and the blessing here is "peace".

"*Hail ye, lords of truth,*" says the Osiris to the "*followers of Hept-skhes.*" "*Let me come to you without fault.*" This reminds us of the greeting of the risen returning Christ, who hails the troubled followers with "*Peace unto you.*" It happens that *hept* signifies peace, and *skhes*, means trouble. The Christ offers peace to the troubled.

Further, he demonstrates that he returns without fault, and is, in a phrase especially Egyptian, "sound"; and submits to a physical examination of the mummy. "*I am one of ye, being with you,*" says the Osiris also on coming forth.[264]

The seventeenth chapter of the *Ritual* is the Egyptian gospel. "This," says Dr. Birch, "contains the esoteric explanation of the faith of the Egyptians." It is entitled the "Chapter of conducting the spirit (deceased, of coming in and going out of Hades, and being among the servants of the Osiris, fed with the food of Osiris, the good Being whose word is law. Coming forth as the day, making all the transformations he had desired, being seated in the hall a living soul, as the blessed of the great gods of the west, after he had been laid to rest. The glory of doing it on earth is for mortals to declare." This may be compared with the last chapter of John, in which the Christ is seen coming out of the hades as he pleases, and joining his servants like the good Being whose word is law ; who returns to feed them, making or completing all the transformation or reappearances he wished to make, this being "the third time that Jesus had showed himself after that he was risen from the dead."[265]

The sun-god rearises on the horizon, where he issues forth, "Saying to those who belong to his race '*Give me your arm*": says the Osirified deceased, "*I am made as ye are*. (Let him explain it.) *The blood is that which proceeds from the member of the sun, after he goes along cutting himself. Those gods who are made attached to the generation of the sun, are* TASTE and TOUCH ;*they are followers of their father Tum daily.*"[266] There are reasons for thinking this is the original of the scene in which the Lord returns to the disciples after *his* resurrection. In the *Ritual* it follows immediately after the death of Atum on the cross, or his setting from the land of life with hands drooping. At his reappearance the Christ demonstrates that he is made as they are, like Atum. "See my hands and my feet ; that it is I myself. Handle me, and see." "And when he had said this, he showed them his hands and feet."[267] "Then said he to Thomas, Reach hither thy finger, and see my hands ; and reach hither thy hand, and put into my side!" These descriptions correspond to that of the cut, wounded, and bleeding sun-god, who says to his companions, "*Give me your arm, I am made as ye are.*"

## DOUBTING THOMAS.

It is Thomas, called Didymus, the twin who insists on putting Jesus to the touch ; and the *god Tum, Greek Tomos, has a twin character in Hu and Ka, called his sons, the meaning of whose names is Taste and Touch.*

The pictures in the hades also show the scene that followed the resurrection from the coffin of Osiris. In this the seven gods are seated together. These are the seven great spirits in the service of their lord, who were placed by Anup for the protection of the coffin of Osiris.[268] They who represent the pleroma of seven powers of which he is the manifestor. The legend reads : *Be attentive ; fulfil your functions near Osiris* : *and adore the Lord of the western region.*" The western region is beyond death or the grave ; there stood the mount Manu in the region of spirits perfected. The power of a boat is also visible in this scene.

## FEED MY LAMBS.

In another scene the legend may be read, "Those who are in this locality are the dispensers of the food of the gods in the inferior heaven. The solar god orders this food for them. These gods (or spirits) mount with that great god to the horizon of the east when he distributes the meats of the gods of the lower heaven." The facsimile of this is found in the last chapter of John. After the resurrection Jesus "manifested himself" to the seven. "There were together Simon Peter and Thomas called Didymus, and Nathaniel of Cana in Galilee; and the sons of Zebedee, and two others of his disciples." These are "the dispensers of the food of the gods, "as fishermen ; and the Christ gives repeated orders for food to be given to those who are in the inferior heaven or on earth, according to the words, "Feed my lambs—feed my sheep."

"*The gods or spirits mount with the great god to the eastern horizon,*" and the Christ says "*Follow me,*" after describing what is taken for Peter's death upon the cross. The spirits followed Osiris to the crossing which is here represented by the cross and crucifixion.

"*In our mysteries,*" says Jerome, "we first renounce *him that is in the west, who dies to us with our sin ; and then turning about to the east, we make a covenant with the Son of righteousness, and promise to be his servants.*[269]

The west was the seat of the devil, or the evil Typhon, in Equinoctial Christolatry. So, in the *Ritual*, the god or spirit, when rejoicing over his resurrection, does exactly the same. He not only turns from west to east to salute the rising sun, he also personates it, and becomes the "*man named East.* He exclaims, "*I am the sun, very glorious, seeing mysteries—hating him who dwells in the west, telling his name.*[270]

The gospels do not simply contain the mythos of Equinoctial Christolatry, they render the matter twice over, and thus doubly show it to be mythical. For example, in a previous volume[271] the writer argued that David, the eighth son of Jesse, whose thirty captains were changed, in keeping with the thirty days of the month, was the Hebrew form of the Kamite moon-god Taht-Esmun, the eighth, one of whose titles is "*the begetter of Osiris,* who was so called because the solar régime was subsequent to the lunar dynasty ; as it is in Akkad and Assyria, where Samas, the sun god, is the son of Sin, the male moon.

It has also been shown that the lion and unicorn were two Typhonian types of the dual lunation ; and this typology was also applied by David,—who says, "Deliver me from the lion's mouth ; for thou hast heard me from the horns of the unicorns,[272] —in his lunar or soli-lunar character.

The mythos of the Old Testament has its sequence and fulfillment by repetition in the new. Here the Christ appears not only as a descendant of the lunar race but is expressly the "Son of David." It is asked, "How then doth David in the spirit call him (the Christ) Lord? If David then calleth him Lord, how is he his son? And no one was able to answer."[273] Nor has the question ever been answered. Neither can it be answered, except in one way.

It was an ancient prophecy that the "*horn of salvation*" was to be raised anew in the House of David.[274] In the great day, or at the end of the great year, a new fountain was to be opened in the House of David; and the Kronian Messiah was to come forth from Bethlehem-Ephratah, the city of David.[275]

The prophecy was mythical, and can only be interpreted by the mythos. The Jews at one time mistook it and thought the Messiah was to become human, but they learned to know better, and bequeathed their error to the Equinoctial Christolators. The mythos meant exactly the same in Israel as it did in Egypt or in India, where it can be followed as an astronomical allegory. We have traced the seven Rishis making the circle of precession through the twenty-eight lunar mansions. We have seen that the last of the Buddhas advanced by twenty-eight steps, seven towards each of the four quarters. We also learn from the *Purana* that the incarnation of Vishnu as Krishna was to be in the tribe of Yadu. "*I am born in the lunar race of the tribe of Yadu,*" says Krishna. "*It was prophesied of old by Garga* (he who had learned astronomy from Sesha) *that at the end of the twenty-eighth Dwapara or brazen age, Hari* (Vishnu) *would be born in the family of Yadu.*"[276] The lunar race of Yadu was identical in the Hindu mythos with the lunar tribe of Judah, in the Hebrew, and the Christ that was to be born of both was one in the celestial allegory, the youthful luni-solar god who was to succeed and supersede the earlier manifestors of time and cycle as the Messiah of the great year of precession,—just as the soli-lunar Khunsu had done in the cult of Amen-Ra in Egypt.

Various transactions in the gospels are described not only as prophecies come to pass but as fulfilments of events already transacted. The events are contemporaneous with the earlier writers, and occurring at the time of writing. It is thus with the parturient virgin of Isaiah, who becomes the virgin mother of Jesus in the gospel.[277]

It is thus with the statement, "*Out of Egypt have I called my son.*"[278]

It is thus with the proclamation of the Lord's anointed as the "*beloved son.*[279]

It is thus with the "*own familiar friend* of the speaker, the eater of his bread who "*hath lifted up his heel against*" him.[280]

It is thus with the thirty pieces of silver which had been already cast into the potter's field.[281]

The things that were and had been are quoted as prophecies of things to be, or are repeated because the mythos is worked over once more in establishing the history. The mythos being Æonian was continued by repetition, and by the passage from the lunar into the final solar phase.

The natural genesis of the solar mythos can only be fashioned in the lunar stage. The sun-god, under various names, was held to die and to rise again from the dead in three days ; three days being reckoned for his burial in the cave of the Winter solstice, or his passage in the womb of the fish or hippopotamus. But the primary manifestor who arose from the dead in three days was the moon-god, the lord of light in the lunar orb. The moon is visible during twenty-seven days, and three days were allowed for its resurrection. The Mangaian Tangaroa-of-the-tattooed-face arose from the dead at the end of three days, "*sacred and enfeebled as you see*" him in the shape and complexion of the new moon.[282]

## JESUS RISES ON THE THIRD DAY.

Osiris, who was betrayed to his death by Sut-Typhon, entered the ark of the underworld, or the tomb, on the seventeenth of the month Athyr, and on the nineteenth day at night the priests proclaimed that the lost Osiris was refound.[283] That is, he had risen again on the third day. Here only do we touch foothold in phenomena. When it was discovered that the moon was a mirror to the solar light, the sun-god as Osiris, was reborn monthly in or of the moon! Thus the resurrection in three days became that of the luni-solar god. The same date was afterwards applied to the sun in the Winter solstice, and lastly to the dead, as it is in the Avesta and the Book of Hosea.[284] The three days reckoned for the death, burial, and resurrection of the luni-solar god were celebrated in the mysteries and recorded in the "Scriptures," and such books of wisdom as kept the astronomical chronology. Hence, the rising again in three days was to be according to those scriptures in which the mythos might be found, and the son of man (who, as Anthropos the son of Anthropos, was the latest type of the god that died and rose again) was to be "*three days and three nights in the heart of the earth,*" as "Jonah" (the prophet) was three days and three nights in the belly of the Fish,"[285] or as âan the representative of the moon in its dark lunation was out of sight or blind during three days. *Aan* and *Anpu* were each a form of the prophet earlier than the human type personified in Jonah, and each symbolized the moon that died and rose again before it was known that the solar light was reborn in the moon at the end of three days.

The natural genesis of the doctrine can be traced to the sole known phenomena, and is not left to be derived anew from phenomena that are unknown. The resurrection of the mythical Messiah was pre-extant, and was only reapplied to the Christ of the gospels who could not originate the resurrection on the third day, and consequently nothing depended upon it when it had been reapplied. Here, as elsewhere, the product called historic was the outcome determined by the mould of the mythos, and the foundations thus traceable in natural phenomena leave no room for the supernatural any more than for the human or historical. The Christ who rose again in three days for the fulfillment of scripture must be the Christ according to that scripture which contained the mythos, and the fulfillment of scripture was the completion of astronomical cycles, whether lunar, solar, or Processional. The process of creating prophecy by false interpretation of scripture is very manifest in the treatment of the myth of Sut and Horus who were twin brothers in the lunar phase. The speaker in Psalm xli. "Yea mine own familiar friend in whom I trusted, which did eat of my bread, has lifted up (or magnified) his heel against me." Sut-Anup represented the heel or hinder part of the lunation ; Horus the head and front of light. Indeed the deceased in the *Ritual* when reconstructed for his rearising says, "*Seb has opened my eyes wide, Anup has fashioned my heel.*"[286] These words of David are repeated by Jesus in John's gospel when he says, "I know whom I have chosen : but, that the scripture may be fulfilled, he that eateth my bread lifted up his heel against me,"[287] and he adds, "I tell you before it come to pass, that when it is come to pass, ye may believe that I am."[288]

But it had already come to pass for the speaker of the psalm, in which the words are personal to him who then spoke and the transaction is past *not* future.[289]

## JUDAS ISCARIOT.

The true original of Judas is the evil Sut of the Egyptian mythos, in which Osiris and Sut were not only familiar friends, but had been born twin brothers. Sut with a gang of conspirators (the seventy-two Sami) formed a plot against Osiris, and betrayed him *at a banquet* by getting him shut up in an ark, taken prisoner, and put to death. This happened at the time when the sun entered the sign of the Scorpion (and Orion set as Scorpio arose), which, therefore, represented the one of the twelve that betrayed Osiris to his death. The end of Judas is thus described, "Now this man obtained a field with the reward of his iniquity and falling headlong, he burst asunder in the midst, and all his bowels gushed out." That field was called Akeldama, that is, field of blood." In the *Ritual* when Osiris had been betrayed and is in the coffin, vengeance follows. The betrayer and his co-conspirators are handed over to the "great strangler in the valley" and the noose of the hangman or capturer. "*They do not escape the custody of Seb or Sebek,*"[290] There is a set day of catching and strangling called "*the day of strangling the accusers of the Universal Lord.*"[291] "*They slaughter them before the chief gods,*" and the blood flows from them at "*the festival of digging the earth in Tattu*" "*on the night of manuring with blood,*" which is called the *Haker* (cf. *Acel*-dama) festival of counting the dead. Instead of being strangled by the justifiers of Osiris, Judas strangles himself and manures Akeldama with his blood.[292] At the same time and in the same chapter occurs the "*setting up the brethren of Horus* (the Kamite Christ), *and preparing the issue of Horus with the things of his father Osiris.*" And in the "Acts" the "setting up of brethren" is the reconstituting of the twelve by filling up the place of Judas. Judas is the evil Sut-Typhon of the twelve, just as Sut-Typhon was the Judas of the seventy-two in the Egyptian mythos, and the betrayal was past as matter of the mythos. As mythos it might be reapplied, but could not originate in later human history. As mythos it was continued. Hence the one of the twelve who is supposed to be transformed when *Satan entered him with a sop.*[293]

The Psalms of David contain a substratum of the *Muthoi*, parables and dark sayings of old,[294] which belonged to the hermeneutical Books of Taht, the Kamite Psalmist, and scribe of the gods.[295] Those who were not in possession of the gnosis searched these writings for prophecy—after the fashion of Justin—upon which to establish the history. Thus it is written in the psalms,[296] "Sacrifice and offering thou didst not desire, burnt-offering and sin-offering thou hast not required. Then said I, Lo, I come ; in the volume of the book it is written of me, I delight to do thy will, O my God ; yea, thy law is within my heart." On this the writer of the epistle to the Hebrews remarks, "therefore when he cometh into the world he saith, "Sacrifice and offering thou wouldst not, but a body hast thou prepared for me. Then said I, Lo, I come (in the roll of the book it is written of me) to do thy will, O God."[297] The Lord's anointed, the Coming One, is the same mythical *one* in the psalm as in the epistle, but quite independently of historical prophecy. The same writer also makes the "reproach" of Christ apply to Moses in Egypt.

It is the speaker David in Psalm ii. to whom "the Lord hath said" "Thou art my son ; this day have I begotten thee." But this is taken for prophecy in proof of an historical Christ.[298] The writer of the epistle to the Hebrews applies it to the Æonian manifestor, who may be David in the Old Testament mythos and Jesus in the New. This view is corroborated by the quotation from Psalm cx., "Thou art a priest for ever, after the order of Melchizedek," which he applies to the manifestor now called the Christ ; that Melchizedek who was "without father, without mother, without genealogy, having neither beginning of days nor end of life, but made like unto the Son of God."[299] they are identical inasmuch as the type was Æonian, whether in the stellar, lunar, or solar phase of the mythos ; they are identical because they are mythical and are not historical. In a psalm assigned to David during his great distress the speaker says, "My God, my God, why hast thou forsaken me?" "The assembly of the wicked have inclosed me : they pierced my hands and my feet." "They part my garments among them, and cast lots upon my vesture."[300] And in another psalm (lxix.) the sufferer cries, "They gave me also gall for my meat; and in my thirst they gave me vinegar to drink."

The first of these words are ascribed to Jesus on the cross at about the ninth hour; and according to Luke "they parted his raiment and cast lots." John testifies that they did not part or rend his garment but cast lots for it, that the scripture might be fulfilled which saith, "They parted my garments among them, and upon my vesture did they cast lots."[301] Matthew says of the suffering Christ, "They gave him vinegar to drink mingled with gall."[302] Here, if anywhere, there should be prophecy, as there is according to the current mode of searching the scriptures without the gnosis. But there is one simple fact absolutely fatal to the theory of prophecy. Such sayings do not relate to prophecies that could be fulfilled in any future human history. The transactions and utterances in the psalm are personal to the speaker there and then, and not to any future sufferer. They may be repeated, but the repetition cannot constitute history any more than it fulfills prophecy. The repetition of the words in character points to the reapplication of the mythos in a narrative assumed to be historical. Such utterances in the psalms of David or of Taht were a part of the dark sayings, the secret logia or parables of old; such could be repeated because they belonged to the mythos, and on no other account whatever. That which was appropriate to David as a luni-solar god was likewise suitable for Jesus as the manifestor in the later form of the mythos.[303] A Jesus in the flesh cannot be David in the flesh, nor the "Son of David," but a Jesus in the mythos is not only the son of David according to the divine descent, he also may be identical with David, as Khunsu, the soli-lunar god, is with Taht; and the same events, transactions, utterances, and sayings do apply personally to both characters because the mythos has been repeated as later history and termed a fulfillment of prophecy. As repetition or reapplication of the mythos the matter is intelligible; but as the human experience of David repeated as the history of a personal Jesus it is impossible. This mixture of the lunar and solar mythos which was necessitated by the blending of the two in the luni-solar form may now be shown to have a bearing upon

## THE NOTORIOUS PASCHAL CONTROVERSY.

About the middle of the second century two different divisions of the Salvation Army debouched from the east and from the west and came into contact. Both claimed to be the Christian church, and both were Equinoctial Christolators. But on the banners of the eastern men the date of the 14th Nisan was proclaimed to be the true day of the Crucifixion, whereas they of the western or Roman church were solemnizing the rite on the 15th Nisan. Both parties claimed the warrant of an apostolic tradition.[304] According to the synoptics, Christ died on the 15th of the month Nisan, but in John's narrative the crucifixion occurs on the 14th of Nisan. The 14th was legally possible, whereas the 15th was rather more impossible than that an Irish Fenian should be hanged on a Sunday. The probable origin of the discrepancy may be found in both the dates belonging to the mythos which explains them perfectly on purely mythical grounds.

An English witness testifies that at one time the dead body of Christ was exhibited laid out in the sepulchre on Holy Thursday in all the churches of Rome. There it remained until Saturday, when it was supposed to rise again to the sound of cannons, trumpets, and bells. Thus a death of the Christ on Thursday and a resurrection on Saturday were continued alongside of a crucifixion on Friday and the rising again on Sunday. *Now, the date assigned for the crucifixion is determined by the full moon of Easter.* The day of full moon also determined the celebration of the equinoctial festival. But *there were two different dates for the full moon* according to the earlier lunar and later soli-lunar reckonings. When Osiris was torn into fourteen parts during the dark half of the lunation, the moon was that of twenty-eight days, and *the fourteenth was the date of full moon.* A half moon, *tena*, is the ideograph of a fortnight or fourteen days. This, the earliest date for full moon, was also British. An entry in *Annales Menevensis,*[305] *"Pascha commutata apud Britones super diem Dominicam emendante Elbodo,"* records the fact that in the year A.D. 755, Easter was Christianized by Elvod. It had up till then been observed by the Britons on the fourteenth day of the moon of March. The Kamite god is said to be "*made on the month and perfected on the half month.*" That is, on the 14th or 15th, according to the two reckonings.[306] *Senhru* (Eg.) is a name of the fourteenth Epiphi, the day on which the eye was full, as the day of the Summer solstice; *this shows the date applied to the eye or full moon of a year.* But in the luni-solar reckoning of thirty days to the month *the full moon falls on the fifteenth day.* It is so in the *Ritual*, where the eye of the moon is at full on this day. The mother moon says, "*I have made the eye of Horus when it was not coming on the festival of the fifteenth day.*"[307]

Ishtar as goddess 15 is also representative of this full moon. So that there were two different dates for the festival of the full moon, and when these were applied to the full moon of Easter they would dominate and determine the celebration on the two different days as we find it in Equinoctial Christolatry. Here then is a natural genesis for the two traditions of the crucifixion (passover or crossing) that was reputed to have occurred on the 14th and on the 15th of the month Nisan, as well as for the two celebrations of the death and resurrection of the Christ which survived to so late a period in Rome. The two celebrations of the one event on different days are the exact parallel to the different dates for the crucifixion given in the gospels, both of which were solemnized by the opponents in the great Paschal schism.[308] Also in the lower signs the luni-solar god was reborn of the full moon, two of whose types were the lion and the unicorn. Two other lunar types were Anup, the jackal, and Aan, the dog-headed ape. These two may be seen figured back to back at the place of the Vernal equinox in the zodiac of Denderah.[309] *Each of the two had represented the dark half of the lunation* (the one with Horus, the other with Taht) in two different stages of the mythos; *each had been the thief of the light; the Mercury who was the thief personified. In these two thieves at the crossing we may perhaps identify the two thieves at the cross, as Horus, the solar lord of light in the moon*—in the form of his hawk—*is placed be-*

*tween or just over these two thieves at the crossing, the station of the cross!* The birthplace of the god who was reborn or who rose again at the Vernal equinox is shown by the constellations of the Thigh or Uterus. Anup on one side of Horus, and Aan on the other, are two thieves on either hand of the Kamite Christ upon the cross at Easter.

In the same zodiac the child Harpocrates is portrayed in the disk of the full moon enthroned or seated on the beam of the balance, the sign of the Scales and of the equinox. From this beam of the crossing it was fabled in the Maori mythos that the young god Rupe fell down and filled the western heaven with his life-blood. And according to Jerome, who quotes the gospel of the Hebrews, it was not the veil of the temple that was rent in twain; but the crucifixion was signalized by the *breaking in two of an enormous beam.* The nature of the *beam* is evidently equinoctial. The place of the division, the month of the equinox, and the dividing veil are synonymous in the Hebrew and Assyrian "*Purakku*," so that the breaking beam and rending veil are types which interchange by name in relation to the equinox. Moreover it is a Christian tradition that the beam which the child-Christ sat upon is yet extant in the synagogue at Nazareth; which goes to identify the place with that of birth at the Equinox.

But proof that the Christ of the gospels is a survival of the solar or luni-solar god, known under names that vary according to the cult, does not depend upon the one character of the Christ alone. If the mythos of Equinoctial Christolatry was in very truth continued, it may be expected that other personages were reproduced in the gospels who can be likewise identified as entirely mythical.

It has been shown how the typical twin brothers of light and shade, day and dark, who contended for ever in the dual lunation, were continued in the character of

JESUS AND JOHN, THE INCREASER AND DECREASER, OF whom it is said by John, "He must increase, but I must decrease," as do the alternating twins in natural phenomena. The Akkadian title of the moon-god, Sin, *Enu-zu-na*, the "*lord of waxing*," indicates the increaser in the lunar phase. John and Jesus are born six months apart, and thus are represented in the solar phase of the brothers Horus; but that is not fundamental. They are really a survival of the twins in the more ancient form of the Sut-Horus. Muhammedan writers call John and Jesus the *Two sons of the Aunt.* And of course cousins-german may be called the sons of two aunts. But there is more meaning than this in the phrase, as there is in the original mythos. In the Osirian form which is quoted by Plutarch, the Sut-Horus or twin Anup, the dual child of the light and dark, is born of the two sisters Isis and Nephthys. Isis being the virgin mother. Nephthys, called emphatically "the sister," *is the aunt to the twins.* Isis is called the mother of Horus, Sut-Horus, or Anup, but he (or they) was begotten on Nephthys and brought forth by her as the aunt. Thus the two, as Anup and Horus, were *the Sons of the aunt.* Anup was the announcer of the inundation called the libation; John is the baptizer with water. Anup was the crier of the way and guide through the wilderness of An, the black land. John's is the voice of one crying in the wilderness, "Make ye ready the way of the lord."[310] "*I make way,*" says the Osiris, "*by what Anup*" (the precursor) "*has done for me.*" John was decapitated by the monster Herod, and Anup is portrayed headless in the planisphere just over the Waterman.[311] The Persians represented this by a decapitated figure with its head in its hand, like St. Denis.[312] The headless Anup is a type of demarcation: a sign of the division or solstice. The river of the division is the Iaru-tana or Jordan; and the Mandaites held that the torrents of blood which flowed from the headless trunk of John made the Jordan red. This can be seen in the planisphere, with the beheaded Anup as the original of John.

The Osirian in the *Ritual*, speaking in the twin-character, says "*I am Anup in the day of judgment; "I am Horus, the preferred, the Day of Rising.*"[313] Anup represents the judgment, and presides over the balance at the weighing of hearts in the underworld and Horus, the preferred, over the resurrection. These two characters of the Precursor and Preferred are assigned to John and Jesus. John the Precursor proclaims the judgment to be at hand, and calls the world to repentance. Jesus comes as "the preferred," on the day of rising up out of the waters, and is announced by the voice to be the "beloved son." John says of Jesus, "He must increase, but I must decrease. He that cometh from above is above all, he that is of the earth is of the earth, and of the earth he speaketh."[314]

Sut-Anup was of the earth and the underworld, the voice in the dark valley of eclipse and the shadow of death, called the wilderness. This character was represented by *Aan,* the Kaf, in one mythos, and by Anup, the jackal (or ass), in the other; *An-Apu* being the Guide through the Wilderness of the underworld, the dark, dark, land. Horus the Christ (or Taht in the fellow mythos) was the logos of light. John is not the light itself, but he bears witness to the light, he is the precursor that "*cryeth saying, This was he of whom I said, he that cometh after me is become before me, for he was before me,*" as it was in all other versions of the mythos. Nor is the lunar mother of the twins altogether absent from the gospel version. She was the bride of the lunar light, who is the Horus of one myth and Taht in another; and she is the Bride of the Christ, who comes from above as the light of the world, *i.e.* of the one who always waxes whilst the other ever wanes.[315] John says, "He that hath the bride is the bridegroom; but the friend of the bridegroom which standeth and heareth him, rejoiceth greatly because of the bridegroom's voice." In the Mithraic mysteries the light one of the twins was designated the bridegroom. These three form the trinity that is most easily followed in the lunar phase. The moon at full was the genitrix, the waning moon was her colt, and the new moon was the virile male, the image of Horus, lord of light, the bridegroom with the bride. Now it may be seen how the Messiah could be said to ride on the ass and on a colt the foal of an ass, although it is enough to give one the heartache to expose the pitiful pretences under which this psychotheistic phantom called the Messiah is masked in human form and made to put on the cast-off clothing of the ancient gods and play their parts once more to prove the real presence of a God in the world.

One of the most touching of pathetic appeals is made by

THE STORY OF CHRIST RIDING ON THE ASS IN ORDER THAT the "prophecy" might be fulfilled and Jerusalem know that the Shiloh or the king had come "riding upon an ass, and upon a colt the foal of an ass." *The object of demonstrating the nature of the trinity in lunar phenomena and of identifying the ass in three characters belonging to the moon including those of the "three legged ass" of the Persians, was to interpret this text.* Neither god nor man can actually ride on the ass and her foal at the same time. Such a proceeding must be figurative; one that could not be humanly fulfilled in fact. We have seen how it was fulfilled in the mythos and rendered in the planisphere The ass and its colt are described in the Book of Genesis[316] as belonging to the Shiloh who binds them to the vine; the imaginery is extant in the Persian planisphere and the Egyptian calendar.[317] The vine to which the ass and foal were tethered is portrayed in the decans of Virgo, the ass and colt being stationed in those of Leo;[318] the two asses in the sign of Cancer. A Rabbinical legend has it that the ass on which the Messiah would ride was to be the foal of the ass that was formed during the six days of creation.[319] That was the six-eyed ass of the 6 X 5 or 3 X 10 days of the moon.

The lunar trinity were variously represented by the cow, calf, and bull; dove, snake, and male figure; woman, ape, and ibis; mare, dog, and serpent. The she-ass, foal, and virile male, the chamor, constitute the triad or trinity of the ass-type. It was a mystic saying that the ass once carried immortality in heaven, but that she sold it to the serpent. The mother produced the colt which passed into the third phase at puberty. The woman of the moon brought forth her child as Aan, Anup, or John. The name of John is akin to the Greek *Onos*, and the French *Ane*, for the ass. Under the ass-type of Typhon, the mother is the *Athon*, or female ass (cf. the Arabic "Atan," *contracto brevique passu incessit*, as applied to the female ass or the moon!) the lessening moon is her little one, and the new moon was the Messiah, as the solar god reborn of the moon.

In the process of fulfilling the prophecies or the mythological allegory, it behoved the Christ to parody the riding on the ass *and* foal. John says simply, "*Jesus having found a young ass, sat thereon, as it is written, Fear not, daughter of Zion, behold thy king cometh, sitting on an ass's colt.*"[320] —and as it had been depicted ages before in the planisphere. But Matthew faithfully reproduces *both the ass and her colt*, the two asses placed by the Greeks in the decans of Cancer, where "*two ways met*," as it is stated by Mark, this being the sign of the Summer solstice; or the ass and colt stationed in the earlier sign by the Egyptians and Persians. Justin reproduces the Vine of the planisphere. He declares that the foal of the ass on which the Christ rode into Jerusalem was "*bound to a vine.*"[321]

The first person in this trinity rode on the wings of the dove (in the Persian *mihr*), or on the vulture's wings in the Kamite symbolism, or on the ass. He may therefore be described as riding on the ass and on its colt,—the other two that complete the three-one,—even as the new moon is seen riding upon the old moon from which it is reproduced. Moreover, the old moon *does* include the mother and foal that precede the male manifestor or anointed one of the mythos. The Christ riding on the ass is the figure-head of the trinity, exactly the same as is the pubescent male who is carried by the dove and serpent in the Persian trinity.

The fact of John and Jesus being born six months apart shows a solar phase of the mythos, like that found in the annual combination of sun and moon at Easter, the moon of the year which was represented by the god Khunsu, as it is by Christ.

In the pictures of the underworld the ass-headed god is portrayed as bearer of the sun, whose disk he carries between the two ears of the ass, whilst hauling himself up out of the lower world by means of ropes.[322] In the Greek shape of the mythos Hephaistos ascends the heaven, or to heaven, at the instigation of Dionysus, and is depicted as returning thither riding on an ass. According to Pausanias,[323] it was upon Dionysus that Hephaistos especially relied. The wine-god *intoxicated him and led him heavenwards*; in which condition we have the Hebrew Shiloh, who was to come binding his ass to the vine, with his eyes red with wine; his garments being drenched in the blood of the grape, and he as obviously drunk as Hephaistos.

Neither of the Evangelists describes Jesus in the state of the fire-god, or the red-eyed and purple-robed Shiloh, but he is sufficiently identified with the blood of the grape. He is an impersonation of the vine, whose blood is to be drunk by his followers. He is called a

WINE-BIBBER AND THE FRIEND OF PUBLICANS OR wine-sellers; and according to John his primordial miracle was the turning of water into wine.[324] "*This beginning of his signs did Jesus in Cana of Galilee, and manifested his glory.*" And such was the first miracle of the young sun-god who was *re-engendered at the Summer solstice* to be born at the Vernal equinox, as Har-ur, or Hal-Ul the elder, *i.e.,* the first or elder Horus, who passed into Phœnicia and Syria as El-Ul, Adonis, or Thammuz, who was associated with the grape and the vintage. He came to ripen the fruit of the vine, and to be represented by the vine in the decans of Virgo, where he is found with the virgin, his mother, just as the Christ appears with the virgin, his mother, when he performs the same miracle, only in a much shorter space of time, at the marriage feast of Cana. He came also to suffer as the sun of the Autumn crossing that descended into hades, or, in later language, "was crucified, dead, and buried," to be transformed and to rise again as the Horus of the Vernal equinox, the sun of Easter.

The natural genesis and Kamite origin of the symbolism can be witnessed in the planisphere, and proved by the seasons in Egypt. The vine or tree in the heavens is the sign of grapes in Egypt. The star *Vindemiatrix* in Virgo denotes the female vintager, *Vindemia* being the vintage.

The record in the Egyptian calendar for the date of Abib 22nd (July 28, 1878), is "*abundance of grapes.*" It is curious that the register for the previous days is "*clothes must not be washed for seven days,*"[325] and that the Shiloh who tethers his foal to the vine is said to have "*washed his garments in wine and his clothes in the blood of grapes*"; When the celestial Shiloh came in the heavens it was the time of rest. In Egypt, little work was done. No foundations were laid. it was the time of feasting and of festival. *Uak* (Eg.) signifies idleness, and to be lazy; and this was the time of leisure. Nature was working for them; the waters were flowing, and they rested, being thankful. The signs of Cancer, Leo, and Virgo show by their emblems in the astrological calendar that this was the time of reposing, and the region of rest. Shiloh, in Hebrew denotes rest, peace, to repose, be tranquil, enjoying a rest. The Shiloh personified was the bringer of this peace and rest, the leisure of the inundation. As Iu-em-Hept the young sun-god was the bringer of peace, who tropically was the peace or rest of Egypt when the sun had attained this quarter of the heavens, and that which is symbolical in Genesis or Zechariah was simple natural fact in Egypt, just as it is represented in the astronomical allegory.

The bringer of rest came annually to the land of Egypt, but he could not come once for all to lift the burden from a weary world, whether riding on an ass or on wings; nothing short of the densest ignorance of the mythical meaning eighteen centuries since could think it; and nothing short of the hereditary condition bequeathed by ages of credulity can account for its being accepted now.

Sut-Anup was before Horus in advent, according to the natural genesis of the twins, because of the beginning on the night side and with the dark half of the lunation. Sut was the Opener, the precursor, the first form of the manifestor or Messiah.

So John appears as a sort of Messiah until the coming of Christ. Like Jesus, he had his twelve apostles.

In the scriptures of the Sabeans, who were worshippers of Sut, we have the descent of the guide and savior into the underworld, the preaching to the spirits in prison, and the resurrection to eternal life, but these are all attributed to John instead of to Jesus. In many legends Sut is the genuine Messiah.

The same stories are told of him as of the Christ. He was instructed by angels. He was carried up into the wilderness during the typical forty days. He was the earliest astronomer, and father of all the prophets. He was also credited with being the author of a book about the Star in the East which was to announce the nativity of Christ,[326] that is, as the starry Sut-Horus of the pyramid who was the announcer of the Christ in the decans of the Ram. Sut as Messiah remained supreme in the Typhonian cult, whether in Egypt, Chaldea, Judea, Italy, or Britain. Some of the primitive Christians or Gnostics continued to worship Sut as the Messiah. One of these sects was called by his name, as the Suttites. The *Codex Nazaraeus* affirms that "*Iesu Mesio is Nebu.*" This was the Messiah of a dual nature, who is also described in the feminine phase.[327] Nebu was Sut-Nub or Anubis in Egypt and the *Iao*-Chnubis of the Gnostics. "*Nebu-Mercury, Messiah,*" is the Jesus denounced in the *Codex Nazaraeus* as the "*false, lying Messiah*;" the "*son of the woman*;" the menstruator; and "*one of the seven impostors who wander, having each the command of a sphere*," who is to die upon the cross, or be superseded, that is, as the equinoctial manifestor in the Kronian allegory, as Sut was supplanted by Horus, Enoch by the Son of man, and John by Jesus.[328] Sut as the Messiah was identified in Rome with the ass whose name in Egyptian is *Iu* or *Aiu*, the plural representative of lunar phenomena. The ass, jackal, and dog, are interchangeable types of the one original. Stories are told of the mediæval Jews and their *parodies* of Calvary made by crucifying dogs. But such a representation was only a survival of the primary type. They still crucify Cocks in Syria. The Jews were Suttites from the beginning, and Sut was the ass-god who was reputed to be worshipped by the Christians in Rome. Celsus says to them, "*Put away your vain illusions, your marvellous formulas, your lion and your amphibius, your god-ass and your celestial door-keepers, in whose names, poor wretches, you allow yourselves to be persecuted and impaled.*" In this exhortation we find the lion was another of their symbols; and the twins Sut and Horus were the male lion-gods, who were made the *keepers of the two gates* of the horizon north and south. The solar Atum is "*lighted by the lion-gods*" as he comes forth "*from the great place within the celestial abyss.*"[329] Says the Osirified, "*I have come like the sun from the House of the lions.*"[330] And this form of the twins survived in the two lions of the Christian iconography, which Celsus couples with the ass. They appear as the two gate- or door-keepers in a picture on the inside of a glass cup that was used at the Agapæ of the Christians.[331] The two lions were also stationed at the doors of ancient Italian Basilicas with some symbolical signification.[332] The rivalry of Sut and Horus (or the dual Messiah) has a bearing on the two resurrections of Christ in Rome and the two dates of the 14th and 15th Nisan for the Vernal equinox. The reckoning of twenty-eight days to the moon was Sut-Typhonian, and this was superseded by the moon of thirty days. Sut's day of resurrection or *repetition* was Saturday, and that of Horus or the Christ was Sunday; both were continued in Rome, in the gospels, and in the eastern and western churches, by those who were cunningly acquainted with, and their followers who were completely ignorant of, the mythical origines of Equinoctial Christolatry.

According to Epiphanius, Zacharias caught his death in addition to his dumbness through a vision which he had in the temple. He was offering incense when he suddenly perceived that the divinity was a man in the form of an ass. It came into his mind that he would make the vision known, and ask the Jews whether they knew the nature of the god they worshipped, but the man in the shape of an ass deprived him of speech. On recovering his speech, however, he told the Jews what he had seen in the sanctuary of the temple, whereupon they slew him. He had seen Sut-Anubis, Sut-Horus, Sut-Nubi, or Iao-Sabaoth, as Epiphanius says the gnostic god *Iao*-Sabaoth was portrayed with the face of an ass;[333] and this was the Iao-Sabaoth of the Hebrews.[334] Zacharias, be it remembered, is the father of John. John and Jesus are the euhemerized form of Sut-Anup and Sut-Horus. It is admitted that John was Elias or Elijah come again. Justin affirms that, "*This John was Elias who was to come before the Christ.*" The Christ himself is made to say of John, "*This is*

*Elijah which is to come.*" John was to go before the face of Christ, "*as the spirit and power of Elijah.*"[335] The name of Elijah, signifies El or Al is Jah, which identifies the god Iah or Iao, who reappears as Elias=John. This was the ass-headed deity seen by the father of John. Jah is one with Bâal the opener, and with Bar (Eg.) or Sut, the opener who divided into Sut and Horus. Origen hints that the soul of Elijah was in the body of John Baptist.[336] Also the name of Nazarean John is Jahia, a form of Jah or Iao. The matter of the mythos being so ancient, this may explain a statement made by Nicephorus Callistus,[337] to the effect that when the foundations of the temple were laid the gospel of John was discovered.

Both characters of the Christ survived in the cult of Rome. The *dark* one of the twins, who was the black Sut in Egypt, and Krishna in India, the one who was always a child, is the babe of Mary, the black bambino; and the grown-up Christ is the pubescent Horus (or Balarama), the anointed son of the father.

The first Messiah was the Son of the Woman, the child of the mother alone, called the virgin. This Son of the Woman was followed and superseded by the Son of man. In the *Book of Enoch* one form of the Messiah is the "*Son of Woman*;"[338] this was Enoch or Enos, the Egyptian Sut-Anush, who had been twin with Horus but was superseded by him. John the Baptist is this typical Son of the Woman, who is the natural precursor of the Son of Man on mythical grounds, as it had been in the primitive sociology.. Of him the Christ says, "*Verily I say unto you, Among them that are born of women there hath not arisen a greater than John the Baptist, yet he that is but little in the kingdom of heaven is greater than he.*"[339] John represented the water, the feminine element, as did Anup and the child-Horus,—the child that was born of the mother only; Jesus personated the spirit as paternal source, and the least of those who were god-begotten children of the father were greater than John. This was the gnostic teaching of "Anthropos, son of Anthropos."

In the sayings and discourses of Jesus the name of the "*Son of Man*" occurs eighty-three times. He is Anthropos the son of the divine Anthropos or the Father God in heaven. He is the Anthropos of the Gnostics, who is only to be explained by the Gnosis or Kabalah, not by the history of the *Idiotes*, and the Son of Man is the particular Christ of the gospel according to Matthew.

The superseding of Sut, who had been a lunar manifestor of time in the earlier heaven, by Horus the solar god, is enacted in the gospel history. In one account the number of apostles sent forth by the Christ is twelve; in another the number is seventy. Yet the occasion, scene, and language used are obviously the same. Both the twelve and the seventy are told that "*the harvest is plenteous and the labourers are few; pray ye therefore the Lord of the harvest that he send forth labourers into the harvest.*"[340]

Instead of seventy, various ancient authorities read seventy-two. Both numbers bear witness to the astronomical mythos. Seventy was the number of divisions in the earlier heaven when Sut was the manifestor, Messiah or Metatron.

The angel Metatron was lord over the seventy. He was the Name personified, and was called by the seventy names. One of the Rabbis writes, "*I have asked Metatron 'Why art thou, in common with the creator, designated by the seventy names?'* The answer given is, '*Because I am holy Enoch.*' "[341]

This is corroborated by the *Book of Enoch*, in which the Son of the Woman is superseded by the Son of Man, the Messiah who became the Deo Soli in the later heaven of the twelve signs and seventy-two duodecans, or lord of the seventy-two disciples in the gospel version of the mythos. There is also the same confusion of the seventy with the seventy-two as in the gospel.[342] According to Luke the seventy or seventy-two are those whose "*names are written in heaven.*" They were so written under the two reckonings, seventy being the number in the earlier, and seventy-two in the later, heaven. Once every year the seventy starry servants who warred with the serpent, scorpion, and the evil powers of darkness, came into the presence of their lord to be judged according to their work. In the same manner the "seventy (or seventy-two) *returned again with joy, saying, Lord, even the devils are subject unto us through thy name. And he said unto them, 'Behold I have given you authority to tread upon serpents and scorpions and over all the power of the enemy.*'"[343]

In the Kamite mythos, Sut was cast out to become the devil, and in this scene of the seventy or seventy-two the dethronement is described. Jesus "*said unto them, I beheld Satan falling as lightning from heaven.*" As a matter of course the Twelve implied the Seventy-two, but all that the mythos had here bequeathed to the A-Gnostics was entire ignorance as to whether the number of those whose names were written in heaven should be seventy or seventy-two.

The age and importance of the matter sometimes found in the Apocryphal gospels may be shown by the gospel of James, in which

HEROD SEEKS THE LIFE OF THE DIVINE CHILD, AND HE sent his servants to slay John. "*Herod sought after John and sent his servant to Zacharias, saying, 'Where hast thou hidden thy son? And Herod said his son is going to be the king of Israel.*"[344] Here it is John who is the infant Messiah.

Precisely the same story is told in the case of the Hindu twins, Krishna and Balarama, who correspond to Jesus and John. In this the wicked Kansa is the Herod who slays the children in order that he may include the Christ; and like Herod he pursues the first-born, who is Rama, the elder to Krishna, thinking he may be the child who is destined to be his destroyer.[345]

Balarama is the child of the old man Nanda, who corresponds to Zacharias. It is said that "*Vasudeva found Nanda rejoicing that a son was born to him; he spake to him kindly, and congratulated him on having a son in his old age.*"[346]

Balarama, the child of the old man Nanda, has the same relationship to Krishna that John, the child of the old man Zacharias, has to Jesus. Rama, in addressing Krishna at the river Yamuna as John addresses Jesus at the river Jordan says "*A portion of thee have I also been born, as thy senior. Thou, eternal, hast last of all appeared below.*"[347]

When Taht superseded Sut in the lunar mythos, the Aan or dog-headed ape took the place of Anup the jackal (or ass) as representative of the dark half of the moon. Thus the mythos contains two different Aans or Johns, just as John the beloved disciple who lay in the bosom of Jesus, and who according to tradition testified that when he tried to feel his body at times it was utterly unsubstantial, is second to John the Baptist. Anup and Aan were both forms of the prophet and scribe of the divine words. Both announced and testified to the Lord of Light (*i.e.* the solar source) in the moon. But, Anup testified orally, as the howler, barker, or bråyer, because he was earlier than writing. So John bears witness by word of mouth. But Aan (Taht-aan) is the later writer who carries the stylus or pen of the recorder; and this second phase of the same lunar character is represented by John called the divine, who "*bare record of the word of God.*" Thus the Kamite mythos offers a probable origin for the two Johns who are supposed to have been the authors of the gospel and the book of Revelation; it being the custom to assign typical and divine names to the sacred writings. The inferior first of the twins had a feminine as well as an infantile character. So John the beloved, θιοζ επιστηη θιοζ the one of the bosom, was designated the virgin, παρθεϖοζ; he represented the female nature of the Word or Logos, and as such is twin with Jesus.

The relationship of Anup to Isis the virgin mother, as her guide through all her wanderings, is continued in the connection of *a* John with the Virgin Mary, as maintained in certain legends. One name of Anup is *Tuamutf,* he who adores the mother (*f,* he him, it; *tua,* to worship, and *mut*, the mother). His station is at the cross to which he leads the mother in her search.

IN THE GOSPELS JOHN REMAINS AT THE CROSS with Jesus and Mary the mother. "*When Jesus therefore saw his mother and the disciple standing by whom he loved, he saith unto his mother 'Woman, behold thy son.' Then saith he to the disciple, 'Behold thy mother.' And from that hour the disciple took her unto his own."* so in the *ritual* Horus pleads, *"Do not ye do any evil to my mother."* Isis, the mother of Horus, adopted Anup (the child of Nephthys), as her own son, and John adopts Mary as his mother. Mary is reputed to have dwelt with John after the crucifixion. In the *Ritual* it is said *"by the sun to him who is before him, 'Let him stand unchanged for a month..'"*[348] In John's gospel it is said of *a* John, *"What shall this man do? Jesus saith, 'If I will that he tarry till I come, what* (is that) *to thee? This saying, therefore, went forth among the brethren that that disciple should not die."*[349] Such was one of the *sayings* attributed to the Lord. Hence the legend of John's living on and lying unchanged through a certain course of time, which is but one mouth in the *Ritual.* According to Augustine—JOHN, CALLED THE SAINT, MADE HIS GRAVE AT Ephesus, and in the presence of divers persons entered it *alive*. He is still believed to be alive, and the earth over him is said to boil and bubble up after the manner of a well, *by reason of John's breathing.*[350] Those who know the place, says the Father, *"must have seen the earth heave up and down;"* and this heaving caused by John's breathing is to continue until the Christ shall come. Now the god Anup alternates with Horus the Christ precisely in this way. He waited and watched with the dead in the tomb. He prepares them for their resurrection which occurs when Horus comes. He takes the mummy in his arms, leaning over it with tender solicitude, or sits crouching and huddled up over the coffin as if communicating a brooding warmth to restore the soul of breath, and bring the mummy back to life. He is the preserver in the lower world, as Horus is above. He is the *breather* in the tomb who survives, as John in the fable; he dwelt with the genitrix after the Autumn equinox. Moreover, it is at Ephesus that the Seven Sleepers repose with their dog, who is Anup the dog (jackal) of the Seven Spirits in the *Ritual*, and Ephesus is the place of the heaving grave and the buried breather, John.

## VARIOUS KAMITE DEITIES WERE CONVERTED INTO CHRISTIAN SAINTS.

The fact was pointed out by De Rouge, in a communication to a learned society of Paris, that in the third century the Egyptians worshipped a large number of saints and were in possession of a calendar of saints. Many of these are found to be deities reduced. The well-known story of Christopher shows that he was a survival of Apheru, a name of Sut-Anup. It is related that he overtook the child-Christ at the side of the river Jordan, and, lifting him on his back, carried him across the waters. But all the while the wondrous child grew, and grew, and grew, as they went, and when they reached the other side the child had grown into the god. The genesis of this is the passage of the annual sun across the waters, which reached the other side as the full-grown divinity. Anup, the jackal-headed, is named Apheru as guide of roads; he carries the infant Christ as Horus. "*Apheru dandles me,*" says the Horus. Christ-Apher is just Apher turned into a Christian saint. On the gnostic stones the child-Christ (Harpocrates) is frequently accompanied by Apheru=Anubis.

If John the Baptist be identical with Anup, we may look on "*Bethany beyond Jordan*" as the House of Anup in Annu, the solar birthplace beyond the river in the planisphere, called the double Holy House of Anubis. One name of this place of the equinox and of Anup is *Apheru*, and it is noticeable that Origen renders Bethany by Beth-*Abara*. The "Great House of Annu" is mentioned in the Inscription of Darius at the temple of El-Karjeh; also in the *Ritual* we read: "*Anup addresses the Osiris, he is building his house on earth, it is founded in Annu.*"[351] Bethany is described as being the favorite resting-place of the Christ, in the house of the two sisters. The Osiris finds his green spot and oasis in Annu, under the sycamore fig-tree of Hathor or Meri. "*the Osiris eats under the sycamore of Hathor,*" and says, "*I have made my time of rest there.*"[352] It is noticeable too that one name of the sycamore is *Anahui* (Eg.). The lady of the *Anahui* says to Osiris, "*I have come, I have brought thee food:*" and the reply is, "*Oh, refresher of the dweller in the west, placing thy arms to his arms, place him away from the heat, give refreshing waters to the Osris under the boughs, give the north wind to the meek-hearted in his place for ever.*"[353] Another name of the sycamore and of Hathor, is *Meri*, or Mari.

THE TWO SISTERS, MARY AND MARTHA, WHO DWELT TOGETHER AT BETHANY WITH THEIR BROTHER LAZARUS, correspond perfectly to the two divine sisters, called at times the two dear sisters, Isis and Nephthys, with their brother Osiris, in the House of Annu. It is said: "*I place the two dear sisters, I have made them belonging to Annu.*" Isis, Nephthys, Apheru (Anup), and Osiris, are the chiefs in Annu. Nephthys is the "*mistress of the house,*" she carries a house on her head, and is designated the "*benevolent saving sister.*" This mistress of the house, the saving sister reappears in Martha, who is depicted as the house keeper in character, she is the mistress of the house. Mary takes on the character and relationship of Isis, the anointer of Osiris. Isis in her mystery is said to be "*coiling her hair there,*" as she "*directs the face of Osiris to the gate of his path.*" So, when Mary poured out the ointment on the body of Jesus and wiped his feet with her hair, she is said to have done it in preparation of his burial. "*The lady with the long hair*" (*i.e.* Nut or Meri, the heaven) is also mentioned as being in Annu.[354] In the "Lamentations" of Isis and Nephthys they utter their grief for their dead brother, and Isis says to Osiris, "*Gods and men live because they behold thee.*" Mary and Martha cry alternately, "*If thou hadst been here, my brother had not died.*" At the supper in Bethany six "days before the passover," the relationships of Isis, Nephthys, and Horus, to the suffering Osiris, are represented by Mary, Martha, Lazarus, and Jesus. Lazarus sits at table with the doomed one, Martha serves him. Mary anoints his person and wipes his feet with the hair of her head. This supper was his funeral offering, and the ointment embalmed his body for the coming burial. In the "Lamentations" Osiris takes the place of Jesus, and it is said: "Thy two sisters are near thee, offering libations to thy person; thy son Horus accomplisheth for thee the funeral offering of bread, of beverages."[355]

According to Kircher, the four stars forming the quadrangle of the Great Bear were identified as the bier of Lazarus. The Arabs called the three tail stars the Daughters of the Bier, and these were considered to represent the three women, Mary Magdalene, Mary the sister of Martha, and Martha. We have now the means of showing that this was not the result of an attempt to Christianize the stars of heaven in the eighth century. The Great Bear was the Bier of Lazarus, as the mummy-type, the dead Osiris. It was called his coffin, or sarcophagus. In the *Ritual* the divine sisters are described as "*walking to place themselves behind him (Osiris) when they are mourners.*"[356] Its seven great stars are also the seven cows, or Hathors, each of which is related to the mummy. The first cow, or star, is the *eidoleion,* the "*house of the future self of Osiris*>" The second is the "*turn of heaven, and conductor of the god.*" The third is the "*wise one keeping her place.*" The fourth is the *Amenti, or lower world of the mummy.*" But the most important for the present purpose are the three Mourners who follow the bier. These are (1) "*the Greatly-Beloved, Red-haired;*" (2) "*Giver of life to the skin;*" (3) "*Name strong by work*" For these *are* the three that follow the bier of Lazarus (or the mummy), according to the astronomical tradition. They may be paralleled thus—

| | |
|---|---|
| "Greatly-beloved, red-haired." | Mary, the Magdalene, especially of the legends. |
| "Giver of life to the skin." | Mary the anointer of Jesus. |
| "Name strong by work." | Martha the house-wife. |

Lazarus, the brother, corresponds to the dead Osiris, who when living is the bull of the cows. Lazarus and the Christ answer to the dead and the living Osiris.

It has been shown that the profoundest of all the religious mysteries in the *Ritual,* or *Book of the Dead,* is related to the seven cows, or Hathors, and Osiris, the bull, the male of the cows.[357] According to the *Rubric* no other such was ever or anywhere known.[358] This was not merely in the Kronian aspect of the mythos, but in the psychotheistic phase of the Osirian mysteries. The cows or Hathors were a seven-fold form of the genitrix (corresponding to the seven spirits), who gave annual rebirth to the mummy Osiris, as the moon-did monthly. The seven stars crossing the waters, or the earth, may be likened to the four pall-bearers and three mourners of the mummy being borne for the rebirth at the place and time of the Vernal equinox. They are seven female attendants on the Osiris, who transforms. They bear and bewail the dead, and give nutriment to the living god. They are called the seven who give food and drink to the living. They are invoked: "*Give ye food and drink to the Osiris, feed him, give ye things to him. The Osiris pursues ye. He serves at your side. Give ye food and drink to the spirit of Osiris.*"[359] NOW, IN THE GOSPELS THERE ARE SEVEN WOMEN WHO ARE INTIMATELY ASSOCIATED WITH THE CHRIST: Mary the Virgin; Mary the Mother of Jesus; Mary the Magdalene; Mary the Anointer for the burial; Martha, Salome, and Johanna, who also *ministered to him of* their substance.[360] These women are his attendants, just as the seven Hathors minister to the Osiris in the *Ritual*. The Egyptian goddess *Meri* is a form of Hathor. *Meri* is the cow, and thus the Seven cows are Seven *Meris* as well as seven Hathors. The name of *Meri* denotes love, the beloved. Hathor=Meri was the Egyptian goddess of love; and the Virgin Mary is, or was, worshipped by the Kypriotes under the name of Aphroditissa.[361] Hathor=Meri was the habitation (*hat*) of the child Horus, who is typified as the bird of soul or spirit, and in the Christian mysteries the feminine Holy Spirit was held to be the mother of the seven Houses.[362]

MADONNA MARY IS WORSHIPPED IN ROME AS THE "*House consecrated to God,*" the "*Tabernacle of the Holy Ghost*" the "*dwelling-place*," or *zabulo*[363] (cf. the Hebrew *zabul*, the habitation as the tower of heaven which was a figure of the great mother). Hathor, like Mary was worshipped as the Queen of heaven. Hathor was "our Lady" in Egypt as Mary is in Rome. Mary was portrayed in the tree, like Nut and Hathor. She wore the veil that Isis declared had never been lifted by male nature. She appears as the Black Virgin, although tradition asserts truly that she only changed to that complexion during her sojourn in Egypt.

Now as the "coming child" is the Iusu (Eg.), the great mother Hathor, or Meri, is a prototype of the Virgin Mary who was the mother of Jesus. As already shown, the genitrix takes two other characters in the two divine sisters, and the three compose the feminine triad. Meri-seker has two aspects in Meri-res (south) and Meri-mehi (north). So in the gospels we find two Marys, both of whom are designated the mother of Jesus. This has necessitated the assumption that there were two sisters of one name, which was without Hebrew precedent, and is useless as a solution. Mary the mother of Jesus is absolutely distinguished by Mark from Mary the mother of James the Less and of Joses.[364] The two versions can neither be harmonized nor made historically true. The parallel runs still further, for there ARE THREE MARYS IN THE GOSPELS ANSWERING TO THE THREE *Meris* in Egypt; and whereas Matthew and Mark describe two Marys at the cross, John has reproduced the perfect triad, as Mary the mother of Jesus, and his mother's sister—Mary the *wife* of Cleopas—and Mary Magdalene.[365] Here we meet the two Marys who were sisters, together with Mary Magdalene, out of whom seven devils were cast by the Christ. The ancient great mother was she who gave birth to the seven Elementaries who were cast out as demons by the later solar god; and as *gadol* in Hebrew signifies the great, the very great, whilst *ma* is a prefix for a thing or person, it is not unreasonable if we derive the name from *ma-gadol* as that of the great mother. She is the great one of the three Marys, who is generally put first, even before the Virgin Mary, when these are named together. It was she who *"ministered to Jesus of her substance"* in life; she who was first at the tomb for the embalmment of the body, and first at the resurrection. Mary Magdalene performs the part of the Great Mother in the *Ritual*.

As *Meri* (Eg.) is a form of the goddess Hathor and of the cow, it follows that the seven Hathors may be represented as seven *Meris, Maries, or Marys;* the seven who are attached to the Lord. Nor is the type of the seven *Meris* quite effaced; there are four Marys by name, and "*Martha*" comes from the same root. Salome is likewise a traditional Mary. According to the *Codex Sinaïticus* Salome was a Mary of the sons of Zebedee. Thus there are six of the name out of the seven, and these are the seven givers of food and drink in person to the Christ. Moreover Mary is intimately associated with that number. The church of Rome celebrates her Joys and solemnizes her sorrows as in number, and assigns to her the Seven white Doves. This sevenfoldness is likewise implied in her being the mother of the child whose sign in the catacombs is the star with eight rays, the Jesus who in revelation is representative of the seven stars. Also the ancient Wisdom, or Sophia, was continued in the Virgin Mary, who carries the Book of Wisdom in her hand, always supposed to be open at the seventh chapter. The Seven Hathors, or Meris, are likewise found as the Seven Wise Women of the Persians, and the Seven Women in White (answering to the Seven White Cows) of the Phrygians.[366]

The constellaion of the seven stars—

That watched the buried sun by night,
And kept alive the sparks of light;
or through the winter showed the way
To realms of ever-radiant day—

as it crossed low down in the northern quarter, was also figured over the abyss. It was the bier of the dead, the bearer into a future life, called the coffin of the seven stars and the sarcophagus of Osiris. The region of the Great Bear is the "*region of the coffin of Osiris*," and the dead Osiris rises from the coffin as the living Horus to find himself in the company of the "Seven Great Spirits in the service of their Lord," these Seven "*are behind the constellation of Ursa Major, or the Thigh* (uterus), *of the northern heaven." "Anup places them for the protection of the coffin of Osiris."*[367] These seven servants of the risen Horus are the seven elementaris and kronotypes continued in the psychotheistic phase as spirits or gods that constitute the pleroma of powers whose perfect flower was Horus, or the Christ, whose symbol is the eight-rayed star. The seven are called *planks in the body of the boat,* the ark, *makhen*, which carries the souls out of hades,[368] the ark of salvation, and boat of the shipwrecked. Horus is the oar or good paddle that steers this boat of souls saved from the waters. Here the Seven in the ark with Horus are identical with the British Seven in the ark with Arthur, son of Arth, the Bear. The saved soul rejoiced that he has "*sat where the great ministers are,*" the company of Seven. He says: "*I have come out of the place of the ark; during the passage Horus, son of Isis, has brought me."*[369] It has been shown that Horus was the fisherman, and that two of the Seven are spoken of as fellow-fishermen. "*Says Horus, 'I have let Tuamutf and Kabhsenuf fish with me.'*" Thus the Seven Planks in the Boat of Souls, the Seven Spirits in the service of their Lord of Christ, are also Seven fishers of men, or savers of souls, with and for Horus. "*Come ye after me,*" says Jesus, "*and I will make you fishers of men."*[370] This is said to the "*two brethren,*" who correspond to the two in the *Ritual.*

Now in John's gospel, when the risen Lord reappears, the scene is in a region beyond the tomb, however the matter may be interpreted. And the present suggestion is that we are landed in the region of the coffin and of the Seven servants, planks in the boat, boatmen, or fishermen of Horus. It is said, "JESUS MANIFESTED HIMSELF AGAIN TO THE DISCIPLES *at the sea of Tiberias; and he manifested on this wise. There were together*

*Simon Peter, and Thomas called Didymus, and Nathaniel of Cana in Galilee, and the (sons) of Zebedee, and two other of his disciples.*" These are the Seven fishers, a group of Seven corresponding to the Seven who are the planks in the boat for saving souls, and the Seven fishers of men in the *Ritual of the Dead.* The Seven are spirits or gods in the Egyptian gospel, and the apparition of the Christ "*after that he was risen from the dead*" gives a look of spirit-world to the transaction in the gospel according to John, as if this last scene in the history might have been the first in the conversion of the mythos and the very point of place where it alighted in the earth-life to be humanized for all who were simply believers.[371]

The details of identification might be followed further. For example, Kabhsenuf the hawk-headed is, as the name denotes, the refresher of his brethren, and this office is assigned to Peter as feeder of the sheep. It was Peter who rushed into the water to meet Jesus,[372] and in the *Ritual*—when the dead Osiris has risen and come forth so that "*all the dead should have passages made to them through his embalmment*"—it says, "*It is Osiris! The son lives! The evil one dies!" Kabhsenuf wets his limbs in the streams for them to guard Osiris,*" in the act of greeting the god who reappears in what is termed "*the orientation.*"[373]

Again, the Yonias continued the dove as the bird of soul. The Osirians adopted the solar hawk. Kabhsenuf is hawk-headed, and Simon Peter is the son of the dove. Both represent the source of soul, whether masculine or feminine. The name of Simon agrees with the Egyptian *S'men*, "to establish the son in place of the father." That is the character of Simon who says to Jesus, "*Thou art the Christ, the son of the living God*;" "*Thou art the Christ of God*!"[374] In return for this recognition the Christ calls Simon

## A STONE OR THE ROCK.

*S'men* (Eg.) denotes that which founds, constitutes, makes durable and fixed. The stone is one type. But it also means that which is seminal, in agreement with the Hebrew *Shmen*, and Maltese or Latin *Semen*. Thus Simon Bar-Jonah is Simon, or *S'men*, soul of the dove—the soul once derived from the feminine source as the Kamite *hesmen*, an earlier form of the name. That was changed when Simon proclaimed the son of the father-god. The dove represented the sakti or power of the goddess; the hawk, of the god.[375] In the gospels the bird is changed, but the type substituted is the masculine stone. The gnosis here expounded is apparent when Simon Magus proclaims himself to be the "*entire essence of God*" the word or logos as masculine representative who came to redeem his Helena or the lost sheep, the mother of souls who had been continued from the biological into a theosophical phase.[376]

The four genii of Horus, who are four of the seven great spirits, may account for the different discoverers and revealers of the Messiah. First, the dove descends to constitute him a masculine soul in the river of baptism. Then he is proclaimed by the son of the dove. But in John's version it is Andrew who precedes Simon in finding the Messiah, whilst John claims priority and preeminence as the witness, the announcer, and forerunner of the Christ! There is another important fact. The four genii may be four including Horus; or four independently. For this reason. The solar hawk was also a type of Horus as well as of Kabhsenuf—Horus having been one of the seven elementaries. When Horus represents the pleroma as manifestor he is the eighth, and not merely one of the seven. Thus, as the four brethren, Horus may be one of them, identified by the divine hawk, otherwise the geni Kabhsenuf. Or the four may appear as independent genii of four quarters, or four paddles to the boat, or four of the great gods in the service of their Lord. Now Simon is made the especial *alter ego* of the Christ as his feeder of the flock,[377] and his representative on earth,[378] even as Kabhsenuf is the refresher of his brethren and manifestor of the soul of Horus as the hawk-headed geni. Moreover, the four genii of the four quarters of the mount are recoverable with Horus as one of the original four in the tradition of the transfiguration. THE FOUR IN THE MOUNT TOGETHER ARE JESUS, SIMON, JAMES, AND JOHN; ANDREW, ONE OF THE PRIMARY FOUR witnesses being on this occasion omitted. These genii are also found as the four attendants on Quetzalcoatl, the brethren of the Lord, who accompanied him to the place of his departure and returned to Cholula and told the people what the vanished god had said. The Cholulans then divided their province into four principalities, and gave the government to these four.[379]

Perhaps the most curious comparison remains to be made between James and the geni Amset. One James in the gospels is known as "*the brother of the Lord*." According to Matthew, Jesus had *four* brothers—*Simon, Joseph, Judas*, and *James*. Their mother is called Mary, otherwise the wife of Cleopas. James is also identified with the carpenter in the gospels as well as in the Talmud. *This is the character of Amset*. In addition to the significance of their names—such as Kabhsenuf, the refresher of his brothers; Tuamutf, the adorer of the mother; Amset, the devoured of impurity—each is named as it were professionally in relation to the work of embalmment and burial. Thus Tuamutf is the painter; Kabhsenuf, the bleeder; Hapi, the digger; Amset, *the carpenter*. Amset as devourer of impurity denotes the great purifier; and James has the traditional reputation of having been a great purifier. Amset is the only one of the four spirits who has a human body. He represents the *double* of the dead, the ka-image or celestial self in a human form.[380] Possibly this may account for his special appearance in the earth-life as the brother of the Lord. Jerome says it was related in the gospel according to the Hebrews that, following his resurrection, "*The Lord, after he had given the napkin to the servant of the priest, went to James and appeared to him!*" He "*said unto him, 'My brother, eat thy bread, for the Son of Man is risen from among them that sleep!'*"[381] and Amset, the brother of the Lord, is the geni to whom the risen one first appears on casting aside the bandages; it is he who presents the ka-image of the resurrection, as the Christ presented his likeness on the Napkin.

The "brethren of the Lord" in the gospels suggest the brethren of the Osiris or Horus-Ahi in the *Ritual*, who is called the "*eldest of the five gods begotten of Seb*"[382] —the five being Horus, Anup (Tuamutf), Hapi (or Shu), Kabhsenuf, and Amset. These are equivalent to Jesus, John, Andrew, Simon (Peter), and James; or to Jesus and the four brothers; and to perfect the parallel Jesus ought to be the brother of the four, and all five to be the sons of Seb. In that case Zebedee and Joseph are two forms of Seb. This would explain the brotherhood of Jesus and James. These are the facts. The "*two brethren*" appear in the *Ritual* as two of the family of fishers. Says Horus, "*I have let, Tuamutf*" "*and Kabhsenuf fish with me, they guard my belly* (fish for me or find food) *when I am there where the god of Annu is;*" and according to Matthew, Jesus says to the "*two brethren*"[383] who had been fishing, "*Follow me, and I will make you fishers of men.*" *Tuamutf and Kabhsenuf are two of four brothers who are the genii of the four corners, also called the four paddles of the boat, the four eyes of the sun (cf. the seven eyes in Revelation); and these two correspond to Peter and Andrew.*

"*And going on from thence he saw other two brethren, James, son of Zebedee, and John, his brother, in the boat with Zebedee, their father, mending their nets.*"[384] Here, then, are four brothers called Peter, Andrew, James, and John, who answer to the four genii of the *Ritual,* two of whom are found fishing with and for Horus the anointed, whose name Har signifies lord. Also, the crocodile-god Sebek, the capturer, as lord and fisher of the stream, occupies the place of Zebedee, the father of the fishers. He was an earlier form of Seb the mundane father of the gods, including the four brethren. The five may be compared thus:—

| | |
|---|---|
| *Zebedee* ... | Sebek, the crocodile-headed. |
| *Andrew* ... | *Hapi,* or *Kafi,* the ape-headed. |
| *Simon* ... | *Kabhsenuf,* the bird-headed. |
| *John* ... | *Anup, called Tuamutf,* the jackal-headed. |
| *James* ... | *Amset,* the human-headed. |

Lastly, the four were readapted as particular kronotypes, and, therefore, as the children of Seb (earth) or Sebek-Kronus, out of the family of Seven who had been elementaries, the inferior hebdomad, who were continued one way or another into the final phase of Equinoctial Christolatry. The fishers are the four brethren in Matthew's gospel, and in John's they are "the seven." In the gospel according to Luke, the MIRACULOUS DRAUGHT OF FISHES OCCURS DURING THE EARTH-LIFE OF JESUS, WHEREAS, IN JOHN'S version it happens in his spirit-life or in a region beyond death where the fishermen are seven in number, yet the two events are obviously identical; and the risen Christ with the Seven fishers is one with Horus and the Seven fishermen, paddles or planks in the boat of souls, the bier of Osiris or the ark of Seb. In the chapter of "knowing the spirits of Annu." Horus not only appears in the "*region of the fishes*" there is also a miraculous *take* of fish. "*Says the sun; I have compelled the fishes to go to the place of Sebek, lord of the stream, and his hands find out for him Horus in the region of fishes.*" "*Says Sebek, lord of the stream; I have terrified them* (the fish in the waters) *with mighty terrors, the chasing was terrible.*" "*No secret is this terror; Horus has laid his hands on it, and his face has opened on it, on the* 1*st and on the* 15*th day of the month.*" That is, Horus is the cause of the fish being caught. And so ancient is this legend of the miraculous draughts of fishes, that it is related in the Mangaian mythology as the invention of the art of fishing. Vatea, the god, half fish, half man, the Oannes of Polynesia, prepared an enormous net which was intrusted to six fishermen, the first that ever were. Day after day they sought for fish in vain. At length they invoked the aid of Raka, god of winds, and then the net was completely filled so that it was not in the power of the six fishers to hold the net. But Tane, son of Vatea, came to their help and the seven threw the net on shore to the feet of Vatea, who turned out the fish and counted them, thus originating the art of reckoning at the same time as that of fishing.[385] The seven fishermen are also found as the seven in the boat or ark of the Californian Hohgates, who are connected with the seven stars.

The Seven powers of the pleroma were represented as seven architects (when they work under the god Ptah the typical seven are Operatives or assistant builders), Seven sailors, Seven fishermen, and Seven carpenters, therefore the manifestor of the Seven was bound to be not only the builder of the bridge (cf. Pontifex Maximus), the lord of the boat, and the fisherman, but also the carpenter. The ideograph of divinity, the nuter, is the sign of the stone axe, adze, or plane which has the name of the cutter, maker, and carpenter. The identity of the divinity and the carpenter is a result of the primal Seven powers being *openers* before they were *shapers*; and of the Celt-stone being the first form of the adze and later plane. The Hindu Bribus, or Ribhus, were the artificers who are also carpenters. Buddha was likewise the carpenter; and in his ninth avatar Indra was incarnated as Salivahana, the carpenter. Origen denies that Jesus was a carpenter, but Justin Martyr not only affirms this,[386] he also identifies him as the maker of yokes and ploughs; and one form of the Great Bear constelllation is the plough,—the yoke being a type of the equinox.

THERE CAN BE NO DOUBT THAT THE GOSPEL HISTORY WAS WRITTEN BEFORE AS MATTER OF MYTHOLOGY, AND IT has now to be shown how it was last rewritten. The tradition of the Christian Fathers, accepted by the Church, is that the nucleus of the gospels was a primary collection of logia, or *sayings of the Lord* assigned to one Matthew as the scribe. Papias, Bishop of Hierapolis, who is said to have suffered martyrdom about 165—167 A.D. in the reign of Marcus Aurelius, was according to Irenæus, a friend of Polycarp, and "*one who has heard John;*" he wrote a "*commentary on the sayings of the Lord*"[387] (about the middle of the second century), from which Eusebius extracted what "*seemed memorable*." Papias is named with Clement, Pantæus and Ammonius as one of the ancient interpreters *who agreed to understand the Hexaemeron as referring to Christ and the church*, which aptly describes the work of the earliest translators of mythic material. A surviving fragment of this lost work states that Matthew wrote the sayings in the Hebrew dialect, and every one interpreted them as he was best able, "*Ματθα ο μευ εβ αιοι οιυμλεξτω τα λογια ουνεγπαψατο, ηομηυευαε οε α τα ω εν ονματοτ εξαοτο*" Papias, whom Eusebius calls a man of limited comprehension, was probably a simple believer in these sayings being the oracles of an historical Jesus written down in Hebrew by one of his personal followers. He did not know that the utterer of these sayings was the logos of mythology, who had been previously personified as Iu-em-hept, the Sayer in Egypt, at least 3,000 years earlier, and whom the present writer identifies as the Jesus (or Iusu) of the Apocrypha. The Books of Wisdom show the nature of the sayings and prove that they were pre-Christian. For example, the Book of Ecclesiastics contains the logia of a pre-Christian Jesus. Here are two of *his* sayings "*Forgive thy neighbor the hurt that he hath done unto thee, so shall thy sins also be forgiven when thou prayest.*"[388] "*Lay up thy treasure according to the commandments of the Most High, and it shall bring thee more profit that gold.*"[389] These are assigned to the Jesus of Matthew's gospel. "*For if ye forgive men their trespasses' your heavenly Father will also forgive you.*"[390] "*Lay not up for yourselves treasure upon earth, where moth and trust doth corrupt, and where thieves break through and steal.*"[391] The "sayings" were common property in the mysteries ages before they were ever written down. "*The parables of knowledge are in the treasures of Wisdom.*"[392] and were taught as such to the initiated.[393]

When Simon Magus (or Paul) points out the contradictions in the sayings assigned to the Christ, Peter admits that the apostles do not pronounce the logia as they were spoken by the Lord himself, or they do not affirm that these sayings were spoken by himself, as it is not in their commission so to do, but they have to show that every one of them is based on truth.[394] Whatsoever gospel of Matthew preceded that canonical gospel *according to* Matthew, it is certain that the "*sayings of the Lord*" are the basis of the book. We read, "*When Jesus had ended these sayings*" (Matt.vii. 28). "*When Jesus had finished these sayings*" (Matt. xix. 1). "*When Jesus finished these sayings*" (Matt. xxvi. 1). And in John's gospel he says, "*Verily, verily, I say unto you, if a man keep my saying he shall never see death*" (John. viii. 51). This is the language and doctrine of the Egyptian *Ritual*, in which the sayer was Horus, son of Osiris; or Iu-em-hept, the Word of Atum, but not an historical teacher.

In the *Ritual* the deceased lives and triumphs over all his enemies, by means of the word, the sayings, the gnosis. He exclaims, "*I am the gnostic*," or the "one who knows."[395] The rubric to the first chapter of "*Coming forth as the day*" says, "*Let this book be known on earth. It is the chapter by which the deceased comes out every day as he wishes, and he goes to his house. He is not turned back, when he passes to the Elysian fields.*" Of the 18th chapter the rubric affirms, "*This chapter being* SAID *a person comes forth pure from the day after he has been laid out.*" Keeping the "sayings" was a mode of insuring eternal life. The Egyptian *Ritual* has been recovered because the divine words and sayings, the logia of Horus recorded by Hermes, were inscribed in hieroglyphics on papyri and amulets, linen cartonages, and coffins. These sayings faithfully kept were considered good against death and devils; they opened all gateways and assured a passage through hell or purgatory to the abodes of the blessed. Among the logia of the LORD IS THE SAYING "THE VERY HAIRS OF YOUR HEAD ARE NUMBERED."[396] IN THE RITUAL EVERY hair is weighed, and there is a day of judgment and of receiving the crown of triumph, the night of which is designated that of "*weighing words, or weighing a hair!*"[397]

The "logia" in the twenty-fifth chapter of Matthew reproduce not only the sayings, but also the SCENERY OF THE LAST JUDGMENT IN THE GREAT HALL OF JUSTICE, REPRESENTED IN THE BOOK OF *the Dead*. The scene is that of "*separating a person from his sins*"; and in the gospel it is the scene of "*separating the sheep from the goats.*" The deceased Osirian says, "*The god has welcomed him as he had wished.*" Then follows a passage rendered thus by Dr. Birch—"*He has given food to (my) the hungry, drink to (my) the thirsty, clothes to (my) the naked (ness); he has made a boat for me to go by.*"

*He has made the sacred food of the gods, the meals of the spirits,—take ye them to him, guard ye them for him.*" It is the doctrine of the *Ritual* that offerings made to the gods are returned with interest to the giver; so is it here. The gifts are food, clothes and a boat to go by. This is reproduced in Matthew's gospel, where it is the Son of Man who speaks and says, "*I was an hungered, and ye gave me meat; I was thirsty, and ye gave me drink; I was a stranger, and ye took me in; naked and ye clothed me.*"[398]

As the Osirified had done these things, the judges say, "*Do not accuse him before the lord of mummies; because his mouth is pure, his hands are pure. Come! come in peace, say they,*" the gods; "*he has been let off,*" and is "*justified for ever.*" They say to him, "*Go forth you have been introduced. Thy food is from the eye, thy drink is from the eye, thy meals are from the eye,*" that is, the Eye as a type of eternal repetition.

This is rendered in the canonical gospel, "*Come ye blessed of my Father, inherit the kingdom prepared for you from the foundation of the world,*" and in the *Ritual* the name of the festival by which the triumph of Horus, son of the father Osiris, was celebrated is, "*Come thou to me.*"[399]

The good are passed on into eternal life whilst the wicked are "*Introduced to the ceiling of flame, the circuit of which is of living snakes,*" or the "*worm that dies not' and the hell-fire that is never quenched.*"

The goat was a type of Sut and the sheep of Horus, according to the twin character of the Sut-Horus. In the text Horus is addressed as the "*Sheep, son of a sheep; Lamb, son of a lamb,*" and invoked in this character as the protector and savior of souls. The goat in the zodiac is the type of Sut, who as Anup, is figured in that sign.[400] Thus the goat in heaven is placed on the left hand whilst the Lamb or ram in the east is on the right hand.[401] According to Revelation (xxi. 27), they alone were to enter the renewed heaven whose names were "*written in the Lamb's Book of life,*" and both the Lamb or God and his Book of Life are Egyptian. Horus is the Lamb of God the father, and is addressed by the name of the lamb who is the protector or saviour of the dead in the earth and Amenti.[402] This is the redeemer who is portrayed in the monumental scenes, presenting the souls of the dead to his father after the judgment, with the roll of their names in his hand.

The followers of Horus become his sheep on the right hand of Osiris, the father; and in the *Book of the Dead*, where the great judgment takes place, on the night when the dead are numbered and souls are judged, *i.e.* the night of reckoning, the last account, it is said that the "conspirators of Sut," those who have sided with him against Horus the Christ, are "*transformed into goats*."[403] It should be observed that the scene of the last judgment, which occurs in the Egyptian Hall of the "Two Truths," is reproduced in the gospel according to Matthew, and in that only. Now, in the *Ritual, the lunar-god, Taht-Aan, is the scribe and recorder of the logia of the Lord.* As the penman and lord of divine words, he writes down the sayings or logia that are uttered by Horus, or Osiris the sun-god. "*Says Horus,*" "*Says Osiris*," is a common formula, and much of the *Ritual* consists of the sayings of the lord Horus or Osiris, which sayings were recorded by Taht for men to get by heart so that they might not forget them in death. Taht proclaims himself to be the justifier of the words of Horus. He writes them down to become law in life and the "open *Sesame*" of all doors that close in death. The funeral *Ritual*, called the Hermetic writings or sacred books of Taht, the books of the divine words or logia, opens with an announcement made by Taht himself, as the forerunner and proclaimer of Horus the anointed. As the sun-god's *light by night*, he bears witness to the true light of the world, the solar Messiah, in accordance with natural phenomena.

He contends for Horus, and smites the accusers of the meek one. He exclaims, "*Oh Horus! I have fought for thee. I have succeeded (or passed) in thy name. I am with Horus, the day of clothing tesh-tesh, to wash the heart of the meek one. I am with Horus, the day of the festival of Osiris Un-Nefer, whose word is law, making the solar sacrifice the day of the festival of the 6th and 15th in Annu. I am the priest in Abtu, the day of calling the world. I am the maker of the festivals of the Spirit-Lord of Tattu. I am the blessed of his keeping. O, openers of roads! O, guides of paths to the soul made in the abode of Osiris! open ye the roads, level ye the paths to the Osiris with yourselves*."[404]

So John bears witness and testifies to the Christ, justifies him, fights for him, appeals to his followers on his behalf. He succeeds in the name of the coming one. He is with the Messiah on the day of baptism, and washes the meek one in Bethany. John's is "*the voice of one crying in the wilderness, Make ye ready the way of the Lord, make his paths straight*."[405]

Taht-Aan was the superseder of Sut-Anup in the later form of the lunar mythos. As already explained, one name of Taht is *Aan* (compared with John); and one of his types, the Ibis, is still known in Upper Egypt by the name of "Father *John*." Another if his titles is that of *Mati* or *Matiu;* the *I* having the *u* inherent. *Taht-Aan* appears in the Judgment Hall as *Matiu* by name, and in the special character of Registrar, who keeps the reckoning at the Assize of Souls, or the last Account.

It is said of the deceased and Mati, "*Let him be introduced to Mati in his hour. Explain the god in his hour. Thou art called reckoner of the earth. The reckoner of the earth is Taht.*" Thus Taht in the character of registrar of the deeds done in the body, is *Matiu* or *Mathias by name!*

*Mati* supplied an Egyptian proper name, male or female; *Mathu*, born of Ameni, was a prophetess of Hathor and wife of Ameni in the time of the 11th dynasty.[406]

IT IS NOW INTENDED TO IDENTIFY THE MATTHEW WHO, according to the testimony of Papias, first wrote down the logia of the Lord, as *Matiu*, as Hermes the writer of the sayings in the *Ritual*.

Taht-Matiu was the scribe of the gods, and in Christian art Matthew is depicted as the scribe of the gods, with an angel standing near him, to dictate the gospel. At times he is represented carrying a carpenter's rule, or square. Taht-Matiu was the measurer. He invented geometry, and is called the measurer of earth and heaven.

The lion is Matthew's symbol, and that is the zodiacal sign of the month of Taht-Mati (Thoth), in the fixed year. Tradition makes Matthew to have been the *eighth* of the apostles; and the eighth (Esmen) is a title of Taht-Matiu. Moreover, it is Matthias, upon whom the lot fell, who was chosen to fill the place of the Typhonian traitor Judas. So was it in the mythos when Matiu (Taht) succeeded Sut, and occupied his place after his betrayal of Osiris. In the gospel according to Matthew the "*place of toll*" is substituted for the Hall of Justice, in which Taht is the scribe and registrar. It is noticeable, too, that Matthew is identical with Levi, called the son of Alphæus, and that Levi, to be joined or double, coincides with *Mati* (Eg.), who is the representative of the truth, law, or justice, in its duality.

It is to the Gnostics that we must turn for the missing link between the oral and the written word; between the Egyptian *Ritual* and the canonical gospels; between the Matthew who wrote the Hebrew or Aramaic gospel of the sayings, and Taht-Mati, who wrote the *Ritual*, the Hermetic, which means *inspired* writings, that are said to have been inscribed in hieroglyphics by the very finger of *Mati* himself.[407]

Clements of Alexandria quotes the "*Traditions of Matthias*" twice over. He writes: "*Matthias, in saying to us in his traditions, wonder at what is before you, proves that admiration is the first step leading upwards to knowledge. Therefore, also, it is written in the gospel of the Hebrews, he who shall wonder shall reign, and he who reigns shall rest.*" Further, the same writer says the followers of Carpocrates would appeal to the authority of Matthias as an excuse for giving full scope to their lusts.[408]

Origen asserts that the gnostic Basilides had the effrontery to compose a gospel, and call it after his own name.[409] In writing this gospel, says Hippolytus, Basilides appealed to a *secret tradition*, which he professed to have received from *Matthias*, which claimed to be grounded on "*private intercourse with the Saviour*."[410]

The term *ευαγγελιου* goes to show that the nature of this scripture was mystical and not historical. We learn from Hippolytus that the Basilidians expressly excluded from their tenets the "generation of Jesus." Now all the difference turned on that! They acknowledged the Christ of the gnosis, the Messiah of the mythos, but, as Gnostics, never admitted the Word to have been made flesh. As now shown by the comparative method it was the Gnostics who had faithfully preserved the true traditions.[411] It was they who made the images in the Christian iconography, and reproduced the Iao-Chnubis and the Kamite Horus on the talismanic stones and in the catacombs of Rome; and they also had their gospel according to Matthew, which is not ours.

It follows, perforce, that the secret tradition appealed to by them was likewise Egyptian; and as the typical recorder and divine scribe was *Mati* by name, it further follows that Mati—whose name with the Greek terminals, becomes Matthias—was the original author of the sayings and traditions assigned to Matthias and to Matthew.

The name of Mati denotes the truth, law, or justice, in a dual form and phase. He is the recorder in the Hall of the Twin Truth, the judgment-place of the clothed and naked, or the righteous and the wicked. Thus the gospel of Mati would be also the gospel of Truth in this double aspect. Now, according to Irenæus, the Marcosian and Valentinian Gnostics were in possession of many gospels. He says, "their number is infinite,"[412] and amongst these apocryphal works was one entitled the "*Gospel of Truth*" (*Evangelism Veritas*). This scripture, he says, "*agrees in nothing with the gospels of the apostles*."[413]

We may be sure that the nearer it was to the Kamite original the less would be the likeness to the four gospels that were finally made canonical. This gospel is probably referred to by Tertullian, who says the Valentinians were in possession of "*their own gospel, in addition to ours*."[414]

The "Gospel of Truth" is the Gospel of Mati, *in Egyptian*; and Mati was the registrar in the Hall of Truth, the recorder of the sayings and divine words of the Lord, whose record is more or less extant as the Egyptian *Ritual*, faith, or gospel.

Valentinus, one of the gnostic pioneers in Christian theology, was an Egyptian born. Both he and his Gospel of Truth came from Alexandria, and he was excommunicated by the A-Gnostic Christians as one of the numerous gnostic heretics.[415] Nevertheless, he was a living and visible connecting link between the Egyptian-gnostic Gospel of Truth, that is of Mati, and the gospel according to Matthew, which was canonized at last. This will explain why one of the earliest known scriptures was entitled the "*Gospel of the Egyptians*," and also account for its having been disowned and dropped out of sight as soon as possible by the worshippers of the carnalized Christ.

The gospel used by the Nasseni or Ophites was known as the gospel according to the Egyptians, and A λογιου of Christ, written in this gospel, is alluded to in one of the books.[416] The *Ritual is* the Egyptian gospel, and that is the gospel of *Mati* and of Truth which contains the logia of the Lord, who was Horus by name.

IRENÆUS ASSERTS THAT, FOR MYSTIC REASONS, THE GOSPELS COULD BE NO MORE AND NO LESS THAN FOUR IN number. The limits were prescribed on account of the four quarters, the four spirits, or corner-keepers, and other figures of the four, amidst which the Christ is seated. The four books he says, are in accordance with the four covenants, one under Adam, before the deluge; the second under Noah, after the deluge; the third being the giving of the law under Moses; the fourth that which renews man, and bears him into the kingdom of heaven. In the Kamite Eschatology everything was founded on the astronomical allegory, and can be followed accordingly. Irenæus does not identify the fourfold nature of the writings in keeping with the pre-Christian canon.

The books of the Egyptian Horoscopus were four in number. The first treated of the system of the fixed stars; the second and third of the solar and lunar conjunctions (eclipses and the ends of periods being called deluges and destructions); the fourth was the book of the rising or resurrections of the sun, moon, and stars, and, eschatologically, of the souls of men.

Four books of magic were assigned to Taht or Hermes—the four in a psychotheistic phase. We are told in the magical texts that

"*These are the titles of the four books:—*

(1) *The old book*

(2) *The book to destroy men;*

(3) *The great book;*

(4) *The book to be as a God.*"[417]

No better identification or apter illustration of the four books of the "Magical texts" could be given than the *Book of Adam* for (1) the Old Book; *the Deluge* for (2) the "Book to destroy men"; *the Law* for (3) the Great Book; and the *Book which renews man and bears him into the kingdom of heaven* for (4) the "Book to be as a God." "For mystic reasons" the four gospels were similarly arranged or written. The gospel of Matthew is the "Old Book," the first we hear of, through Papias, as the original logia. Mark begins with the baptism, the conjunction of John and Jesus, the end of a time, "the time is fulfilled"—analogous to the covenant of Noah. If Luke's stands for the "Book to be as a God." No stress need be laid on this arrangement; still one sees the four are cast according to the quadriform gospel, or the four Books of Taht. The Messiah in the gospel after John says, "*In my father's house are many abodes: I go to prepare a place for you.*"[418] But in the Egyptian texts the number of abiding-places for the elect is in accordance with the fourfold nature of the books; "*there are four mansions of life at Abtu* (the abode of the four corners); *each is built four stories high. There are four mansions of life. Osiris* (the father) *is master thereof. The four outer walls are of stone. Its foundation is sand, its exterior is jasper, one is to the south, another to the north, another to the west, another to the east. It is very hidden, unknown, invisible, nothing save the solar disk sees it. It escapes men that go there. The sun's librarians, the treasure-scribes, are within*" (answering to the twelve apostles, including him who carried the treasure in a bag). This quadrangular is the house of the writings, the scribe and librarians of the manifestor. "*The writer of his divine books is Taht* (Mati-Aan), *who is vivifies it* (the house) *each day; its excellency is neither seen nor heard.*" "*O, thou daily hidden one,*" is written in front of the house, and in the chapter to open the gate of this house it is said "*I have opened heaven, I have opened earth, I enter.*"

IN THE GOSPEL THE LORD IS ABOUT TO GO THE HIDDEN WAY TO PREPARE A PLACE FOR HIS FOLLOWERS IN THE house of many mansions. The scene in the "Texts is that in which Horus is about to be betrayed by the Egyptian Judas and is protected against Sut and the wicked conspirators. "*The souls of the sun are around; this great god approaches them to kill his enemies. Those that dwell there are the sun's librarians. The sun's servants protect his son daily.*" The scene in the gospel is where the twelve are gathered around the Lord, and Satan enters Judas with the sop. The Lord announces that he is about to enter the secret place where they cannot follow. The disciples have just been called the servants of the Lord, and Peter has offered to lay down his life in protecting his Lord, just as the "*Son*" is said to be protected by his servants daily. These "servants" are called to be the scribes and preachers of all that the son had heard of the father, and made known to them. *I have given unto them the words which thou gavest me and they have received.*"[419] Therefore they answer to the "Librarians of the Sun," the "*Souls of the Sun*" the protectors and proclaimers of the son of the sun, or of Osiris the father.

Several Aramaic words, left untranslated in the Greek, point to a collection of the "sayings" in that language as an intermediate link between the Egyptian and the Greek. The same link is observable in the "Magic Papyrus." Among the spells for giving power over all reptiles and animals there is a list of Aramean magic names.[420] The Aramean or Aramaic language, which was supplanted by Arabic, was not merely Semitic; hieroglyphics papyri were amongst its monumental remains as well as the "Inscription of Carpentras." Some of these Aramaic words are likewise Egyptian. For instance, the word *Raca* [421] is the Egyptian *Raka*, for the scorner, culpable, profane, a rebel in religion. The statement that "*whoever shall say, Thou μωρε* (rendered "fool") *shall be in danger of the hell of fire*"[422] is a reminder that the Kamite phlegethon, or hell of fire, is the *murbu*, the place (*bu*) of the *mur*; and that the *mur* may be a reptile, blindworm, &c., as well as the condemned dead.

In the account of Christ giving Sight to the blind man, the healer "*said unto him, Go, wash in the Pool of Siloam* (which is by interpretation, Sent)."[423] Now the *shent* is the typical pool and source in Egyptian, whilst *sunnt* (later *sennt*) *signifies a medicated or healing bath.*

There is no need to strain a single point for the purpose of making ends meet, but it may be remarked that the words assigned to the sufferer, both in the psalms and gospels, "*Eli, Eli, lama sabachthani*,"[424] are also Egyptian. Lama, or *Rama*, denotes weeping; *Remi*, was the weeper in Rem-Rem. *Sabak* means to be prostrate and utterly subdued. *Tani*, is to bow down to the forehead. Instead of those words John says, "*When Jesus had received the vinegar he said, It is finished; and he bowed his head, and gave up his spirit.*" Now it is noteworthy that *the one version should be a rendering of the other, according to Egyptian. Heli* (heri) means it is finished, ended, to fly away, give up the ghost, ascend as a spirit. Any Egyptologist will know that *heli-lama-Sabaktani* contains and conveys the sense of *heli*, to *be ended* (in giving up the ghost); *lama*, to weep; *sabak*, be prostrate; and *tani*, to *bow down the forehead*. He will also know that as such *it is a description by another speaker and not a dramatic utterance of the sufferer;* and John's version *is* a descriptive narrative except in the words "*it is finished*," which as "*Heli-heli*" might express the giving up of the spirit by whomsoever they were said. If the words were Egyptian, *heli* would naturally become *eli*, as Semitic form.

In some of the ancient Egyptian temples the Christian iconoclasts, when tired with hacking and hewing at the symbolic figures incised in the chambers of imagery, and defacing the most prominent features OF THE MONUMENTS, FOUND THEY COULD NOT DIG OUT THE HIEROGLYPHICS, AND TOOK TO COVERING them over with plaster; and this plaster, intended to hide the meaning and stop the mouth of stone word, has served to preserve the ancient writings as fresh in hue and sharp in outline as when they were first cut and colored. In a similar manner the temple of the ancient religion was invaded and possession gradually gained by connivance of Roman power; and that enduring fortress, not built but quarried out of the solid rock, was stuccoed all over the front and made white a-while with its look of brand-newness, and reopened under the sign of another name—that of the carnalized Christ. And all the time each nook and corner was darkly alive with the presence and the proofs of the earlier gods, even though the hieroglyphics remained unread. But *stucco* is not for lasting wear; it cracks and crumbles, sloughs off, and slinks away into its natal insignificance; the rock is the sole true foundation, the rock is the record in which we reach reality at last.

Such has been the reversal of cause and outcome according to the non-evolutionary view that the Substance and the Shadow have had to change place and relationship. All that was foundational, all that was substantial in the past has been held to be the foreshadow of that which was to come. The long procession of fetishism, typology, and Kronian mythology is looked upon as if it were like that representation of Adam in the German play, who is seen crossing the stage whilst *going to be created*. Wilkinson, the Egyptologist, has actually said of Osiris on earth, "*Some may be disposed to think that the Egyptians, being aware of the promises of the real Saviour, had anticipated that event, regarding it as though it had already happened, and introduced that mystery into their religious system!*"

We are told by writers on the catacombs and the Christian iconography, that one figure is Apollo, *as a type of Christ*. This is Pan or Aristæus, *as a type of Christ*. This is Harpocrates, *as a type of Christ*. This is Mercury, but, *as a type of Christ*. This is the devil (for Sut=Mercury became the devil), *as a type of Christ*. Until long hearing of the facts reversed, perverted, and falsified, makes one feel as

IF UNDER A NIGHTMARE WHICH HAS LASTED FOR eighteen centuries, knowing that Truth has been buried alive and made dumb all that time, and believing that it has only to get voice and make itself heard to end the lying once for all, and bring down the curtain of oblivion at last upon the most pitiful drama of delusion ever witnessed on the human stage.

The Christ who was only portrayed by mythical types must remain a mythical Christ, even as the Crucifixion and Resurrection that are only represented by symbols (in the Catacombs), remain symbolical.

It has often been said that if there were no historic Christ then the writers who represented such a *conception* of the divine man, must have included amongst them one who was equal to the Christ! But the mythical Christ was not the outcome of any such conception. It was not a work of the individual mind at all, but of the human race; a crowning result of evolution *versus* any private conception of a hero. This was the hero of all men, who never was and was never meant to be human, but from the beginning was divine; a mythical hero without mortal model, and equally without fault or flaw. This was the star-god who dawned through the outermost darkness; this was the moon-god who brought the message of renewal and immortality; this was the sun-god who came with the morning to all men; this in the Kronian stage was the announcer of new life and endless continuity at the opening of every cycle; and in the psychotheistic phase the typical son of the eternal, as manifestor and representative in time.

As a mental model the Christ was elaborated by whole races of men, and worked at continually like the Apollo of Greek sculpture. Various nations wrought at this ideal, which long continued repetition evoked from the human mind at last as it did the Greek god from the marble.

EGYPT LABORED AT THE PORTRAIT FOR THOUSANDS OF YEARS BEFORE THE GREEKS ADDED THEIR FINISHING TOUCHES TO THE TYPE OF THE EVER-YOUTHFUL SOLAR GOD. It was Egypt that first made the statue live with her own life, and humanized her ideal of the divine. Hers was the legend of supreme pity and self-sacrifice so often told of the canonical Christ. She related how the very god did leave the courts of heaven, and come down as a little child, the infant Horus born of the Virgin, through whom he took flesh, or descended into matter, "*crossed the earth as a substitute*,"[425] descended into Hades as the vivifier of the dead, their vicarious justifier and redeemer, the first fruits and leader of the resurrection into eternal life. The Christian legends were first related of Horus or Osiris, who was the embodiment of divine goodness, wisdom, truth, and purity; who personated ideal perfection in each sphere of manifestation and every phase of power. This was the greatest hero that *ever lived in the mind of man—not in the flesh*—to influence with transforming force; the only hero to whom the miracles were natural *because* he was *not* human. The canonical Christ only needed a translator not a creator; a transcriber of the "sayings" and a collector of the "doings" already ascribed to the mythical Christ.

The humanized history is but the mythical drama made mundane. The sayings and marvellous doings of Christ being pre-extant, the "*spirit of Christ*," the "*secret of Christ*," the "*sweet reasonableness of Christ,*" *were* all pre-Christian, and consequently could not be derived from any "personal founder" of Christianity. They were extant before the great delusion, had turned the minds of men, and the figure-head of Peter's Bark had been mistaken for a portrait of the builder.

THE CHRIST OF THE GOSPELS IS IN NO SENSE AN historical personage or a supreme model of humanity, a hero who strove, and suffered, and failed to save the world by his death. It is impossible to establish the existence of an historical character *even as an impostor*. For such an one the two witnesses, astronomical mythology and gnosticism, completely prove an *alibi*. The Christ is a popular lay-figure that never lived, and a lay-figure of Pagan origin; a lay-figure that was once the Ram and afterwards the Fish; a lay-figure that in human form was the portrait and image of a dozen different gods.

The imagery of the catacombs shows that the types there represented are not the ideal figures of the human reality. They *are* the sole reality in the centuries after A.D., because they had been in the centuries long before. The symbolism, the allegories, the figures and types, remained there just what they were to the Romans, Greeks, Persians, and Egyptians. The iconography of the catacombs absolutely proves that the lay-figure, as Christ, must have sat for the portraits of Osiris, Horus the child, Mithras, Bacchus, Aristæus, Apollo, Pan, the Good Shepherd. The lay-figure or type is one all through. The portraits are manifold, yet they all mean the mythical Christ, under whatsoever name.

The typical Christ, so far from being derived from the model man, has been made up from the features of many gods, after a fashion somewhat similar to those "pictoral averages" portrayed by Mr. Galton, in which the characteristics of various persons are photographed and fused in a portrait, a composite likeness of twenty different persons merged in one that is not *anybody*.

It is pitiful to track the poor faithful gleaners who picked up every fallen fragment or scattered waif and stray of the mythos, and to watch how they treasured every trait and tint of the ideal Christ to make up the personal portrait of their own supposed real one. His mother, like the other forms of the queen of heaven, had the color of the *mater frugum*, the complexion of the golden corn; and a Greek Father of the eighth century cites an early tradition of the Christians concerning the *personnel* of the Christ to the effect that in taking the form of Adam he assumed features exactly like those of the virgin and his face was of a *wheaten color*, like that of his mother.[426] That is he (the seed) was *corn-complexioned*, as was the mother of corn, like Flava Keres, Aurea

Venus, the Golden Lakshmi, the Yellow Neith; and the son was her Seed which in Egypt was the corn brought forth at the vernal equinox, and which was continued in the cult of Rome as the "Bread-Corn of the elect."

In the chapter of "knowing the spirits of the east" the Osirified assumes the types of the virile and hairy Horus, the divine hawk of the resurrection. This is called *the type under which he desires to appear before all men;* and it is said, "*his hair is on his shoulder when he proceeds to the heaven.*"[427] This long hair of the adult Horus reaching down to the shoulders is a typical feature in the portraits of the Messiah, the copy of the Kamite Christ made permanent by the art of the Gnostics. The halo of Christ is the glory of the sun-god seen in his phantom phase when the more physical type had become psychotheistic. Hence, it is worn by the child-Christ as the *karast* mummy. It is the same halo that illumined Horus and Iu-em-hept, Krishna and Buddha, and others of whom the same old tales of deliverance and redemption were told and believed. Yet the dummy ideal of paganism is supposed to have become doubly real as the man-god standing with one foot in two worlds,—one resting on the ground of the fall from heaven, and the other on the physical resurrection from the earth.

It has been confidently declared by some that the ancient traditional belief in a life beyond the grave was raised to an incontrovertible fact by the resurrection of Jesus Christ. As if a physical resurrection and the ascent of a corporeal body to heaven could demonstrate a future spiritual existence! Such a resurrection is at once non-spiritualistic, anti-scientific, and altogether nihilistic. It is the natural antithesis of all that is spiritualistic. Thus, when phenomenal spiritualism (whether true or untrue is not the question here) is put forth in our days as a scientific basis for the continuity of existence, the mytholators immediately rush to arms to defend their faith against the alleged facts. The Christian DOCTRINE OF A RESURRECTION FURNISHES ABSOLUTELY CONCLUSIVE *evidence of the astronomical and Kronian nature of the origines.* Every time the worshipper turns and bows to the east it is a confession that the cult is solar, the Christolatry Equinoctial,—the confession being all the more fatal because it is unconscious. And the resurrection is Kronian accordingly only the cult has become dateless. Christian Revelation knows nothing of immortality except in the form of a periodic renewal dependent on the *coming* Savior, who is reincarnated at the end of the world. It does but continue the Kronian typology without the gnosis, by which alone it could be explained. At the last time of the *coming* there was a resurrection of the dead. According to Matthew "*the tombs were opened, and many bodies of the saints that had fallen asleep were raised;*

*and, coming out of the tombs after his resurrection, they entered into the holy city and appeared unto many;*"[428] since which time the dead sleep on, and are spoken of as being "no more," or as lying at rest awaiting *the next coming of the Christ*. The doctrine is identical with that of the underworld as the savior of the dead, and the resurrection followed for those who were worthy of a future life. Our own festivals of "all souls" is an extant relic of the yearly collection and resurrection.

The Christian revelation reveals nothing of a spirit world, knows nothing of the natural and sequential continuity of life. The renewal that it teaches belongs, as of old, to the end of the cycle, called the world; and the resurrection of the dead depends upon the day of judgment at the termination of an indefinite time. It is the resurrection for which the men of the mounds and caves first sought to protect and preserve the bones of their dead; the resurrection of the Egyptian mummy at the end of 3,000 years, or the Great Year. All who have ever died "in the Lord" have had only the hope of a resurrection at some future time, when the next great cycle should be completed and the coming one return, or the phœnix transform once more on the scale of the Great Year—a resurrection once in 26,000 years! At root it is reliance on this ancient doctrine of Kronian repetition and the absence of all spiritual foothold in the infinite that caused the millenarians to keep on "prospecting" for the second coming of the Messiah, who is to finally effect all that the earlier ones left unfulfilled.

THE ANCIENT WISDOM OF EGYPT AND CHALDEA LIVED ON WITH THE MEN WHO KNEW, CALLED THE GNOSTICS. They had directly inherited the gnosis that remained oral, the sayings uttered from mouth to ear that were to be unwritten, the mysteries performed in secret, the science kept concealed. The continuity of the astronomical mythos of Equinoctial Christolatry and of the total typology is proved by the persistence of the types—the ancient genitrix, the two sisters, the hebdomad of inferior and superior powers, the trinity in unity represented by *Iao*, the tetrads male and female, the double Horus, or Horus and Stauros, the system of Æons, the Kamite divinities, Harpocrates and Sut-Anubis, Isis and Hathor. Theirs was the Christ not made flesh, but the manifestor of the seven powers, and perfect star of the pleroma. The figure of eight which is a sign of the Nnu or associate gods in Egypt, who were the primary Ogdoad, is reproduced as a gnostic symbol, a figure of the pleroma and fellow-type of the eight-rayed star.[429] The "Lamb of God" was a gnostic sign. "*Lord, thou art the Lamb*" (and "our Light") was a gnostic formula.[430] The "*Immaculate Virgin*" was a gnostic type. On one of the sard stones Isis stands before Serapis holding the sistrum in one hand, in the other a wheatsheaf, the legend being "*Immaculate is our Lady Isis*,"[431] which proves the continuity from Kam.

It was gnostic art that reproduced the Hathor-Meri and Horus of Egypt as the Virgin and child-Christ of Rome, and the Icons of characters entirely ideal, which served as the sole portraits of the *historical* Madonna and Jesus the Christ. The report of Irenæus sufficed to show the survival of the true tradition. He complains of the oral wisdom of the Gnostics, and says rightly they read from things unwritten; *i.e.* from sources unknown to him and the Fathers in general. Chief of these sources was the science of astronomy. He testifies that Marcus was skilled in the form of the gnosis, and enables us to follow the line of unbroken continuity, and to confute his own assertion that gnosticism had no existence prior to Marcion and Valentinus;[432] which shows he did not know or else he denied the fact that the Suttites, the Mandaites, the Essenes, and Nazarenes were all Gnostics; all of which sects preceded the cult of the carnalized Christ. Hippolytus informs us that Elkesai said the Christ born of a Virgin was æonian. The Elkesites maintained that Jesus the Christ had continually transformed and manifested in various bodies at many different times.[433] This shows they also were in possession of the gnosis, and that the Christ and his repeated incarnations were Kronian. Hence we are told that they occupied themselves "*with a bustling activity in regard to astronomical science*." Epiphanius also bears witness that the head and front of the gnostic boast was astronomy, and that Manes wrote a work on what was at the time termed astronomy; astronomy being the root of the whole matter concerning Equinoctial Christolatry.

Nothing is more astounding, on their own showing, than the ignorance of the Fathers about the nature, the significance, the descent of gnosticism and its rootage in the remotest past. They knew nothing of evolution or the survival of types; and for them the new beginning with Christ carnalized, obliterated all that preceded. Such a thing as priority, natural genesis, or the doctrine of development, did not trouble those who considered that the more the myth the greater was the miracle which proved the Divinity.

Also, it has been asserted from the time of Irenæus down to that of Mansel that the gnostic heretics of the second century invented a number of spurious gospels in imitation of or in opposition to the true gospel of Christ, which has descended to us as canonical, authentic, and historic. This is a popular delusion, false enough to damn all belief in it from the beginning until now. The ignorance of the past manifested by men like Irenæus is the measure of the value of their testimony to the origines of Equinoctial Christolatry. They who pretend to know all concerning the founding and the founder know nothing of the foundations. Hippolytus, in quoting a passage from Irenæus respecting the tetrad of the Valentinians, personified the *doctrine of "kolarbas" as another of those heretics whose name was Colarbasus!* Like the vigilant "Watch" in Shakespeare's drama who knew "that deformed" and "*remembered his name.*"[434] Gnosticism, according to those who are ignorant of its origin and relationships, was supposed heresy developed from a primitive Christianity through a perversion of the true faith in an historic Christ. Nothing could be falser, and all that has been based on such falsehood falls with it. When Tertullian used the word προβογη he asserted that heresy had taken the phrase from truth to mould it after its own likeness. Mansel calls the gnostic trinity a "*profane parody of the Christian doctrine of the holy trinity,*" and he asserts that its value consists in its testimony to the "*primitive existence of that article of the Christian church from which it was borrowed.*"[435] This is an utter reversal of the facts and relative positions; and so it has been all through.

The Docetæ sects, for example, are supposed to have held that the transactions of the gospel narrative *did occur*, but in a phantasmagoria of unreality. This, however, is but a false mode of describing the position of those who denied that the Christ could be incarnated and become human to suffer and die upon the cross. The Christians who report the beliefs of the Gnostics, Docetæ, and others, always *assume the actual history and then try to explain the non-human interpretation as an heretical denial of the alleged facts*. But the docetic interpretation was first, was prehistorical, and those who held that with knowledge could not discuss the human, even as a possibility; they knew better. Whereas the A-Gnostics charge them with denying the established facts and trying to explain the reality away by a perverse interpretation of the same data. The data were docetic, gnostic, mythical; Mithraic. Osirian, anything but humanly historical.

The alleged heresy of the Gnostics, which is supposed and assumed to have originated in the second century, the first being carefully avoided, only proves that the A-Gnostics, who had literally adopted the pre-Christian types, and believed they had been historically fulfilled, were then for the first time becoming conscious of the cult that preceded theirs, and face to face with those who held them to be the heretics. Gnosticism was no birth or new thing in the second century; it was no perverter or corrupter of Christian doctrines divinely revealed, but the voice of an older cult growing more audible in its protest against a superstition as degrading and debasing now as when it was denounced by men like Tacitus, Pliny, Julian, Marcus Aurelius, and Porphyry. For what could be more shocking to any sense really religious, than the belief that the very God himself had descended on earth as an embryo in a Virgin's womb, to run the risk of abortion and universal miscarriage during nine months *in utero*, and then dying on a cross to save his own created world or a portion of its people from eternal perdition? The opponents of the latest superstition were too intelligent to accept a dying deity. Porphyry terms the Christian religion a blasphemy barbarously bold (*Βαρβαρου τολμγμα*). "A pestilence," cries Suetonius. "*Exitiabilis superstitio*," says Tacitus. "*Certain most impious errors are committed by them*," says Celsus, "*due to their extreme ignorance, in which they have wandered away from the meaning of the divine enigmas*."[436] Which is true as it is temperate. The "primitive Christians" were men whose ardor was fierce in proportion to their ignorance, as the narrower chimney makes the greater draught, and turns the radiation of heat into an upward roaring; guide as blind in theosophy as in geology.

When Peter, Philip, and John, as preachers of the new creed, were summoned before the Jewish hierarchs to be examined, the council decided that they were only ignorant men, unlearned in the oral law, unskilled in the tradition of interpretation, believers who did not know the true nature of that which they taught. They were not punished, but dismissed with warnings, or contempt, as δνθρωπο αγραμματοι αι ιδῶτοι or as we have the word in later language, idiots.[437] They were *idiotai*, whether judged by Kabalist or Gnostic, Jew or Gentile. When judged they were found to have laid hold at the wrong end of things. This was the position of the believers in a Christ carnalized when tested by the Gnostics.

NEVER WERE MEN MORE PERPLEXED AND BEWILDERED than the A-Gnostic Christians of the third and fourth centuries who had started from a new beginning altogether, which they had been taught to consider solely historic, when they turned to look back for the first time to find that an apparition of their faith was following them one way and confronting them in another; a shadow that threatened to steal away their substance, mocking them with its aerial unreality; the ghost of the body of truth which they had embraced as a solid and eternal reality, claiming to be the rightful owner of their possessions; a phantom Christ without flesh or bone; a crucifixion that only occurred in cloud-land; a parody of the drama of salvation performed in the air; with never a cross to cling to; not a nail-wound to thrust the fingers into and hold on by; not one drop of blood to wash away their sins. It was horrible. It was devilish. It was the devil, they said, and thus they sought to account for Gnosticism and fight down their fears. *You poor ignorant idiotai*," said the Gnostics, "*you have mistaken the mysteries of old for modern history, and accepted literally all that was only meant mystically." You spawn of Satan*," responded the Christians, "*you are making the mystery by converting our accomplished facts into your miserable fables; you are dissipating and dispersing into thin air our only bit of solid foothold in the world, stained with the red drops of*

*Calvary. You are giving a Satanic interpretation to the word of revelation and falsifying the oracles of God. You are converting the solid facts of our history into your new-fangled allegories.*" "*Nay,*" replied the Gnostics, "*it is you who have taken the allegories of mythology for historic facts.*" And they were right. It was in consequence of their taking the allegorical tradition of the fall for reality that the Christian Fathers considered woman to be accursed and called her a serpent, a scorpion, the devil in feminine form.

Whether Jews, Greeks, or Romans, those who were versed in the gnosis, and acquainted thus far with the origines of the doctrines, could not, and they could not, and did not, accept historic Christianity; the Gnostics were its bitterest opponents because they knew. On the one hand we have the Salvation Army of the first century, who were so ignorant of all that preceded them that they redated everything from their own indefinite epoch A.D. So ignorant they believed everything that is impossible in nature to be true because that proved the miracle of the supernatural. On the other side we find in serried ranks, that form a solid, stolid, blank wall of opposition, the Romans, Jews and the Gnostics of various races. The Romans are simply ignorant of the alleged historic transactions. The total intelligence of Rome treats the new religion as a degrading superstition founded on a misinterpretation of their own dogmas. The Jewish race, the supposed oracles of divine revelation and sole *receptaculum* of the living God, whose communication of his own nature culminated in the rebegettal and rebirth of himself as the Christ, after the fashion of Sut-Typhon, Khem-Horus, and Heitsi-Eibib, the husband of the virgin mother, have either modestly begged leave to deny the divine honor, or been fiercely opposed to the Christian rendering of the Messiahship, and the doctrine which was based on an utterly different ground in the Hebrew writings and oral teaching. The Gnostics not only deny that such things were; they explain *how* they were not, could not be, but were only misbelieved. These are supported by all that is now made known by science, mythology, types, and symbols; by the pre-Christian status and significance of the same doctrines; by all that is gathered from the past, all that is cognizable in the present, all that human experience, practical reason, and common sense becoming prophetic, warrant us in thinking true for the future.

The general assumption concerning the canonical gospels is that the historic element was the kernel of the whole, and that the fables accreted round it; whereas the mythos, being pre-extant, proves the core of the matter was mythical, and it follows that the history is incremental. The myths of the gospels are not fabulous in the sense of the false reports that seek to magnify the true. The essential substance belongs to the genuine mythos which cannot be resolved into the falsehood of a later fable. The *logia* were the *true* fables; not the fable that is half a truth, but that which is doubly true according to the gnosis. That which was pre-extant all through as mythos cannot become historical in a last confused rendering of the same subject, found in four gospels which were concocted from a hundred previous ones. And here *the worst foes of the truth have ever been the rationalizers of the mythos*. They have assumed the human history as the starting-point, and accepted the existence of a personal founder of Christianity as the fundamental fact. They have done their best to humanize the divinity of the mythos by discharging the supernatural and miraculous element from the history in order that it might be accepted. Thus they have lost the battle from the beginning by fighting it on the wrong ground.

M. Renan, for instance, claims to be historical before all things, yet he fully admits the legend and illusion, and then proceeds to convert the mythos into history by rationalizing the miracles. As historian he accepts the scene of the Pentecost for fact: it did undoubtedly occur, but in the guise of a thunderstorm; his only misgiving is as to whether the electric fluid penetrated the chamber itself, or whether the apostles thought the Holy Ghost entered in a dazzling flash of lightning.[438]

But it is the miraculous that shows the mythical nature of the history; the identical miracles of Christ the healer that prove him to have been the same character as the healer Iu-em-hept, or Æsculapius, and the caster-out of dæmons, Khunsu. It was the human history that accreted round the divinity, and not a human being who became divine.

On the theory of an historic origin and interpretation the discrepancies may be paralleled for ever with no possibility of attaining the truth; the matter can never be moulded into coherent consistency. But the mythical origin explains all. When once we start with that, it is like introducing the creative principle into chaos, or the theory of gravitation as an explanation of planetary law. This view alone serves to read the riddle of the root. The natural genesis of Equinoctial Christolatry, or Christianity, and the initial point of an embryonic unity, are not to be discovered in the life and teaching of a personal founder or historical Christ. On the other hand, all that is impossible as human history is not only possible as mythos but is the essence and creative cause of the history. The mythical orgines only can explain the Messianic prophecy. The mythical origines only can explain the birth of the child that was begotten without the fatherhood; the virginity of the motherhood—an unknown human factor—beg the natural status of the most ancient genetrix in mythology, who was earlier, than God the father. The virgin mother is nothing if not divine, and being a divinity she cannot become humanly historical. The most ancient, gold-bedizened, smoke-stained Byzantine pictures of the virgin and child REPRESENT THE MYTHICAL MOTHER, AS ISIS, AND NOT A HUMAN MARY OF NAZARETH.

The mythical origines only can explain why there are two Marys both of whom are described as being the mother of Jesus. The mythical origines only can explain why Jesus should have been rebegotten as the anointed son at thirty years of age, the time of full adultship according to Egyptian reckoning, in the likeness of the fatherhood. The mythical origines only can explain why there is no history furnished from the time when the child-Christ was about twelve years of age to that of the adultship of thirty years. The mythical origines only can show how the Word, or Manifestor, from the first could be said to be made flesh. The mythical origines only can explain why Jesus the Christ of the catacombs should have been persistently portrayed in the two distinct characters of the beautiful Youth and the little ugly old child or elder Horus. The mythical Christ could have two birthdays like the dual-natured Horus, one at the solstice and one at the equinox. The mythical Christ could be crucified on the 15th Nisan, all Jewish laws and prejudices notwithstanding, because that was the day of the crossing, of the cross, and therefore of the crucifixion of the Christ. He descended into Hades because that was the way of the underworld first travelled by the solar god. He rose from the dead on the third day because that had been the length of time allowed in the mysteries, and because it took three days, measured by visible phenomena, for the lunar Messiah to rise again and reappear. Easter, determined by the full moon, is the time of the resurrection, because the sun-god was born, or reborn,—these being identical in the true mythos, though necessarily untrue in the false—each year at the place of the Vernal equinox, where the sun "crossed the line," made the transit, and marked the period of the passover. He rearose as Ichthys, the Fish, because Pisces was the sign of the cross after 255 B.C. and as the Lamb, or Ram, because Aries had been the previous sign.

And here it may be pointed out that Equinoctial Christolatry has falsified the time of the world. The mythical Christ was born as Ichthys in the year 255 B.C. That was a true date.

At the end of this century the Vernal colure will pass into the sign of Aquarius, and the year 1901 will be the year 1 of the Waterman. And at that date the time of the world ought to be made astronomical once more. Then Equinoctial Christolatry might resume its chronological course, and no longer falsify the time kept in heaven with a reckoning that is wrong by 255 years on earth. After Ichthys comes the Deluge of the Waterman.

The ready Waterer in heaven,
Stands waiting till the sign be given
To break the clouds of sterile Creeds,
And free in flowers the fruitful seeds.

Christianity commenced absolutely without criticism or inquiry concerning the foundational facts, and its history was manufactured from mythology called prophecy. The cardinal "facts" of the New Testament are *founded* on an illusion regarding the nature of the *Old*, and the latest form of Equinoctial Christolatry was based upon traditions falsely interpreted. The authors of this unparalleled imposition of ignorance had crossed a chasm on a mist of the night in the past, and lo.! by the light of day in the present we behold no bridge! The primary foundation-stone for a history in the New Testament is dependent upon the fall of man being a fact of the Old, whereas it was only a fable that had its own mythical and unhistorical meaning. When we try over again that first step once taken in the dark, we find no foothold because there was no stair. The fall is absolutely non-historical, and the first bit of standing-ground for an actual Christ the Redeemer is missing in the very beginning, consequently any one who set up, or was set up for, an historical Savior, from a non-historical fall could only be an historical impostor.

The "history" in the New Testament has been accepted by those who were ignorant of the mythos in the Old. From the first supposed catastrophe to the final one the figures of the celestial allegory were taken for matters of fact, and thus the Equinoctial Christolator has to climb to heaven with one foot resting on the ground of a fallacious redemption, and the other on the ground of a fictitious fall. Salvation through the blood of Jesus Christ is based on the geology of a world created in six days, and the fable of a heaven lost in one. An aberration from the course of natural development and from scientific knowledge previously extant has been accepted as a supernatural Revelation, and this impossible faith constitutes the greatest obstacle visible on the surface of the whole earth to any possible unification of the human race.

## THE HISTORICAL JESUS.

### BUT ARE THERE NO HISTORICAL DATA FOR A PERSONAL JESUS IN THE TALMUD?

It has been generally allowed that the existence of a Jehoshua, the son of Pandira (whom Porphyry calls Panzerius), acknowledged by the Talmud, proves the personal existence of Jesus the Christ as an historical character in the gospels. But a closer examination of the data shows the theory to be totally untenable. The personal reality of Jehoshua ben Pandira, is undoubtable.

One account affirms that, according to a genuine Jewish tradition "*that man* (who is not to be named) *was a disciple of Jehoshua ben Perachia.*" It also says "*he was born in the fourth year of the reign of Alexander Jannæus, notwithstanding the assertions of his followers that he has born in the reign of Herod.*"[439] That would be more than a century earlier than the date of birth assigned to the Jesus of the gospels. This fact has to be emphasized in order that we may secure the first bit of historic foothold in the vast bog whose quakings have virtually made all negative criticism as wavering and infirm as are the Christian apologetics. But it can be shown that Jehoshua ben Pandira must have been born considerably earlier than the year 102 B.C.

Jehoshua, son of Perachia was a president of the Sanhedrin, the fifth, reckoning from Ezra as the first; one of those who in the line of descent received and transmitted the oral law, as it was said, direct from Sinai.[440] Ben Perachia had begun to teach as a Rabbi in the year 154 B.C. We may therefore reckon that he was not born later than 180—170 B.C., and that it could hardly be later than 100 B.C. when he went down into Egypt with his pupil Ben Pandira. It is related that he fled there in consequence of a persecution of the Rabbis, conjectured to refer to the civil war, in which the Pharisees revolted against King Alexander Jannæus, consequently about 105 B.C. If we put the age of his pupil at fifteen years that will give us an approximate date, extracted without pressure, which shows that Jehoshua ben Pandira may have been born about the year 120 B.C.

According to the Babylonian Gemara to the *Mishna*, Tract "Sabbath," Jehoshua, the son of Pandira and Stada, was stoned to death as a wizard in the city of Lud, or Lydda, and afterwards crucified by hanging on a tree on the eve of the Passover. It says "*there exists a tradition that on the rest-day before the Sabbath they crucified Jehoshua, on the rest-day of the Passah*" (the day before the Passover).[441] The year of his death, however is not given, but there are reasons for thinking it could not have been much earlier nor later than B.C. 70. King Jannæus reigned from the year 106-79 B.C. He was succeeded in the government by his widow, Salome, whom the Greeks, called Alexandra, and who reigned for some nine years.[442] Now the traditions, especially those of the first and second "*Toledoth Jehoshua*,"[443] relate that the *Queen of Jannæus and mother of Hyrcanus*, who must therefore be Salome in spite of her being called *Oleina*, showed favor to Jehoshua and his teaching; that she was a witness of his works and powers of healing, and tried to save him from the hands of his sacerdotal enemies, *because he was related to her*, but that during her reign, which ended 71 B.C., he was put to death.

The Jewish writers altogether deny the identity of the Talmudic Jehoshua and the Jesus of the gospels. This, observes Rabbi Jechiels, which has been related of Jehoshua ben Perachia and his pupil, contains no reference whatever to him whom the Christians honour as a God. Another Rabbi, Salman Zevi, produced ten cogent reasons for concluding that the Jehoshua of the Talmud was not he who afterwards was called Jesus of Nazareth,[444] and that (as we find) the Christ of the gospels is the *God* of the mythos, not the *man* of the Jewish history.

The "blasphemous writings of the Jews about Jesus," as Justin Martyr[445] calls them, always refer to Jehoshua ben Pandira, and not to the Jesus of the gospels. It is he they mean when they says they have another and a truer account of the birth and life, the wonder-working, and death of Jesus. This repudiation is perfectly honest and soundly based. The only Jesus known to the Jews was Jehoshua ben Pandira, who had learned the arts of magic in Egypt and who was put to death as a sorcerer. This was likewise the only Jesus known to Celsus, who affirms that he was not a pure Word, a true Logos, but a man who learned the arts of sorcery in Egypt. So in the Clementines it is in the character of Ben Pandira that Jesus is said to rise again as the magician.[446] But here is the conclusive fact. The Jews know nothing of Jesus as the Christ of the gospels, and when the Christians of the fourth century trace his pedigree by the hand of Epiphanius, they are forced to derive their Jesus from Pandira. Epiphanius gives the genealogy of the canonical Jesus in this wise—

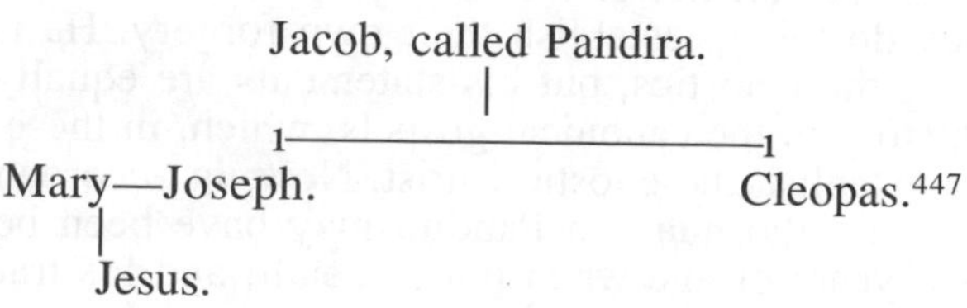

This proves that in the fourth century the pedigree of Jesus was traced to Pandira the father of that Jehoshua who was the pupil of Ben Perachia, he who became one of the magi in Egypt and was crucified as a magician on the eve of the passover by the Jews, in the time of Queen Alexandra, who had ceased to reign in the year 70 B.C. Thus the Jews do not identify Jehoshua ben Pandira with the gospel Jesus, but protest against the assumption as an impossibility, whereas the Christians *do* identify their Jesus as the descendant of Pandira. It is not the Jews, but the Christians, who fuse two supposed historic characters in one. There being but one history acknowledged or known, it follows that the Jesus of the gospels (*plus* the mythical Iesu) *is* the Jehoshua of the Talmud. This shifts the historic basis altogether; it antedates the human history by more than a century, and destroys the historic character of the gospels, together with that of another Jesus. In short, the Jewish history of the matter corroborates the mythical; and both combine to show that the Jesus of the gospels is the mythical Iesu=Jesus. Jehoshua ben Pandira was a mage and adept in the mysteries, a mental Thaumaturge, and what in our day would have been termed a spiritualistic medium. His death was in strict accordance with the Jewish laws and customs. He was first stoned and then hung on a tree to become accursed, which is in agreement with the description that occurs twice over in the "Acts," of him who was slain and hung on a tree, and consequently not crucified after the Roman fashion.[448]

As Epiphanius knew of no other historical Jesus than the descendant of Pandira, it is probable that this is the Jesus whose tradition is reported by Irenæus. Irenæus was born in the early part of the second century between 120 and 140 A.D. He was Bishop of Lyons, France, and a personal acquaintance of Polycarp; and he repeats a tradition testified to by the elders, which was directly derived from John, the "disciple of the Lord," to the effect that Jesus "*passed through every age*," and lived on to be an oldish man! he repudiates the man or god of thirty years who was lord of the æon (a title of Osiris) or of the annual cycle, who suffered death in the twelfth sign, that of Scorpio, at the end of the lunar, equinoctial year. He is replying to those who set forth the lord of the æon, or one year, lesser or greater, as the fulfiller of the "*acceptable year of the Lord*," and says they do this to establish their own forgery. He is ostensibly answering the Gnostics, but his statements are equally applicable to the history in the canonical gospels, which, in these particulars, tends to establish the gnostic Christ. Now, in accordance with the dates given, Jehoshua ben Pandira may have been between fifty and sixty years of age when put to death; and his tradition alone furnishes a clue to the nihilistic statement of Irenæus.[449] When the true tradition of Ben Pandira is recovered, it shows that he was the sole historical Jesus who was hung on a tree by the Jews, and authenticates the claim made by the astronomical allegory to the dispensational Jesus, the Kronian Christ, the mythical Messiah of the canonical gospels.

This reading will account for the total absence of contemporary testimony or recognition, and explain how it is that no voice breaks the blank silence outside the gospel narrative, save one or two forgeries that may be laughed into oblivion. The existence of THE PASSAGE IN TACITUS CONCERNING THE NAME OF CHRIST WAS OBVIOUSLY UNKNOWN TO THE CHRISTIAN FATHERS, AND THEREFORE NON-EXTANT. THE ALLUSION IN JOSEPHUS'S HISTORY IS MANIFESTLY INTERPOLATED BETWEEN THE TWO CALAMITIES THAT BEFEL THE JEWS. BESIDES WHICH, PHOTIUS states explicitly that Josephus made no mention of Jesus Christ. Another Jewish historian, Justus of Tiberias, "does not make the least mention of the appearance of Christ, nor says anything whatever of his miracles."[450] Philo, who was an Essene, born in the year 20 B.C., and who lived to the year 50 A.D., knew nothing of Jesus or his works. The *Mishna*, a collection of writings ranging from B.C. 400 to A.D. 200 which were edited by the Rabbi Jehuda, A.D. 219, at Tiberias, beside the Sea of Gallilee, where the patriarch lived, contains no allusion to the gospel Jesus or his works, his life or his death. There being no other Jesus than Ben Pandira, that will satisfactorily explain for the first time how it is that Paul, the sole distinct Personality of the New Testament writings, has made no report of one, and left no record of his miracles; how he should have instituted no inquiry concerning him during his visits to Jerusalem, nor learned anything of him, nor been able to corroborate the gospel history by one single word—*there having been no personal Jesus of that* TIME. It becomes possible even for Paul to have made his second journey to Jerusalem, in company with Barnabas, to carry the offerings of the faithful to those who had suffered from the great famine in the year 44 A.D.; and for *his conversion to have occurred either in the year* 30, *or* 27, as the different statements imply;[451] because it did not depend upon the death of an historical Jesus.

This view alone enables us to understand the position of Paul, or comprehend the mystery of his gospel, which was opposed to that of the Christ made flesh, the "*other Jesus*" of the gospel preached by the Sarkolatræ, who were his deadly enemies. A difference the most radical divided Paul and the historical James, John, and Cephas. They had nothing in common with him from the first, and never forgave him to the last. They did not preach the same gospel, nor set forth the same Christ. Both started on two sides of the same gulf, that could not be closed and never has been bridged by the Pontifex Maximus established in Rome. The *Praedicatio Petri*[452] declares that Peter and Paul remained unreconciled till death. That gulf can be partly gauged by the treatment of Peter and Paul in the Clementines where Paul is portrayed as the arch-enemy of the new religion and the author of some great *future* heresy (see the passage especially in which Peter comments upon Paul's conversion through his abnormal vision and questions whether his revelation comes from the genuine Christ); but it cannot be completely bottomed except on the ground that there was no personal historical Christ, and that Paul opposed the setting up of a Christ carnalized, and fought the Sarkolators tooth and nail. As a matter of course his writings have not been allowed to come down to us in their doctrinal and textual integrity; writings that withstand Cephas behind his back as Paul had withstood him to his face were not kept concealed for a century without being worked over by the secret weavers of the web in Rome, the men who forged the faith of the Christ made flesh, and damned all disbelievers.[453] And if the writings of Paul were retouched by the carnalizers, that will account for the two voices heard at times in his Epistles and the apparent *duplicity* of his doctrine, which has never been unified and still remains in direct contrast with his own force of character and singleness of purpose. The Christology of Paul is fundamentally opposed to the human personality of the Christ. His doctrine at root is not that of the Word made flesh, a few added touches of subtle seeming on the surface and the opening paragraph of the Epistle to the Romans notwithstanding, Paul *had* preached a gospel of the flesh which was *not* that of the Sarkolatræ; not that of the humanity of Jesus, nor the Christ carnalized, but that of the fleshly and Kronian type of the Messiah, which elementary doctrine he afterwards repudiated on behalf of a spiritual interpretation of the mystery of manifestation. Paul was at one with the Gnostics in rejecting the genealogies of the carnalized Christ. The Docetæ and Ebionites discarded the genealogies in the gospel after Matthew.[454] Tatian, the pupil of Justin, who left the Christian church as a non-believer in the Christ carnalized, also struck out the genealogies of the human descent. From Luke's gospel Marcion removed "*all that was written respecting the generation of the Lord.*"[455] So Paul warned Timothy against giving "*heed to fables and endless genealogies*;"[456] and instructed Titus to "*shun foolish questionings and genealogies.*"[457]

It is recorded that certain apostles saw the risen Christ ascend into heaven as a veritable being of flesh and blood. But Paul taught that "*flesh and blood cannot inherit*" the kingdom of God. According to Chrysostom, Theophylact, and Æcumenius, the philosphers who heard the preaching of Paul took the "resurrection" to be a new goddess Anastasis.

Paul's doctrine of the resurrection is entirely opposed to that which was preached by Hymenæus and Philetus, whose word, he says, *will eat as doth a gangrene*;" men "*who concerning the truth have erred, saying that the resurrection is past already*,"[458] and thus have overthrown the faith of some in the doctrine as it was preached according to the gospel of Paul. Now the only way in which the resurrection could be preached as already past was the same then as it is to-day, namely the resurrection of a personal and historical Saviour who was held to have died and risen again, and this brought immortality to light. Paul's resurrection was not assured by any risen Christ, it was something to attain in the gnostic sense. *If by any means I may attain unto the resurrection of the dead! Not that I have already attained, or am already made perfect; but I press on.*"[459] This resurrection was neither past nor was it assured for the future on account of its having passed once for all, but had to be striven for by seeking perfection like the Hindu Siddhas.

PAUL'S IMMORTALITY WAS CONDITIONAL; A FUTURE STATE TO BE ATTAINED BY GROWTH IN THIS. Such was the universal doctrine of the Gnostics who identified immortality with *Nous* and Wisdom, thence with the gnosis. The writer of the *Wisdom of Solomon* says "*by means of her* (Sophia) *I shall obtain Immortality*." Paul said by means of the Christ (the male type) evolved within (this the Sivaist terms the Linga in the soul), or "*the stature of the fulness of Christ*," who was the perfect flower of the gnostic pleroma, not the divine flower of humanity *attained by one man*, but the flower of humanity in the eighth degree of ascension, which was represented by the eight-rayed star of the preceding seven powers; the summit of attainment on the peak of the perfected.

Paul proclaims that he derived this gospel from no man, and that he was instructed by none. He received his revelation direct from heaven by spiritual manifestation of what he called the Christ, as typical manifestor. Only the phenomenal spiritualists who have known the "other world" to demonstrate its existence by becoming ocular or palpable; only those who have had proof that the human consciousness persists in death, and emerges in a personality continued beyond the grave, are really qualified to understand the mystery or the message of Paul. The secret of the spiritual logos is theirs in Paul's sense, but having no relationship save that of an antithesis to a carnalized Christ. Paul, according to his own testimony, was an abnormal seer, subject to conditions of Trance. This was the source of his revelations, the cause of his "thorn in the flesh," his infirmity in which he gloried. he shows the Corinthians that his abnormal condition, ecstasy, illness, madness, or what not, was a phase of spiritual intercourse in which he was divinely insane—insane on behalf of God; but he was sober-minded, sensible, sane, normal enough in his relation to them. Modern science would say he suffered from hallucination; phenomenal spiritualists that he saw spirits. Either way this was the origin and ground of his conversion.

If a spirit demonstrated its existence in apparition to Paul, that proved a rebirth; the spirit, being one of the twice-born, was a form of the Christ. For Paul had continued the type of rebirth at puberty in his mystery of the Messiah. Hence his conversion was a rebirth, a change in which the Christ was born within as the pubescent soul, a son of the father of God. There is nothing for it but laying fast hold of the primary types when we are befogged and befooled in the metaphysical phase.

Paul was a Hebrew Gnostic learned in the Kabalah, a master in the mysteries, one who spoke wisdom among the perfected. He knew the nature of the typical Christ from the genesis, as the anointed one of puberty, whose symbol was the stone or rock; also as the Kronotype; and he *continued the type*, not merely in a vague psychotheistic phase like that of the Gnostic *Nous* but as the Christ of spiritual manifestations that were objective, visible and audible to himself. A manifestor had been entified in apparition for him! Hence he spoke the "*wisdom of God*," the knowledge revealed to him "*in a mystery*,"[460] or according to the mode of the mysteries. His own especial mystery was made known to him by revelation [461] abnormally, or in trance. By aid of this he understood and interpreted anew the "mystery of Christ" which "*in other generations was not made known unto the sons of men*," as it had now been revealed to him "*in the spirit*."[462] His work is to "*fulfil the Word of God*," the "*mystery which hath been hid from all ages and generations*,"[463] he himself being the Christ or Makheru (Eg). Paul's gospel was founded on a new application of the ancient gnosis to the facts of his own abnormal experience for the purpose of creating belief in a spiritual existence. Also the Word that had been manifested and tabernacled in time could not be clothed in flesh, but the type could serve to represent renewal or the new man in a spiritual sense. Clement Alexander states that Paul designated the "*fulness of the blessing of Christ*" which he would bring to the Romans the communication of the gnosis, or the hidden tradition of the mysteries which was unknown to the Romans, and which, according to this Christian Father, was revealed by the Son of God, "*the teacher who trains the Gnostic by mysteries*."[464]

Paul passed away and his writings remained with the enemy, to be withheld, tampered with, reindoctrinated, and turned to account by his old opponents who preached the gospel of Christ carnalized. But we know that his Jesus and his gospel were not theirs; we know that he warred strenously against their false interpretaion of mythology; and it now appears probable that the never-yet fathomed "*mystery of lawlessness*" which Paul described as being already at work was none other than the gospel of the carnalized Christ which was being foisted on the world by James, Cephas, and John; one of the three being the Man of sin, the Lawless one (Anomos), "*the son of perdition, he that opposeth and exalteth himself against all that is called God or that is worshipped, so that he sitteth in the temple of God, setting himself forth as God.*" He is no outsider, but a mortal enemy within the gates! In that case Paul was the one who restrained them for the time being, until he himself should be taken out of the way. Thus interpreted, Paul foresaw what would come to pass through the pernicious teaching of James, John, Cephas, and the other Sarkolatre when he himself should be removed; and we have seen what he foresaw.

Now the second Toledoth Jehoshua represents Bed Pandira as being a Nazarene, on account of which the Rabbis cut off his hair and washed his head with the water Boleth, so that the hair might grow no more. And the book *Abodazura* has a comment on James, in which it says he was "*a follower of Jehoshua the Nazarene.*" Further, in the second chapter of the Clementines there is a letter of Peter to James, in which the sobriquet of "*the lawless*" is flung at Paul! On the present reading of the data the epithet thus cast back identifies it, together with the original at whom it was first aimed by Paul. It was Jehoshua the magician and wizard whose advent had been made as the worker of signs and wonders; and it looks as if Paul's "*mystery of lawlessness*" may have been connected with the followers of "*that man*" who were engaged in converting him into the veritable son of God, according to their gospel of the Christ made flesh. Jehoshua the Nazarene is demonstratedly historic; not so the Jesus of Nazareth. According to Matthew, the child was brought to dwell "*in a city called Nazareth, that it might be fullfilled which was spoken by the prophets that he should be called a Nazarene.*" Whereas he could not have become a Nazarene by merely living at Nazareth, nor have been named "*of Nazareth*" by being a Nazarene. The Greek *Ναζωραιοζ* neither renders the *Ναζιιοζ* of the Seventy, nor the Hebrew. The supposed prophecy is interpreted by means of false philology to establish the geographical locality, and thus the alleged historic fact has to be founded on a manifest fiction.

From the Gnostic standpoint the true Christ could not be "of Nazareth" as a mundane locality, consequently no "Jesus of Nazareth" appears in Marcion's Gospel. It was a neck-and-neck question, however, in a race that was run for two or three centuries between the Christ corporeal and the Christ incorporeal; and the fleshy Messiah beat the phantom, even as the belief in a physical resurrection triumphed over the older belief in a spiritual survival after death which had been inculated in the pre-

Christian cultus. The Gnostics were conquered by the carnifiers of the Christ, who made God flesh to eat him as a redeeming sacrifice, and with whom the cult of Equinoctial Christolatry entered its final phase.

HOW WAS IT THEN THAT THE RELIGION OF THE IGNORANT OVERTURNED AND SUPERSEDED THAT OF THE learned? One explanation is because the ancient wisdom had been concealed; because the hidden gnosis was only communicated in secret, and the initiates received it under the seal of secrecy. The religion of mystery was doomed to die of the secrecy in which it had been self-enshrouded. It was buried alive with its own seal on its own mouth. It was an unpublished religion. And when the new sect put forth the same dogmas, doctrines, tenets under the same types, accompanied by the same rites and ceremonies, they became the first publishers of the ancient religion with a new interpretation of the Christ made flesh. The Gnostics did try to say, with the suppressing hand on their mouths, "*You are only publishing our secrets with a lying gloss put upon them*," but this slight protest was unheard amidst the loud clamour of the fanatically ignorant. Also the mythical and typological had everywhere prepared the way for the alleged historical Christ. The astronomical mythos, extant in many lands, appeared to authenticate this new revelation when it was announced. So ingrained in the human mind were the types and symbols of paganism, that a doctrine ridiculous as that of a triangular God who divided all things into three, himself included, could be accepted because such a type had already been made mental.

Las Casas relates how easily the converted Indians, who could not read Spanish and whose books had been destroyed, would portray the Christian legend and dogmas from their own symbols and characters, and says he had seen a large portion of the Christian doctrine written in their figures and images. When the Scriptures were first made known to the Arawaks of Guianâ as the word of God, they observed "*The word is good, but we knew most of it before*." What chiefly arrested their attention was the statement of the Word having been made flesh to die for the salvation of men. Mythology had everywhere prepared the way for the belief, in the absence of the gnosis.[465]

When the story of the Christian Messiah was first told to the natives of New Zealand, the missionaries and the Maoris were equally amazed to find the likeness of Jesus to the character of Tawhaki, a Messiah already known to them, of whom the selfsame incidents were related as those now retold of the later Christ.[466] The connection between Tawhaki and Osiris (or Horus) is shown by *his death having been effected by the reptile gods*, the Apophis and conspirators in the *Ritual*. The Buddhist is able to prove that the history of Jesus is one with that of Buddha, called Gautama. This is not mere parallel but identity. Such history cannot be personally true twice over, once in India and once in Judæa. Nor was the gospel narrative drawn from Buddhist sources any more than the Buddhist was derived from the Christian. Both had a common origin as mythos, but not as human history. Astronomical mythology claims and accounts for thirty thousand years of time at least; and this alone goes down to the source of the whole matter; this only can explain the relationships found on the surface by an original identity at root.

THE TRANSFORMATION OF THE ANCIENT RELIGION INTO THE NEW WAS MADE WITH SUFFICIENT SECRECY to imply consciousness. The sloughing was chiefly out of sight, but the real truth of the origines must have been concealed amongst the *arcana imperii* or secrets of the management in Rome. The re-beginnings are not only shrouded in mystery, they are the mysteries, and the same mysteries at root as those that were pre-extant. The three degrees of purification, initiation, and perfection corresponded to those of the Greek Eleusinia, and the three degrees in Masonry. Certain of the Christian Fathers came to see the likeness of their mysteries to those of the Mithraic religion which, as Plutarch testifies, had been especially established in Rome about the year 70 B.C.

Augustine says, "*I know that the priests of him in the cap- (istius pileati) used at one time to say our capped one is himself a Christian*," or a Christ. Which means that the Mithraists identified the Christ with Mithra, the Christ of the "*Bonnets rouges*" in the catacombs. The Mithraic mysteries were so like those of the Christians that Justin Martyr declared the devil had stolen them to deceive the human race.[467] Peter, in his epistle to James, urges the necessity of taking extreme precautions to prevent the secret doctrine from being promulgated or divulged. Clement Alexander, who calls the gnosis the "*Apprehension of things present, future, and past*,"[468] affirms that the mysteries hidden until the time of the apostles were those that had been concealed in the Old Testament.[469] He also says, "*Not enviously said he* (*i.e.* Barnabas), *the Lord announced in a certain gospel, 'My mystery is unto me and the sons of my house*.'"[470] The Carpocratean Gnostics, who quoted the traditions and logia of Matthias as the authentic gospel, declared that Jesus spoke in a mystery to his disciples and followers *privately*, who requested and obtained permission to hand down the sayings and teach them to others who should be worthy by believing.[471] This privacy according to the gnostic doctrine was *within the pleroma* where the disciples were the twelve æons.

The position of the gnostic Jesus who expounds the mysteries to the twelve æons within the pleroma is occupied and acknowledged by Jesus, when he is asked why he speaks in parables and he replies, "*It is given you to know the mysteries of the kingdom of heaven.*"[472] *The secret doctrine of Christ was the secret doctrine concerning the Christ*, the interpretation only known to the initiated. It was absolutely necessary that this should be kept concealed from the people if the historic interpretation of the mythos was to be believed. It was maintained by some that the apocrypha ought only to be read by those who were perfected;[473] and in the fifth century these scriptures were limited to a few adepts. According to the *Clementine Homilies*, the "mystery of the scriptures" taught by Christ was identical with that which from the beginning had been secretly communicated to those who were worthy,[474] that was to the initiated in the mysteries, the adepts to whom Paul spoke *wisdom*, when he uttered his "*revelation of the mystery which was kept in silence through times eternal.*"[475] In the same writings Peter asserts the existence of a secret doctrine or gnosis, and states that Christ had given instructions for the true gospel, that of the hidden mysteries, not to be proclaimed until after the destruction of Jerusalem; and then it was only to be taught covertly. He says the true prophet has told us the false gospel must come first from a certain misleader who is Paul under the guise of *Simon Magus*), and after the destruction of the holy place the true gospel is to be *transmitted secretly for the correction of future heresies*.[476] This affords a glimpse of the Arcana in Rome, and of the way in which the mythical was turned into the historical and the Christ made flesh. The end of the æon or world, being the new point of departure in the mythos, this end in Jerusalem was afterwards made to prove and establish the mythos as history; then it was declared that such was the teaching of Christ himself when in the flesh. Hence the merging of the mythos into history when it had occurred, and the connection of the coming Christ with the fall of Jerusalem.

What the Jews had believed through misapplying the mythos of the ending and the coming one was continued as veritable and verifiable revelation by the Christolators. We find in the epistle to the Hebrews that the Christ had come as High Priest of good things, "*through the greater and more perfect tabernacle, not made with hands*," which was the new temple of the heavens that followed the tabernacles of old.[477] This coming on the grand scale of the Great Year could only follow the fall of Babylon; and Jerusalem above would descend in place of Jerusalem below. Hence, according to Jarchi, *the Hebrews believed that on the last day of the destruction of Jerusalem by the Romans the Messiah was born.* The Messiah being Kronian, a lord of the æon or age, he could only come at the end of the world (or æon) as it was interpreted, that is at the time of a deluge or destruction. In the Books of Enoch and Revelation the end is figured as the destruction of the old temple of time in the heavens which was replaced by a new tabernacle or ark of the eternal in the psychotheistic phase of the typology. And thus the fall of Jerusalem and the end of the Jewish temple were made typical to authenticate that end of the æon, age, or world which always occurred at the coming of the Messiah. The statement of Mallebranche that "*the end* (as object) *of creation was the incarnation of Christ*," also affords a good example of the way in which the Kronian allegory had been converted into a metaphysical mystery, by the manufacturers of patristic theology.

The cult of Equinoctial Christolatry substituted faith for knowledge as the guiding principle. Valentinus said the Christians had faith, but his followers possessed knowledge. The best believers (actually called "*the better believers*") were those who knew the least;—and this ignorance extended to all the supposed facts on which their faith was founded. The European mind is only just beginning to recover from the mental paralysis that was consequently induced; and what is most required at the present time is a *New Gnosticism* which shall include and comprehend *all the sources of experimental knowledge*, and let Belief take its proper place in the rear.

The existence of a conscious, creative, and eternal Cause, and the persistence in death of the force full summed in the individual human life, must needs be based on different and more enduring grounds than those of the expiring faith.

The cult of Equinoctial Christolatry is responsible for enthroning the cross of death in heaven with a deity on it doing public penance for a private failure in the commencement of creation. It has divinized a figure of human suffering and a face of piteous pain; as if there were nought but a great heartache at the core of all things, or a veiled sorrow that brings visibly to birth in the miseries of human life. But "in the young pagan world men deified the beautiful, the glad;" as they will again upon a loftier pedestal, when the tale of the fictitious fall of man and false redemption by the cloud-begotten God has passed away like a phantasm of the night, and men awake to learn that they are here to preclude poverty, to wage ceaseless war upon sordid suffering and preventable pain, and not to apotheosize an effigy of sorrow as a type of the eternal; for the most beneficent is most beautiful; the happiest are the healthiest; the most Godlike is most glad. Equinoctial Christolatry adopted and sanctified the savage doctrine of blood sacrifice and vicarious expiation, which is a complete reversal of the common law of civilization, that all sane persons shall be held responsible for their deeds and not acquitted because the innocent may have suffered for the guilty. A doctrine so cowardly and immoral must have rotted the backbone out of all manhood if men were no better than their professed beliefs, and had not been fed from other and healthier fountains of life.

The vivisection of the Dog, man's first friend and foremost ally, is a natural outcome of the unnatural doctrine of vicarious suffering. The cowardly cruelties of its practitioners, and their shameless expositions intended to abash, appall, and terrorize the conscience of others, would have been impossible with any race of men who had not been indoctrinated by the worship of a vivisecting deity whose victim was his own son. The Red Indian and other savages will vivisect and torture *their conquered enemies* for *minutes* or *hours*. But it was reserved for races civilized by Christian culture to vivisect and inflict nameless torments on their *helpless* fellow creatures and *harmless* familiar *friends* for weeks and months, or years, together. This must have been unbearable to a nation of animal-lovers unless the motor nerve of the race had been paralyzed by the *curare* of vicarious suffering which confers divine sanction on the doctrine of saving ourselves by means of the suffering inflicted upon others. Our national religion is the fetishism of primitive man in the last stage of perversion. Eternal Cause is treated as if were a weather-vane at the summit of creation that might be forced to veer round at every breath of selfish prayer. The very existence of a God has been made dependent upon his personal manifestation in Judæa; consequently he is non-extant if not historical and a Jew; those for whom the historical evidence fails find themselves without a God in the world as the natural result of such atheistic teaching, and the poor Jews have to suffer for the imposition that has been practised in their name.

Atheism is at times and in some natures the necessary revolt of the higher consciousness, as if the real god within was at war against the sham set up for worship without.

Equinoctial Christolatry boasts of having put an end to individual sacrifice; but it is compatible with the masses of the toiling people being offered up for ever in one great sacrifice. The other world has been held as a lure in front of that beast of burden, the Producer, in order that the scent of future food in another life might make him forego his right to the common grazing-ground in this world. The cult has been made compatible with a state of society which shows more repulsive extremes of wealth and poverty, splendor and squalor than any in the pre-Christian world; in which the slayers of men still win the great rewards; in which intelligence may be legally turned to the chief account by taking every advantage of the ignorant; and in which *the standard of conscience is the* STATUS QUO *of things as they are; and not a test of the result of things as they are.*

The equinoctial christolators are responsible for postponing to a future stage of existence the redress of wrongs and the righting of inequalities which can only be rectified in this. Their profession is the cure of souls by a spurious theology and a false faith founded on cloud-shadows offered us for stepping-stones across the waters of the river of death, not the healing in this life of ills and ailments in the body politic, or the running sores of the social state. False believing is ever the worst enemy of true doing; and every Sunday the teaching of these legalized kidnappers of the children, for compulsory inoculation of their minds with the old theological virus, tends to nullify the good done by education during the other six days of the week.

They want to have the children's souls in pledge
That these shall only bear their kind of fruit
Who are but dead sticks in the living hedge,
Rotting for lack of root.

Ever ready to fight with shadows like the "primal curse" or to promise the "lost paradise" to those who have faith (in defiance of facts) that it once existed, they leave it for Communists and Nihilists to force into the sphere of practical politics the discussion of reforms that have to be effected before humanity can be saved. They remind us of those Greek heroes who deserted their native city when it was on fire, and found immediate solace in watching a theatrical representation of the "*burning of Troy.*" In relation to this world their teaching is a failure; in relation to the other it is a fraud. They have exalted the lot of Lazarus for the needy and miserable, as if the diseased starveling and cowering outcast of earth were the model man for the heavens! They have promised that those who remained sufficiently poor and worm-like in spirit during this life should rise erect from their grub-condition in death, to soar up for the next life as ready-made angels, full-fledged or full-statured.

Equinoctial Christolatry has fanatically fought for its false theory, and waged incessant warfare against Nature and evolution—Nature's intention made visible—and against some of the noblest human instincts during eighteen centuries. Seas of human blood have been spilt to keep the bark of Peter afloat. Earth has been honey-combed with the graves of the martyrs of free thought. Heaven has been filled with a horror of great darkness in the name of God.

Eighteen centuries are a long while in the lifetime of a lie, but a brief span in the eternity of truth. The lie is sure to be found out or fall at last:

No matter though it towers to the sky
And darkens earth, you cannot make the lie
Immortal; though stupendously enshrined
By Art in every perfect mould of mind:
Angelo, Rafaelle, Milton, Handel, all
Its pillars cannot stay it from the fall.

And at length the long delusion on misinterpreted mythology is drawing near its end.

The only way to dispose finally of the false history in the Old Testament or the New was by recovering the true tradition. This has now been attempted to the depth. The natural genesis and continuity of the typology have been traced from the beginning to their culmination in Equinoctial Christolatry; the supremest verities of revealed "truth" are proved to be only falsifications of ancient fables; and the facts adduced in evidence suffice to confirm the long-suspected flaw in the title-deeds of Christianity; they demonstrate the non-historical nature of the gospel records, and show them to be the work of virtual forgers who obtained possession of sacerdotal authority upon pretences entirely false.

The pyramid of imposture reared by Rome,
All of cement, for an eternal home,
Must crumble back to earth, and every gust
Shall revel in the desert of its dust;
And when the prison of the Immortal Mind,
Hath fallen to set free the bound and blind,
No more shall life be one long dread of death:
Humanity shall breathe with fuller breath;
Expand in spirit and in stature rise.
To match its birthplace of the earth and skies.

## GLOSSARY

AAN. An Egyptian lunar god in the form of a dog headed ape.

AAHENRU. The field of heaven.

ABBA-UDDA. The month of December.

ABODAZURA. A book of the Talmud.

ABTU. The passion week of Osiris.

ABYDUS. A town in upper Egypt where was the famous temple of Osiris.

ACHAMOTH. The Gnostics mother with the issue of blood.

ADONIA. Festivals in honor of Adonis celebrated at Byblos in Phœnicia.

ADONIS. A Phoenician personification of the sun.

ÆONIAN. The period assigned to an event.

ÆONS. Inferior deities proceding from the one incomprehensible God.

ÆSCULAPIUS. The god of medicine, son of Apollo.

AGAPÆ. A love feast, or feast of charity, which, among the early Christians usually accompanied the Eucharist. It closed with the holy kiss.

AGIA PSYCHE. An abstract form of the Holy Ghost.

AGION PNEUMA. Ditto.

AGNI. Lambs or rams.

AHURA-MAZDA . A Persian God.

AMENHEPT. A Pharaoh of the 18th Dynasty, who reigned about 1600 B.C.

AMENI. A Pharaoh of the 11th Dynasty, about 2400 B. C.

AMENTI. The under-world; Hades.

AMEN-RA. An Egyptian god of the sun: the king of the Gods.

AMMONIUS. The founder of Neo-Platonism, who taught at Alexandria, Egypt in the 2d century.

AMSET. A god of the underworld, connected with embalming.

ANBU. Eyelashes or hair.

ANDROGYNOUS. Having two sexes; being male and female.

ANKHBA. Life of the soul.

ANNECDOTI. Fishmen.

ANNU. Heaven.

ANOMOS. The lawless one.

ANUBIS OR ANUP. An Egyptian god, jackal-headed, son of Osiris. He presided over mummification; he also weighed the souls in the balance and executed the sentence of the judge in Hades.

ANS-RA. The sun bound up in linen.

ANTHROPOS. The son of man.

*A Ω* Alpha and Omega. The flrst and last letters of the Greek alphabet; the all.

APATOR. Without father.

APER or APERTO. The god of things funereal.

APHERU. Another name for ANUP, the son of Osiris.

APHRODITE. The Grecian name of Venus, the word meaning froth, because the goddess was said to have been born from the froth of the sea.

APHRATHAH. The fruitful wife or genetrix.

APIS. The sacred bull of Egypt, the living emblem of Osiris and thus connected with the sun and the Nile.

APOCHRYPHA. Books of the Bible whose authority as inspired writings is not admitted by Christians.

APOPHIS. The evil powers. The Devil.

APT. Place or person.

APTU. The typical birth-place.

ARIES. The ram,(the first of the 12 signs of the Zodiac,) which the sun enters on the 21st of March.

ARISTÆUS. A divinity largely worshipped in ancient Greece. He was a benevolent deity who introduced the cultivation of bees, vine and olive.

ASCALON. One of the five chief cities of the Philistine, 12 miles N of Gaza, on the coast of the Mediterranean, now Askulan.

ASEB. A title to Osiris.

ASSUR. An Assyrian god.

ASTERISM. A cluster of stars.

ATEN. The disk of the sun. This god was worshipped under the representation of a large circle.

ATHRGATIS. A divinity among the Syrians, often considered the same as Venus.

ATHOR. A goddess of the under-world: Eg. Venus.

ATUM. The setting sun in the western horizon.

AU. A calf-headed god of Egypt.

AVESTA, or ZENDAVENTA. The scripture of the Zoroastrian faith, the ancient religion of Persia.

AZI-DAHAKA. The destroying serpent.

BAHMAN YASHT. Sacred book of the Parsees—ancient Persians,

BALAK. A King of Moab: see Numbers 22-24.

BAMBINO. A Roman catholic carven image, which is claimed to possess power to heal the sick in Rome. It is under the special care of the Virgin Mary.

BASCILICAS. Palaces of the ancient Roman kings.

BASILIDES. One of the most celebrated of the ancient Gnostics. He flourished about 120 A. D. Born in Syria: studied in Alexandria.

BEROSUS. A Chaldean priest, who lived in the time of Alexander the Great.

BRIBUS. Hindoo artificers or carpenters.

BRUGSCH PASCH. A noted writer upon ancient Egypt .

BUNSEN. A famous German scholar, born in 1791, the intimate friend of Niebuhr.

BUDDHA. One of the beings, worshipped by the Buddhists in India.

CÆSAR AUGUSTUS. Emperor of Rome, born about 63 B. C.

CARPOCRATES. A Gnostic of the 2d century.

CASSINI. A distinguished astronomer of the 17th century, director of the observatory of Paris.

CHRISTOLATRY. Idolatry of Christ, Christianity.

CHRYSOSTOM. The most famous of the Greek Christian fathers, born about 347 A. D. at Antioch in Syria.

CLEMENTINE HOMILIES. Writings of Clement of Alexandria.

CLEMENT of Alexandria, Egypt: a noted Christian father of the 2d century.

CODEX-SINAITICUS; an ancient manuscript of the New Testament found in a convent on Mount Sinai. It is of the 4th century.

COPTIC. Egyptian.

COPTS. Egyptians.

CURARE. The treatment or care.

DAG. The fish.

DAMASCIUS. A celebrated Neo-Platonic philosopher, born about the middle of the 5th century. He studied at Alexandria, taught at Athens.

DECANS. Tens.

DECUSSATE. To cross in the form of an X.

DENDERAH. An Arab village in upper Egypt, about 28 miles north of Thebes: the site of the ancient city of Tentyra and the seat of the famous temple dedicated to Athor, the Egyptian Venus. Here was found the "Zodiac" about the close of the last century.

DE-ROSSI. An Italian poet, born in Rome, 1754.

DIDRON. A French archæologist born in 1806.

DIODORUS. A Greek historian born in Sicily. He lived in the 1st century before the Christian era.

DOCETÆ. A Christian sect who held that Christ during his life had not a flesh body, but only a phantom one.

DUODECANS. Twelve.

EG. Egyptian.

EIDOLON. Image.

ELEUSINIA. A great festival observed every fourth year at ELEUSIS in Greece.

EMANING. Flowing forth.

EMPHE. An ancient god.

EPICENE. A name common to both sexes.

EPIPHANIUS. A celebrated father of the church, born at the beginning of the 4th century, in Palestine.

ERIDANUS. A river in Italy; now called the Po.

ESCHATOLOGY. The "doctrine of last things," or Christian speculation on what the scriptures reveal concerning a future life.

ESDRAS. The supposed writer of the apocryphal book of Esdras.

ESHTA. absolve, to propitiate.

ESMEN. The eighth.

ESSENES. A sect of the Jews who were ascetics and held their property in common.

EUHEMERIZED. Humanized.

EUSEBIUS. "The father of church history" who flourished in the 4th century and was contemporary with Constantine the Great.

FIRMICUS. A Latin writer of the 4th century.

FOMALHAUT. A star of the first magnitude in the constellation Pisces Australis, or Southern Fish. The word means mouth of the large fish.

GAUTAMA BUDDHA. The founder of Buddhism.

GEMARA. The second part of the Talmud, or the commentary on the Mishna.

GENETRIX. She that produces; a mother.

GNOSIS. The things known.

GNOSTICS. Those who knew; a sect of the first centuries of the Christian era.

HABER. The great serpent of darkness.

HAPI. The digger, one of the four genii who presided over the grave and also over embalming.

HAR-KHUTI. Lord of the lights, or the great Pyramid.

HAR-MAKHU. An Egyptian dual deity.

HARPOCRATES. Horus considered a child of the mother alone.

HAR-SEBTI. Horus of the pyramid.

HARTHOR. A female counterpart of Osiris.

HARTHOR-MERI. The Egyptian Virgin Mary.

HEBDOMAD. Seven.

HELI. It is finished.

HEPHAISTOS. The Greek god of fire used in art, like the Latin Vulcan.

HEPTANOMIS. Seven-named.

HERAKLES. Hercules, the Greek god of strength.

HERMES. The Egyptian Thoth. To him is ascribed the writing of the 42 sacred books of Egypt; among them the "Book of the Dead."

HEXAMÆRON. The title of a work on the creation of the world by Ambrosius.

HIERONYMUS. A christian writer called St. Jerome.

HIPPOLYTUS. A writer on Gnosticism.

HOMME FAIT. A made man.

HOR-APOLLO. A celebrated author of a Greek treatise on the Egyptian Hieroglyphics, who lived probably in the 5th century, A. D.

HOROSCOPUS. A book that kept the hours.

HORUS. Son of Osiris and Isis. He is hawk-headed, and thus a solar god connected with Ra. Osiris being identified with the sun of the night. Horus is naturally the sun of the day. Horus was the Egyptian Jesus.

I A O-SABAOTH. A Gnostic god portrayed with the face of an ass.

ICHTHON. The sign in the Zodiac now called Pisces.

ICHTHYS. The fish.

ICONOGRAPHY. The description of ancient images or representations, statues, or paintings in fresco, mosaic, etc

ICONS. Images or representations.

IDEOGRAPH. A symbol which is intended to represent the object to be described.

IDIOTES. Ignorant persons.

IGNATIUS. One of the apostolic fathers.

INDRA. A Hindu god of storm and thunder.

IRENÆUS : Bishop of Lyons in the end of 2d century.

ISIS. The wife of Osiris and mother of Horus.

IU EX-HEPT. The youthful Messiah; the Egyptian Jesus.

JAMBLICUS: or IAMBLICUS; the chief representative of Syrian-Neo-Platonism. He flourished in the 4th century.

JUSTIN MARTYR: an able and eloquent advocate of Christianity who lived in the 2d century.

KABALAH: the technical name for the system of theosophy which began to be developed among the Jews in the 10th century, and which has played an important part in the Christian church since the Middle Ages.

KABALIST; a Jewish doctor who professes the study of the Kabalah.

KABHSENUF: one of the four genii who presided over the grave and of embalming.

KAM; Egypt.

KANSA: the Herod of Purana.

KAMUTF; the male mother.

KARAS: To embalm.

KARAST: a mummy.

KERES and KERES FLAVA: Ceres, the Roman goddess of corn and of harvests.

KHEM-HORUS; the Horus of thirty years of age.

KHEMT: Horus at thirty years of age.

KHEPR-RA. Ra in the form of twin born. He becomes two children.

KHNUM-AB-RA: an ancient Egyptian god.

KHNUM-HEPT-; an ancient Egyptian god.

KHUNSU; a luni-solar god of Egypt.

KHUNSU-NEFER-HEPT: A god who gives oracles, and expels obsessors.

KNEPH: the Spirit or Holy Ghost. The creator of mankind. The Lord of the water.

KRISHNA: the Hindoo Christ;.

KRONIAN; pertaining to time.

KURIOS. Lord or master.

KYHAK: In the Egyptian calendar a month corresponding nearly to December.

LAKSHMI. The Hindu goddess of wealth: the wife of Vishnu. She is said to have sprung from the churning of the ocean.

LAS CASAS. A Spanish missionary who preached to the Indians in Hispaniola in the 15th century.

LEGENDA-AUREA; Golden Legend.

LEX PAPPIA: the laws of Pappius man Tribune.

LOGIA: sayings.

MACROBIUS :A Roman grammarian and philosopher who wrote toward the beginning of the 6th century, A. D.

MA-KHERU: The word made truth or become law.

MAMZER: the fatherless.

MANEROS: Men-Horus.

MANSEL; He was born in 1820 in England. He wrote lectures on the gnostics heresies.

MANUS. Buddhas.

MAORI. New Zealanders.

MARCION. The founder of the Marcionites, a sect of the 2d century, by some called Christians, by others, Gnostics.

MARCUS AURELIUS. Emperor of Rome from 161 to 180 A. D.

MATHU. A prophetess of Hathor.

MATI. An Egyptian proper name.

MATIU. Another name for Taht, the registrar of deeds, done in the body.

MERU. The mount of the birthplace in the North.

MITHRAIC. Pertaining to the worship of the Persian god Mithras.

MITHRAS. A Persian god whose worship spread over the Roman world during the 2d and 3d centuries.

MONOGENES. In the Gnostic faith, an Æon or spirit who stood between the Father and the lower æons or spirits.

MUNTER. Born in 1791 a bishop of Seeland, a great oriental scholar.

MURBA. The place of the reptile or of the condemned dead.

MUT-EM-UA. The Virgin mother.

MUTHOI. Parables and dark sayings of old.

MYTHOS . A myth, a fable.

NABLOUS. A city of Samaria, 33 miles north of Jerusalem.

NANDA. Half-brother to Gautama Buddha.

NASSENI. Snake worshipers.

NAZARENE. A sect among the Gnostics.

NEFER-HEPT. The god of peace and good luck. The giver of life; the expeller of demons.

NEITH. The goddess who was a personification of wisdom, like the Greek Athêné.
NEPTHYS. The sister of Isis.
NERYOSANG. An angel or friend of Ahura-Mazda.
NETERT. He who hides himself—a title of Ra.
NISON. The month of April.
NNU. The sign of the associate gods in Egypt.
NOUS. One of the Gnostic Æons.
NU. The firmament; the sky.
NUM-RA. An Egyptian God.
NUT. The mother heaven; the goddess of the firmament.
NUTER-KAR. The nether world.
OAN. The fish man.
OANNES Fishmen.
OGDOAD. The eight primary associate gods in Egypt.
ONOMATOPŒIA. The forming of a word to resemble in sound the thing it signifies.
OPHITES. Snake worshippers.
ORANTE. The beseecher.
ORIGEN. One of the Christian fathers.
OSIRIS. The most universally worshipped god in Egypt. He was a form of the sun, and especially the sun god of the underworld or Hades.
OSIRIS-UN-NEFER. Osiris, the Rood-helper.
PACHONS. The name of a month corresponding to a part of April and May.
PAN. The god of the woods and shepherds.
PARACLETE. The intercessor. A term applied to the Holy Spirit.
PARACLETUS. The comforter; one of the aeons of the Gnostics.
PARAPHRAST. Explanation.
PEBLUM. An upper garment.
PHLEGETHON. A hell of fire.
PISCINA. A fish pond.
PISCICULI. Little fishes.
PHALLIC. Pertaining to the male organ of generation.
PHALLUS. The male organ of generation.
PLEROMA. The full heaven of the Gnostic æons, (spirits).

PLUTARCH. An ancient writer, the author of "Plutarch's Lives."
POLYCARP. A famous Greek writer of the first century A. D.
PONTIFEX-MAXIMUS. The chief pontiff. The Pope of Rome.
PORPHYRY. A Platonic philosopher of Tyre.
PRŒSEPE. A small cluster of stars in the sign of Cancer.
PTAH. The god who shaped and formed the universe.
PURANA. Brahaminical writings.
QUETZALCOATI. A Mexican deity.
RA. The sun or the God of the sun
RA-HAR-KHUTI. The Lord of Lights and of Spirits, or glorified elect ones.
RAKA. A god of the winds. A scorner: a rebel in religion.
REMA. An Egyptian name of the fish.
RENEN. The virgin, the gestator.
REPLICA. Reflection, duplicate.
RERIT. The Sow.
RIBHUS. Hindu carpenters.
RITUAL The Book of the Dead.
RUACH. The spirit.
SABAK. To be prostrate and subdued.
SAHU. The constellation, Orion.
SALEVAHANA. A Buddhist god, the carpenter.
SALOME. A queen of Judea.
SARKOLATRÆ. Worshippers of a flesh add blood god.
SAROSH. One of the messengers of the god Ahura-Mazda.
SEB. An Egyptian God; the head of the family of Osiris.
SEBEK. A God of the river or water.
SEBEK-RA. A title of Ra.
SEMIRAMIS. A celebrated queen of Assyria.
SENEKHER. Ra as shining face.
SENNT. A medicated or healing bath.
SERAPIS, The defunct Apis who has become Osiris.
SEVEKH . An Egyptian deity.
SHENT. A typical pool and source.
SHEPHERD OF HERMES. One of the apocryphal books of the New Testament.
SHEPI. The god who lights the sacrophagus.

SHERON. The youth.
SITON. The gesator.
SHUS-EN-HAR. The great pyramid.
SHU. A god of light, probably the light of the sun, and a type of celestial force.
SISTRUM. A metallic rattle which was used by the Egyptians in celebrating the rites of Isis.
SOSHYANS. The last of the prophets in the Persian religion.
SOTHIS. Egyptian name of the constellation Sirius which received divine honors.
STAUROS. A stake for supporting.
SUNNT. A medicated and healing bath.
SUT. The exil deity.
SUT-ANUBIS. See Anubis.
SUT-ANUP. The god who attended on the dead.
SUT-HORUS The double Horus.
TAHT. The Egyptian lunar-Mercury.
TAHT AAN . A lunar god.
TAHT-MATIU. The Egyptian god who wrote the Ritual.
TANE. Son of Vatea.
TANEN. Ra, as the god of the earth.
TANI. To bow the forehead.
TARGUM. A translation of the sacred scriptures into the Chaldee dialect.
TAT. An Egyptian god.
TATTU. The under world.
TAWHAKI A New Zealand god. A Messiah like Jesus Christ.
THOTH. A moon god. It was his special office to record the result when souls in Amenti, (the underworld), were judged and their deeds weighed in the balance. He is believed to have composed the "Ritual of the Dead."
TOTUM. The whole.
TOUBEH. A month corresponding to the last six days of December and part of the month of January.
TUAMUTF. One of the four genii who presided over the grave and embalmment.
TUM. The setting sun.

TYPHON. The evil god of the Egyptians.
UAK. idleness.
URÆUS. A lamp emitting globes of flame.
USHA The doctor.
USHTA. To absolve, to acquit.
UTERUS. The womb.
VALENTINUS. A pioneer Gnostic.
VATEA. A god of Polynesia, half man, half fish.
VENUS AUREA. The golden Venus.
VENUS PISCES. Venus of the fishes.
VERONICA. True image.
VESICA PISCES. The bladder of fishes.
VISHNU. *A* Brahman deity.
WITOBA. The Mexican Messiah.
ZARATUSHT. A Persian seer.
ZENDAVESTA.. The Bible of the ancient Persians.

# INDEX

[1] Wake, Genuine Epistles of the Apostolical Fathers, p 198. Smith, Epistles of St. Ignatius.
[2] Jowett, Epistles of St. Paul, vol i. p. 102
[3] Rev. ch. x. 9—11.
[4] Ch. xii. 4. In explanation if this description it may be pointed out that if the seven stars of the lesser Bear be taken to represent the seven heads of the Dragon as previously suggested, then the tail of the Dragon sweeping round to the stars Etanin describes exactly one-third of the circle of the Precision, including the ancient polestars from Etanin, which was the polestar 11,051 B.C., to a Draconis (say) 2500 B.C.
[5] Vend. Fargard, xix. 18.
[6] Bund. ch. xxx 7.
[7] Ch. lxxi. 1.
[8] Ch. lvi. 5. Ch. lxviii. 39 Ch. lxix. 1—3.
[9] 2 Edras vii.
[10] Rev. xxi. 2, 9, 10.
[11] Tischendorf, (1) Acta Apostolorum Apocrypha; (2) DeEvang. Apocryphorum Origine et Usu; Gospel of Nicodemus, pt. ii. ch. ii. , iii., and vii.; Latin Gospel of Nicodemus, ch. iii., iv., vii., and xii. Cowper. Bartoloc. Bib. Rab. tom. i. pp. 228, 229.
[12] The Acts of the Pilate.

The great judge of the dead in Amenti was designated the Rhat (Eg.), whence the Greek Rhadamanthus. The Rhat with the letter L instead of R is the Lat, and with the masculine article Pi becomes Pilate, for the judge in Amenti. Now as Pilate is found to be one of the saints canonized by the Abyssinian church, his day being that of the summer solstice, it is possible that this Pilate was the judge in Amenti. The Christian theory of the "Acts of Pilate" is that there once existed an official report of the trial, condemnation, and crucifixion of Jesus, which was made by Pontius Pilate and forewarded by him Tiberius in Rome. Justin and Tertullian appealed to such a document. This is supposed to have perished and to have been replaced by the apocryphal gospel that has come down to us. But the extant "Acts of Pilate" are related to the Amenti, or underworld, into which the crucified descends to conquer death and Hades, and effect the Resurrection of the dead; and my suggestion is that the extant opens "Acts" were derived from the mythical original which supplied the supposed history.
[13] Eclogue, iv.
[14] Dabistan, vol. i. p. 218: Shea and Troyer.
[15] Colebrook, Essays, vol. i. p. 190.
[16] Stanley, Hist. Jewish Church, app. iii. pt. i.
[17] Didron, fig. 86.
[18] Ritual ch. xxiii. Champ. Gram. 95.
[19] See the constellation "Triangula," plate, vol. i.
[20] Ann. of Ramesis, iii.
[21] Triangle. This figure in a dual character also forms the six-pointed star or figure of space in six directions, the hexagram of the heaven that followed the heptanomis: a change that was likewise indicated by the dragon losing one of his seven heads.
[22] Planisphere, previous vol. In Egypt the seven spirits are also described in a more abstract phase, as—

1. Khuti, the brilliant triangle (or pyramid) in shining place.

2. The mysterious spirit form the mysterious place.
3. The blessed place from the blessed place.
4. The destructive from the place of destruction.
5. The revealing spirit from the opening.
6. The elevated spirit from the high place.
7. The hidden spirit from the Ament.

The seven spirits were also continued in the seven doves of the Christian iconography, supposed to symbolized the seven gifts of the Holy Spirit.

The elemantary spirit, whether in external or in human nature, did not rise beyond the number seven.

As human constituents, the sixth was created spirits, the ruach of puberty, and the seven attained a summit in the soul. Lastly, divinity or godhead was reached by the eight, the repeater of or to the rest. In the Ritual the seven elementary can be identified as the soul of Sevekh. The deceased exclaims, "Shu causes me to shine as a living lord, and be made the seventh when he comes forth:" "I am the one born of Sevekh the Lord." Sevekh signifies the number seven. the seventh was the highest elementary force. Sevekh the seventh was the crocodile type: he attained the dignity of the first god as Sevekh-Kronus, the dragon. In the Kaffir dialects the crocodile and the soul are synonymous, as they were in Sevekh on account of his superior intelligence.

It should be observed that the soul of Seb, the ithy-phallic father of the fifth Creation, is identified with the Buddhist "fifth-principle" or element, as the animal soul: that of Putah, the sixth, is one with the Buddhi, as the sixth principle: whilst Atma, the seventh, is the same by name and nature as Atum, of the seventh creation in whose keeping is the "reserved soul," as the seventh in the series.

*Irenæus, b. i. ch. xiv. I.

*See the Typology of Numbers, vol. i. pp. 206-214.

*Hippoiytus, vol. iv. pp. 13, 14; preface. Wake, par. 19.

*Ch. lxix. †2 Edras xiii. 25, 26. ‡Berosus, from Alexander Polyhistor. Cory, Ancient Fragments. §2 Esdras xiii. 52. Matthew viii. 23. ¶2 Esdras xiii. 52. ¶¶Matthew xiv. 25; Mark vi. 48; John xii. 36. "Farther still, the aquatic in divine natures indicates a providential inspection and government inseperable from water. Hence also the oracle calls these gods water-walkers." —Proclus in Timæ, b. iv.

23 John iv. 32—34.

24 Matthew xvi. 4.‡Luke xi. 30.§Irenæus, b. iii. ch. xvi. I. ‡See the vivid figure in vol. i. kircher.

25 Garrucci, Storia della Arte Christiana, pl. 105. Didron, Icon. Chret. p. 353.

26 Roma Sott. pl. 16.

27 Monumental Christianity, p. 369. fig. 169.

28 Keane, Towers and Temples of Ancient Ireland. ‡DeRossi, Roma Sotterranea, vol. i. p. 348. Lundy, p. 139.

29 Vossius, De Idolatria lib. i. cap. xxiii.

30

31 History of Egypt, vol. ii. p. 299: Eng. tr.

32 Munter, Sinnbilder. Lundi, Monumental Christianity, p. 132.

33 Inscription of Khnun-Hept, Records, vol. xii. pp. 42, 43.

34 Inscription of Hatasu, Records, vol. xii. pp. 3, 4.

35 Micah v. 2: Matt. ii. 4—6.

36 Is. xxviii. 28.

37 i Chron. 2 ii. 19 and 50. *On Exodus, xii. 42.
38 Great Mendes Stele, Museum at Boolak. Records, viii. 92.
39 Sanhed. 98a.
40 Revelation xi. 8.
41 Jones, Finger-ring Lore, p. 199.
42 Or Roma in Cambodia, cf. vol. i. p. 167. * Apocryphal Gospels, ch. vvviii,; Cowper,
43 Select Pap, iv, 3, Birch, Dict, p, 347,
44 Movers, p, 210,
45 P 366
46 Syria and Palestine, p. 467; 2nd ed
47 1600 B.C.
48 Strom, i
49 Trans Soc B A, vol. iv pt ii p 234. Les Zodiaques de Denderah.
50 Of Isis and Osiris
51 Egytpian Calendar, p 62, 1878
52 Ch. i. 3
53 Luke ii. I, 2.
54 Josephus, Antiq b. 18 ch. i ii.
55 Bunsen, Egypt's place, v iii 77.
56 De Trin lib iv cap v
57 Ch. 18
58 Ch. 13 and 14
59 Ch. 7
60 Ch. ii
61 Justin Dialogue cum trypho, pp. 240 and 304.
62

63 Chrysostom, Monitum in Hum de Natal Christi. Gieseler, vol. i p 54 †Neander, Church Hist. vol. iii. p. 437: Bingham, b 20 ch. iv.
64 Vishnu Purana, ch. iii. p. 503: Wilson.
65 Luke 21 27.
66 1/2 Rit ch. 145.
67 Line 2
68 John 10 30; 14 7.
69 Line 5
70 Lines 3 and 6
71 Line 6 and 7.
72 Lines 17 and 18
73 Line 20
74 Line 75
75 Line 36
76 Line 36
77 Mark 16 18
78 Fresco, 2nd or 3rd century Aringhi, vol i p 322 Bosio, p 257
79 John 12 7
80 Line 62
81 Line 73
82 Line 74
83 Ch 64
84 Ch 75
85 Line 29

86 Luke 24 26
87 Line 24
88 Mark 12
89 Lines 39, 40
90 Lines 39, 40
91 Line 40
92 Line 59
93 Line 65
94 Ch iii II
95 Luke 12 49
96 Matt iii II 12
97 Ch 13 42
98 Ch 25 41
99 Line 41
100 Line 42
101 ‡Acts i 9
102 Ch. i 18.
103 B. i. 1 10
104 Cited by Renouf, Hibbert Lectures, p 252.
105 He is my own good beetle, not so much because he is only begotten (God), not because he himself, the author of himself has taken on the form of mortals, but because he has rolled himself in our filth and chooses to be born from this filth itself.himself has gotten (God), not b
106 Ch. xiviii; Birch
107 Rit. ch. 31.
108 See Roma Sotterranea: or Didron, figures 18 and 66.
109 Cf. ch lxviii and ixix of the Ritual, for Seb and Aseb.
110 Ch cxlii.
111 "Tale of Setnau," Records, vol iv p 137.
112 John xiv 27: xx 21.
113 Matt. x 34.
114 Rit ch lxiii.
115 Ch. xiv.
116 Clement Alexander, Stromata, iii 12. Clement of Rome, 2 Ep c xii.
117 John 16 25.
118 John 16 13.
119 John 16 8.
120 I John i 6.
121 Ch iii 21.
122 Ecclesiasiasticus xlii 15.
123 Ch ii 42—25.
124 Matt iii 17.
125 Pierrett, Pantheon Egyptien, fig p 77.
126 Denkmaler, iii 243, 250; iv. II.
127 Ephesians ii 14.
128 Denkmaler, iv II.
129 Amen. In the Roman Litany of the Mass the worshippers are taught to pray in these words: "God Hideen, and my Savior, have mercy upon us."
130 Luke iv 32.
131 Records of the Past, vol iv pp 53—60.
132 Lines 19—22.

133 Not only does the full moon still rule at Easter, the pig also suffers, is sacrificed and eaten. Bacon is the prescribed accompaniment of the eggs of easter; and a gammon of bacon, even with many of the poor, is still the correct sign of the season. In a sermon preached at Blandford Forum, Doretshire, January 17, 1570, dedicated to Ambrose, Earl of Warwick, it is stated, on p 18, by William Kethe, minister, that "on Good Friday the Roman Catholics offered unto Christe egges and bacon, to be in favor till Easter day be past."
134 Records of the past, vol x pp 112—114. Ritual, ch cxii. Herodotus, ii 47, 48. Of Isis and Osiris.
135 Luke viii 29—33.
136 Ritual, Cadet.
137 Ch ixxxiii.
138 Luke viii 27.
139 Luke ix 38.
140 Matthew xii 22.
141 Luke viii 43.
142 Ch 118; Birch.
143 Plate in preceding vol.
144 i 32.
145 Legenda Aurea, "De Ass. Beatæ Virginis Mariæ."
146 Matt iii II, 12. Luke iii 16, 17.
147 Goodwin, Cambridge Essays, p 275; 1858.
148 Ritual, ch cxivi; in the Fourth Gate of Elysium.
149 cxv.
150 Ch cxv.
151 Another version from Pap. 9900, Brit. Museum, appended by Birch to ch cxv.
152 Chs 117 and 118.
153 John iv 14; ch vii 37, 38.
154 Ch 78.
155 Ritual, ch 125.
156 Eusebius, b ii c xvii.
157 Ch 115.
158 Matt 9 37, 38.
159 Matt 13 36—43.
160 Ritual, ch 17.
161 Records of the Past, vol 10 pp 116—119.
162 Ch lii.
163 Ch liii.
164 Rit ch 140; Rubric.
165 Records, vol 10 p 116.
166 John vi 9.
167 Matt 15 34.
168 Bosio, Rom Sott. Lundy, fig. 171.
169 Mark 6 44. John 6 10.
170 "Revolt in Heaven," records, vol 7 p 128.
171 John 6 15—21.
172 Ritual, ch 57; Birch.
173 John viii 59.
174 John 10 39.
175 Ch 145.

176 Ch 145.
177 John 10 22—40.
178 Luke 4 29.
179 John vii 8
180 Irenæus, b i ch vii p 2.
181 Ritual, ch 21 2—6. Litany of Ra, ch ii 4.
182 Matt xiv 23.
183 Matt xv 29, 30.
184 Matt xvii 1,2, 5.
185 Matt xxiv 3.
186 Acts i 9.
187 Vol i p 165. The annual celebration being "upon the kalends of the month Phamenoth."—Plutarch, Of Isis and Osiris.
188
189 Matt xvii II
190 Matthew xvi. I—13.
191 Pymander, b vii.
192 Eusebius, iii 3.
193 John viii. 56—58.
194 Ch 136.
195 Matt 12, 34.
196 Verse 44.
197 John viii 23.
198 Iren b i ch viii 4.
199 Luke xv 4, 6.
200 Matt x 6, 7; xv 24.
201 Luke ix I.
202 Irenæus, b i ch xxiii. 1—3.
203 Irenæus, b i ch ii 2—4; ch iii 3—5; ch iv I.
204 "Story of Veronica," Apocryphal Gospels, Cowper, p 223.
205 Luke viii 41.
206 John ix i.
207 Irenæus, b ii ch xvii. 9.
208 Giving sight to the blind. The bak-hawk, the Lord of vision, a symbolical bird of Light was a type of Horus. Plutarch repeats an Egyptian superstition concerning the hawk to the effect that in flying over the dead bodies of men it dropped its dirt upon their eyes. And because the hawk symbolled sight, says Hor-Apollo, "Physicians use the herb hawkweed for the cure of the eyes.'
209 Ephesians v 32.
210 Irenæus, b i ch i 2.
211 John xiv 26.
212 B i ch iii 6.
213 Records of the Past, vol. x. pp. 91, 96, 100, 106, 115, 128.
214 Records of the Past, Vol x p 91.
215 Ibid. p 100.
216 Ibid. p 95.
217 Book of the Underworld, Deveria; a variant of the Book of Hades.
218 Matthew 27 45.
219 Matthew 27 52.
220 Matthew 27 34

221 Rit ch cxivii.; Birch.
222 P 18 69
223 B i 58.
224 Apud Photium; Bibliotheca Cod. 242 p 343. Luke xxii 44; Matt xxvi 36.
225
226 Biblia Sacra No. 6328; cited by Didron.
227 Of Isis and Osiris.
228 Ch xv.
229 Bancroft, iii 271, 272.
230 Matt 27 51; 28 2.
231 2 Esdras x 1, 2.
232 Sophocies,Œdipus Col. 1049.
233 Ch lvii.
234 Ch 35.
235 John xviii 2.
236 John xiii 26, 27.
237 Rit ch 35.
238 Ritual Ch 64.
239 Matt 26 62, 63; 27 12.
240 Luke 23 9.
241 Ch 18.
242 Ritual Ch 18.
243 Ch 19.
244 Ch 19.
245 Ch 28.
246 John 19 40: 20 7.
247 Ch xix.
248 John 20 1.
249 John 20 11, 12.
250 Ch xivi.
251 Ch 28 2.
252 Litany of Ra, line 42.
253 Irenæus, b i ch iv 1.
254 Ch xlii.
255 Luke 24.
256 Book of Sen-Sen, i. Records, vol iv p 121.
257 Sahu-Ra was a Pharoah in the third dynasty, named after Orion the star of Horus, or Ra. A star and eight points annexed to the Sahu sign idnetify the eight stars in Orion, which are equivalent to the eight-rayed star of the manifestor. In the time of Sahu-Ra, Orion was the representative of the sun in the sign of Taurus. Orion was connected with Sothis-Sut, because Sut and Horus were twins, but it is the especial star of Horus or Ra on the upper horizon, as that of Sut was in the lower heaven.
258 Rit. Ch. 152.
259 Bosio, Rom. Sott. p 579. Lundy, fig. 88.
260 Plutarch, Of Isis and Osiris; also Herodotus.
261 Vol. i p 119.
262 Lepsius, Todt. xv 28; 20 42; 26 71—76.
263 Asiatic Researches, vol x p 124.
264 Rit ch 58

265 Verse 14
266 Ch 17
267 Luke 24 39 40
268 Ritual, ch xvii.
269 Cited by Bingham, Christian Antiquities, vol i p 517; ed. Bohn.
270 Ch xliv.
271 Book of Beginnings, vol ii.
272 Ps 22 21
273 Natt 22 43, 47
274 Luke 1 69 70
275 Micah 5 2
276 Vishnu Purana b v ch 23 p 567; Wilson
277 Isaiah 7 14 Cf Matt 1 23
278 Matt 2 15 Cf Hosea 11 1
279 Psalm 2 7 Cf Matt 3 17
280 Psalm 41 9 Cf John 13 18
281 Zech 11 12, 13 Cf Matt 27 9
282 Gill, Myths and Songs, pp 68, 70.
283
284 Of Isis and Osiris Ch vi 1, 2.
285 Matt xii 40.
286 Rit ch 26.
287 Ch xiii 18.
288 Verse 19.
289 John 17 12.
290 Ch 19.
291 Ch 18.
292 Ch 18.
293 John 13 27.
294 John 17 12.
295 Ps lxxviii. See Book of Beginnings, vol ii.
296 xl. 6—8.
297 Heb x 5—7.
298 Ch xi 26.
299 Acts 13 33.
300 Psalm 22 1, 16—18. See Book of Beginnings, vol ii p 35
301 Luke 24 34; Psalm 22 1—18.
302 John 19 24.
303 See "Egyptian Origines in the Hebrew Scriptures," vol ii Book of Beginnings.
304 Eusebius, H. E. iv 14—26; v 23, 24.
305 No. 836, Har. MSS. Brit. Museum. See also Bede, ii. c. xix.
306 Rit ch 145.
307 Ch 80.
308 Book of Beginnings, vol i p 274. The ceremonies were seen in the years 1817 and 1818 by the authoress of Rome in the Nineteenth Century.
309 Plate 1, vol ii Book of Beginnings.
310 Matthew iii 1—3.
311 Zodiac of Denderah.
312 Salverte, Des Sciences Occultes, p 47.
313 Ritual ch 31.

314 John iii 29—32.
315 John iii 29—32
316 Ch 49 10, 11.
317 Plate in preceding vol.
318 Drummond, pi 16.
319 Eisenmenger, vol ii p 697.
320 Ch 12 14, 15.
321 Apol. 32.
322 Records of the Past, vol x p 130.
323 i 20
324 John ii 11.
325 Egyptian Calendar, p 19, Alexandria, 1877.
326 Fabricius, J A, Codex Pseudebigraphus Vet Testamenti, i 139 and fol
327 Codex Naz Onomasticon, p 74.
328 Codex Nazaræus Liber Adami Appellatus a M Norberg, vol i pp 55—57.
329 Rit ch iii.
330 Ch 78.
331 Lundy, fig 130.
332 Ciampini, Vetera Monimenta, vol i ch iii p 35.
333 Adv. Hæres, 26.
334 Tertullian, Apol 16.
335 Luke i 17.
336 Origen in Evang. Johan, tom. ii p 180.
337 Lib 10 c. 33.
338 Ch 61 9.
339 Matthew 11 11.
340 Matt 9 37. Luke 10 1—20.
341 Menachem Racanatens, in Legem, f 26 c 3. Stehelin, vol ii pp 94, 95. Kad Hakkemach, f 42, c1. Stehelin, vol i p 182. Bartol tom i pp 335, 336. Bechai in Legem, f 9, c 3. Nachman, in Legem, f 59, c 3. Shepha Tal f 23, c 3. Stehelin, vol i p 185.
342 Book of Enoch, ch 69 1—3
343 Luke 10 17—19.
344 Cowper, Apoc Gospels, p 24.
345 Vishnu Purana, b v ch iii p 503; Wilson.
346 Ibid b v ch vi p 506.
347 Ibid.
348 Ch 115.
349 John 21 21—23
350 Vide Fabricii, Codice Apocrypho, tom ii p 590.
351 Ch cliii; Birch
352 Ch lii
353 Ch ciiii.
354 Ritual, ch 115
355 Records of the Past, vol ii p 124.
356 Ch 17
357 Section 9
358 Ch 149
359 Ritual, ch 149; Birch
360 Luke vii 3
361 Lohber, Cyprus, p 105

362 Beusobre, tom i p 418
363 The Golden Manual; also the Garden of the Soul
364 Mark 15 40 See also Eusebius; H E ii 1
365 John 19 25.
366 Epiphanius, c 49.
367 Rit ch 17; Birch.
368 Ch xcix.
369 Rit ch civ.; Birch. Also Papyrus 9,900, B. M.
370 Matt iv 19.
371 John xxi 1—3.
372 John xxi 7.
373 Ch clxii; Birch.
374 Matt xvi 16. Luke ix 20.
375 Hawk and Dove. It is related of Gautama-Buddha, that in a former incarnation he gave his blood and body to a hawk to save the life of a dove.
376 De Tillemont, Hist. Eccles. tom ii 5.
377 John 21 15—17.
378 Matt 16 18.
379 Bancroft; vol iii 252—259.
380 Hapi presides over th heart; Tuamutf, over the soul; Kabhsenuf, over the mummy )the mundane image); and Amset, over the ka-image (or celestial self). In the Apostolic Constitutions the designation of James as the brother of the Lord, according to the flesh, is not found in the two Vatican MSS.: he is simply called "Brother of the Lord," just as Amset was brother of Osiris. Both are missing from the Coptic, Syriac, and Oxford MSS., chapter 35 being omitted altogether.
381 Jerome, St Hieron, De Viris Illustribus, c 2. Also History of the Apostles, by Abdias.
382 Rit ch lxix.
383 Matt iv 18, 19.
384 Matt iv 21.
385 Gill, Myths, p 100.
386 Dial, ch 88.
387 Eccl. 28 2.
388 †.
389 Eccl 29 11.
390 Matt vi 14.
391 Matt vi 19.
392 Eccl i 25.
393 The "Lord's Prayer," assigned to Jesus as a teacher, is found almost verbatim in the Jewish Kadish, a player to the Father. "Our Father which art in heaven, be gracious to us, O Lord our God; hallowed be thy name; and let the remembrance of thee be glorified in heaven above, and upon earth here below. Let thy kingdom reign over us, now and for ever. Thy holy men of old said, 'Remilt and forgive unto all men whatsoever they have done against me. And lead us not into temptation, but deliver us from the evil thing. For thine is the kingdom, and thou shalt reign in glory, for ever and for evermore."
394 Recog. ii 33.
395 Matt x 30.
396 Ch vii.
397 Ritual, ch 19.

398 Matt 25 35.
399 Ritual, ch 18; Birch. Hibbert Lectures,
400 Renouf.
401 Planisphere in preceding vol.
402 Chabas, Bulletin Archeologique, p 44, Juin, 1855. Sharpe Eg. Inscrip. pis. 9—12, fol. 1837. Wilkinson, pl. 88.
403 Ritual, ch 18.
404 Ritual, ch i; Birch.
405 Matt iii 1, 3.
406 "Inscription of Ameni," Records of the Past, vol vi p i.
407 Chapter 64 is described in the Rubric as being one of these Sayings. It was among the sayings of Har-ta-tef.
408 Clement Alexander, Stromata, i 9.
409 Hom i in Lucan.
410 Hippolytus, Adv Hær. vii 20.
411 Hippolytus, Ref Om Hær vii 27.
412 Irenæus, b i ch 20 1.
413 Irenæus, b iii ch 11 9.
414 Tertullian, De Præscrip. 49.
415 Suum præter hæc nostra."—Terull. De Prœscrip. 49.
416 Bunsen, Hippolytus and his Age, vol i p 35.
417 "Magical Texts," Records, vol vi p 122.
418 John xiv 2.
419 John xvii 8.
420 "Magic Papyrus," Records, vol 10 pp 157, 158.
421 Matt v 22.
422 Matt v 22.
423 John 9 7.
424 Matt 27 46.
425 Rit ch 48.
426 Cited by Didron.
427 Ch 109; Birch.
428 Matt 27 52, 53.
429 King, Gnostics, pp 103—128, 534.
430 Ibid p 104.
431 Ibid p 71.
432 B iii ch iv 3.
433 Hippolytus; Ante-Nicene Library, vol vi p 389.
434 Much Ado About Nothing, act iii scene 3.
435 Gnostic Heretics, p 98.
436 Origen, Cont Celsum, b vi ch xlii.
437 Acts iv 13.
438 Les Apotres, ch iii.
439 Abraham Zacuth in Juchasin, p 16, c 2. Wagenseil Sota, pp 1057, 1058
440 Mishni, Treatise 12 ch i 6.
441 Babylonian Gemara, Tract, "Sanhedrim," 43 1.
442 Josephus, Ant. b 13 ch 15 5; ch 16 1—6; ch xiv 2.
443 Wagenseil, Altdorf, 1681. Huldricus, Leyden, 1705.
444 Eisenmenger, Entdecktes Judenthum, vol i pp 231—237.
445 Dialogue cum Trypho, ch 17.
446 Recog. ch i 42.

447 Epiphanius, Adv. Hær lib. iii; Hær 68 7.
448 Acts v 30; x 39.
449 Irenæus, b ii ch 22 5.
450 Tacitus, Annal. 15 44. Josephus, Ant. b 18 c 3. Photius, Bibliothec, cod 33.
451 Acts xi 30; xii 35. Gal. i ii.
452 In Cyprian, De Rebapt.
453 1 John ii 22; iv 3.
454 Epiphanius, Hær 29 9.
455 Irenæus, b i ch 27 2.
456 1 Tim i iv.
457 Titus iii 9.
458 2 Tim ii 18.
459 Philippians iii 11, 12.
460 1 Cor ii 6, 7.
461 Eph iii 3.
462 Eph iii 5.
463 Col i 26.
464 Strom vii.
465 Brett, Indian Tribes of Guiana, p 109.
466 Te Ika a Maui, pp 101, 102.
467 Justin, Apol i 66. Dial. 70—78.
468 Stromata, vi 7.
469 Ibid v.
470 Ibid vi 17.
471 Irenæus, b i ch 25 5.
472 Matt 13 11.
473 Credner, Geschichte des N. T. Canon, c cxi 279.
474 Homily iii 19.
475 Rom xvi 25.
476 Homily ii 17.
477 Ch ix 11.